# ESTHER ROSS,
# STILLAGUAMISH CHAMPION

Esther at age eighteen with her lustrous dark hair cascading over her shoulder. Her long hair was worn various ways but rarely braided in the typical Indian fashion.

# Esther Ross, Stillaguamish Champion

By Robert H. Ruby and John A. Brown
Foreword by LaDonna Harris
Introduction by Alan Stay and Jay Miller

University of Oklahoma Press : Norman

ALSO BY ROBERT H. RUBY AND JOHN A. BROWN

*Half-Sun on the Columbia: A Biography of Chief Moses* (Norman, 1965)
*The Spokane Indians: Children of the Sun* (Norman, 1970)
*The Cayuse Indians: Imperial Tribesmen of Old Oregon* (Norman, 1972)
*Ferryboats on the Columbia River* (Seattle, 1974)
*The Chinook Indians, Traders of the Lower Columbia River* (Norman, 1976)
*Myron Eells and the Puget Sound Indians* (Seattle, 1976)
*Indians of the Pacific Northwest: A History* (Norman, 1981)
*A Guide to the Indian Tribes of the Pacific Northwest* (Norman, 1986, 1992)
*Dreamer-Prophets of the Columbia Plateau: Smohalla and Skolaskin* (Norman, 1989)
*John Brown Bibliography* (1989)
*Indian Slavery in the Pacific Northwest* (Spokane, 1993)
*John Slocum and the Indian Shaker Church* (Norman, 1996)

Publication of this book is made possible through the generosity of Edith Gaylord Harper.

Library of Congress Cataloging-in-Publication Data

Ruby, Robert H.
    Esther Ross, Stillaguamish champion / by Robert H. Ruby and John A. Brown; foreword by LaDonna Harris; introduction by Alan Stay and Jay Miller.
    p. cm
    Includes bibliographical references and index.
    ISBN 978-0-8061-6272-4 (paper)

    1. Ross, Esther Ruth, 1904–1988. 2. Stillaquamish Indians—Biography. 3. Stillaquamish Indians—Government relations. I. Brown, John Arthur. II. Title.

E99.S75 R677 2001
979.5'00497—dc21

2001027135

The paper in this book meets the guidelines for permanence and durability of the Committee on Production Guidelines for Book Longevity of the Council on Library Resources, Inc. ∞

Copyright © 2001 by the University of Oklahoma Press, Norman, Publishing Division of the University. All rights reserved. Paperback published 2019. Manufactured in the U.S.A.

To
Tiffany, Stephanie, Caleigh, Aleksey, and Jeanne
and to
Kathryn

# Contents

| | |
|---|---|
| List of Illustrations | ix |
| Foreword, by LaDonna Harris | xi |
| Introduction, by Alan Stay and Jay Miller | xv |
| Preface | xxi |
| List of Abbreviations and Acronyms | 2 |
| 1. The California Years | 3 |
| 2. Stillaguamish: The Land and the People | 13 |
| 3. The Stillaguamish: A Tribe Reborn | 23 |
| 4. Duality: Tribal and Domestic Affairs | 26 |
| 5. The Nomadic Years | 33 |
| 6. Claims: Land Losses and Family Losses | 43 |
| 7. Fish Wars: The Courts and the Rivers | 58 |
| 8. Esther Meets the Rebel General | 64 |
| 9. The Poor People's Campaign | 74 |
| 10. War Cry along the Stilly | 79 |
| 11. Legacy of the Dead, Land Base for the Living | 87 |

| | |
|---|---|
| 12. Organization, Disorganization, and Militancy | 95 |
| 13. Mrs. Ross Goes to Washington—Again | 103 |
| 14. Half the Salmon: The Boldt Case | 109 |
| 15. The Boldt Court: The Fallout | 124 |
| 16. The Push for Recognition | 136 |
| 17. The Chief and the Wagon Train | 145 |
| 18. While Waiting for Recognition | 157 |
| 19. The Case of the Flying Fish | 166 |
| 20. The Wait Goes On | 170 |
| 21. A Celebration at Muckleshoot Hall | 180 |
| 22. Recognition Brings More Troubles | 185 |
| 23. Calling the Roll: A Troublesome Task | 198 |
| 24. A War of Words and Wills | 208 |
| 25. Stratagems for Leadership | 216 |
| 26. Exit and Exile | 226 |
| 27. Debility and Denouement | 235 |
| 28. Epilogue and Retrospect | 246 |
| Notes | 253 |
| Bibliography | 293 |
| Index | 301 |

# ILLUSTRATIONS

### MAPS

| | |
|---|---:|
| Important places in Esther Ross's life | 14 |
| Stillaguamish lands and environs in Washington | 17 |

### PHOTOGRAPHS

| | |
|---|---:|
| Esther at eighteen | *frontispiece* |
| Infant Esther, her mother, and her father | 4 |
| Esther's mother's family | 5 |
| Esther and her mother | 6 |
| Esther's mother and stepfather | 7 |
| Esther as a teenager and her mother | 8 |
| Esther's first husband, Fletcher Carlton, and her first child, Margaret Ruth | 11 |
| Stillaguamish Indians in a dugout canoe | 19 |
| Esther's second husband, Walter Allen | 30 |
| Truck that carried the Allen family to California | 34 |
| Walter, Ruth, and Marion at the Ketchikan waterfront | 36 |
| Esther in her fur coat | 42 |
| Wedding party at Esther's marriage to Arnold Ross | 49 |
| Esther and Arnold on her fifty-second birthday | 53 |
| Demonstration at the federal courthouse, Seattle, 1965 | 60 |

| | |
|---|---|
| Retired Gen. Herbert G. Holdridge | 66 |
| Political cartoon, Esther and Gov. Daniel Evans | 72 |
| Esther and Frank on their way to the Poor People's Campaign, 1968 | 75 |
| Esther hunting for Stillaguamish burial sites | 88 |
| Esther and her cigar box full of Stillaguamish bones | 92 |
| Charles Trimble, executive director of the National Congress of American Indians | 105 |
| Esther and David Getches, attorney, Native American Rights Fund | 111 |
| John Silva, Stillaguamish tribal chair; Esther; Toddy Smith, tribal elder; and Gus Smith, tribal member | 126 |
| Esther and Rod Sayegusa, tribal consultant | 134 |
| Bicentennial Wagon Train, June 12, 1975 | 150 |
| Esther outside the Island Crossing office, addressing members of the Bicentennial Wagon Train | 152 |
| Esther in Washington, D.C., with Joe DeLaCruz, Quinault tribal chair | 163 |
| Esther at a Department of the Interior meeting | 164 |
| Esther with Sam Cagey and Roger Jim at an Americans for Indian Opportunity meeting, March 1976 | 168 |
| Esther at December 4, 1976, banquet in her honor | 182 |
| An aging Esther in Indian regalia | 196 |
| Tribal office at Island Crossing | 213 |
| Esther and former governor Dan Evans | 231 |
| Esther with Frank and his children, 1987 | 233 |
| Billy Frank, Jr., of Northwest Indian Fisheries Commission, and Esther | 237 |
| Esther and Frank | 241 |

# Foreword

When President Clinton appointed me to serve on the Commission on the Celebration of Women in American History, I was honored and excited to do so. Being a Comanche woman, I have always been aware and proud of the role played by women in our tribal society and our history. What I am also aware of is the lack of public knowledge about Indian women's contributions to American history. One can easily count those few women whose legacies have been written about, and the even fewer biographies about Indian women. Because these stories are not being told, people are not accustomed to thinking of Native women as feminists, leaders, and contributors to social change. Their songs are unsung.

Women who serve as tribal chiefs and in other leadership roles have profound influence that extends far beyond the tribe. Their efforts to protect and better their communities' health, welfare, education, and cultures have an influence on the larger population of American Indian people and also make an impact on American society as a whole. The telling of their stories provides models for students and women in pursuing their own aspirations. These stories are not only interesting and entertaining, but instructive.

If one were to judge by the scarce resources detailing the lives of these Native leaders of distinction, one could come to the conclusion that such women were exceptions. The truth is that these women have always existed and flourished within tribal societies, even though writers have not explored their lives. Ask the general public to make a list of outstanding Native women and chances are thay can name but two well known in literature, the daring and heroic Pocahontas and the brave and celebrated Sacagawea. Yet these same citizens would have no trouble making a list of prominent and powerful historic Native males.

Because most people have little understanding of tribal societies they are unaware that women are the keepers of the culture in all tribes. The roles of women are highly treasured and honored. The fact is feminism is not new to Native cultures.

Esther Ross's story covers an era in contemporary American Indian history that until now has gone unexplored. Finally, here is her story, a story about taking risks. As Esther's life demonstrates, the achievements of Native women in the 1960s were generally based on taking great risks, and sometimes brought much pain.

We need stories about the movers and shakers, such as Esther, who got things accomplished. The truth is we need everyone's account, not just to learn about what they did but to know how they did it.

I knew Esther Ross and I worked with her. She was an original. She had her own method of operating and she forced the United States Congress to adhere to her "rules." She demolished barriers and broke protocol to gain federal recognition for her tribe, the Stillaguamish of the Pacific Northwest. By doing so, she brought her people back from near extinction. By 1919 the community had dwindled to a mere twenty-nine people. When Esther became involved with the tribe, the Stillaguamish were dispersed and without tribal organization. Esther stood up to the government and challenged the arbitrary excuses offered by the Department of the Interior for delay and sidestepping. She forced the government to change its policies in dealing with tribes. She became involved with almost every Indian office and movement in the Pacific Northwest in the last century, all of which are described and portrayed in this volume. While it is difficult to convey the emotion and power of traditional oral history, this book is an excellent portrayal of Esther Ross's impact as a leader of her people and a woman of her people. Most important, it conveys her story, an interesting, valuable, and informative addition to the literature of achievements of Indian women.

LaDonna Harris
*President and Founder*
*Americans for Indian*
*Opportunity*

# INTRODUCTION

Esther Ross was an extraordinary woman. Lacking most advantages and resources, she dedicated herself to badger, cajole, and finally convince the federal government to grant recognition to the Stillaguamish tribe. With that recognition came the benefits and rights that would help bring prosperity to her people, such as their new community near Arlington. This was her all-consuming mission in life.

Her most effective weapon was persistence. At every public gathering, whether of Native people or state or federal officials, she made her presence felt. She remained convinced that America should be a democracy and was sure that elected officials would help her. She also knew and lived the maxim that the most effective politics was the most dramatic. Indeed, today that hearing aid she used so selectively—for Esther, the issue was not so much what an official might have to say to her as what she might have to say to the official—is almost as well remembered today as is her sense of the moment in achieving her ends. She entertained by her very presence, without being threatening or unjust. Above all, she was extremely fortunate to be born among the Coast Salish, where rank and determination far outweigh gender in the course of life. Today, as in the past, both women and men routinely hold public responsibilities as equals.

Despite grinding poverty, repeated "abandonment issues" involving her family and friends, and sometimes dubious allies, Esther carried on. This was not often easy. She never learned to drive, so she had constantly to involve others just to get around. Usually, these drivers were her husbands, her son Frank, or her close friends, but urgent needs called for prompt response from whomever she could conscript.

Famous in her own day, Esther is still recalled with a broad smile throughout Indian Country, but she was not a traditional Indian steeped in tribal religion and its practice. Her own fundamentalist religious upbringing may have made her cautious of any religion, including the traditions of her own people. Perhaps her religion was more the passion she felt for her tribe and the knowledge that without federal recognition it might perish, as had so many tribes and Indian people before. To be a member of one of the smallest tribes in America, to fight the federal government's never-ending rejections of the Stillaguamish claims left little room for other pursuits or passions. While some might be puzzled that she never appeared at traditional tribal gatherings, in accounts of day-to-day Native struggles in the Northwest, her name was often foremost.

Throughout the Puget Sound area, a distinct tribal community occupied every river drainage, and those rivers are still known by names of the communities that occupied them for millennia. Skagit, Snohomish, Snoqualmi, Puyallup, Nisqually, and Stillaguamish persist as such river-tribal names.

Yet "Stillaguamish" itself stands out from these others because it alone derives from the generic Lushootseed word for "river" and, as such, implies that these people had a very strong orientation to the river. Such commitment to their river homeland would play an important role in the injustice suffered by the Stillaguamish over decades—an injustice that Esther would make right some one hundred and fifty years later. In 1855, the United States negotiated treaties with the tribes in what would become Washington State. The plan crafted by the federal government was to send the Indians to various reservations scattered along Puget Sound and along the Washington coast. Because Stillaguamish members had broad kinship ties, many could have moved to various reservations. Some did move. But more refused to leave their homes and the lifeways that they had known for generations. Working as loggers and fishers, applying for homesteads, and avoiding much of the outside world, these people remained where their ancestors were buried. Over the decades that followed the treaty signings, promises made to the Stillaguamish were ignored by the United States. Indeed, the federal government forgot that it had once recognized the Stillaguamish as a sovereign tribe when they negotiated the Indian treaties. Considered an unrecognized tribe, the Stillaguamish were left to fend for themselves. It was into this breach that Esther Ross strode.

Though it seems incongruous that a tribe known to be a signatory of the 1855 Treaty of Point Elliott should be forced to seek affirmation of its sovereign status a hundred years later, the Stillaguamish shared this fate with several other so-called landless tribes in western Washington simply because they chose to stay in their homelands. It must be remembered that the lack of federal recognition did not mean a tribe did not "exist." Rather, without federal recognition the ability of a tribe to implement the treaty promises and use its sovereignty in a modern age was rendered virtually impossible. Each tribe would follow the Stillaguamish to fight for their sovereign rights and for federal recognition in the latter part of the twentieth century. The success of these other tribes, as well as of the Stillaguamish, is in no small measure due to the efforts of Esther Ross, who, to the end of her life, continued to raise this issue on behalf of all landless tribes.

During the years when these landless tribes struggled to survive, they continued to gather together by season. In summer, there were and still are canoe races and "first food" feasts. In winter, there were and still are religious expressions of family and personal ties with immortal beings conducted in "smokehouses" derived from ancestral communal households.

The spark that would turn the tide for the Stillaguamish and provide the momentum for Esther's final victory and the recognition of her tribe was the unprecedented federal court decision affirming the treaty fishing rights of those tribes that had signed the treaties of 1854 and 1855. It was in that decision that Judge George Boldt affirmed the sovereign status of the Stillaguamish. And it was in that case that Esther and the Stillaguamish enlisted strong allies in the fight for sovereignty. From Seattle, a small band of Legal Services lawyers began working for a variety of local tribes, including the "Stilly." There were few lawyers and many tribes, so work hours were long and personnel spread thin. As described in this book, David Getches took the initiative to guide Stillaguamish efforts. Later, lawyer Alan Stay and others helped implement the decision and assisted in the last efforts toward recognition. But throughout this struggle it was not the lawyers who carried the day, rather it was the determination of the Stillaguamish people and, in particular, Esther Ross. What courage it took for the tribe, in 1976, to stand as a physical and spiritual barrier to the Bicentennial Wagon Train as it attempted to cross ancestral lands of the Stillaguamish people. This effort brought the injustices experienced by the Stillaguamish to a national audience. Like many of the people who had the good fortune to cross the path of Esther Ross, Alan Stay came to appreciate her fine sense of theater. Among her most effective strategies was never letting him know ahead of time what her next dramatic gesture would be. In consequence, he became as caught up in the moment as everyone else.

Since the 1970s era of "Red Power," several neighboring tribal communities have achieved federal recognition and tiny reservations for themselves. Much of their argument relied on evidence (in written documents acceptable to officious outsiders) of ongoing political leadership and cohesion. In a somewhat unique legal situation, the right of Natives to file for homesteads had enabled many to stay in their homelands, though not on prime waterfront real estate, and thereby establish court-compelling claims.

For some tribes, recognition only came twenty-five years after Esther Ross's triumph. The Stillaguamish preceded them all because they were led by this daunting figure—a one-woman dynamo of persistence and, in the long run, of success.

ALAN STAY

JAY MILLER

# Preface

Our initial awareness of Esther Ross came out of the research we did in writing our *Guide to Indian Tribes of the Pacific Northwest* (University of Oklahoma Press, 1986 and 1992). Our interest in examining her life story took root then, though our opportunity did not come until April 1993, when Esther's son, Frank Allen, proposed that we write his mother's biography. When we visited Allen's home on the Lummi Reservation, we found it filled with Esther's personal papers—a treasure trove of material, but in total disarray. He told us that the papers had been offered to the federal archives at the Sand Point Naval Station in Seattle, but had been rejected because of their unindexed state. Allen had then approached the Lutheran Church Board, an organization that frequently funded projects affecting Indians, but they declined the job of organizing and preparing the papers for deposit in the federal archives. The papers were also rejected when offered to the History Department of Western Washington University in Bellingham. That archive declined because it could not meet the requests of the family regarding certain conditions in storing the papers. In the end, Esther Ross's papers found a home at the Eastern Washington State Historical Society in Spokane, where they now reside.

But standing that day in 1993 in Frank Allen's home, we gave each other long quizzical looks, fully aware of the magnitude of the task. The primary documents and secondary sources filled five footlockers. Several large cardboard boxes contained newspapers and clippings. And there were many photographs. Once we began the work, we used all of these materials and rounded out Ross's story with nearly one hundred (mostly telephone) interviews with non-Stillaguamish Indians; local, county, and federal government personnel; church officials; officers of Indian organizations; various business owners; attorneys; and friends and family members. All those interviewed had vivid memories of Esther. The word most frequently used to describe her was "persistent," the second most frequently used, "tenacious."

During the fifty years Esther devoted to re-creating and bringing recognition to the tribe, she sacrificed her time and money with little support and no financial help from tribal members. However, many others offered their help in bringing her dream to reality. Monetary support came from the pockets of outside Indians, from government grants and assistance, and from churches. Sadly, the tribe itself was reluctant to provide input or assistance in her quest—or in our preparation of this story.

The role of women in American Indian history, similar to that of women in the larger American community, has only recently been fully recognized. As for Esther Ross's role in history, it provides an example of the frequent conflict between a woman's concern for her larger community and for her family. We find it difficult to judge her; in the end we can neither explain nor condemn her choices. The same holds true in judging the actions of people who are tribal members and some outside the tribe, the ones who would deny her the celebrity status that we believe she deserves. We leave judgment of Esther Ross to powers higher than ourselves.

Quotations from Esther's writings have been edited as necessary to avoid misreading, but her voice remains intact.

We thank Ursula Smith and professors Susan Armitage and William Lang for their wise and helpful consultation on this manuscript.

ROBERT H. RUBY,
*Moses Lake, Washington*
JOHN A. BROWN,
*Wenatchee, Washington*

# Esther Ross,
## Stillaguamish Champion

# ABBREVIATIONS AND ACRONYMS

| | |
|---|---|
| AIM | American Indian Movement |
| AIO | Americans for Indian Opportunity |
| ANA | Administration for Native Americans |
| APS | Adult Protective Services |
| ATNI | Affiliated Tribes of Northwest Indians |
| BAE | Bureau of American Ethnology |
| BIA | Bureau of Indian Affairs |
| CETA | Comprehensive Employment and Training Act |
| DSHS | Department of Social and Health Services |
| GIAC | Governor's Indian Advisory Committee |
| HEW | Department of Health, Education, and Welfare |
| HIP | Housing Improvement Program |
| HUD | Housing and Urban Development |
| ICAI | Intertribal Council of American Indians |
| ICWW | Inter-tribal Council of Western Washington Indians |
| IRA | Indian Reorganization Act of 1934 |
| NAIA | National American Indian Association |
| NARF | Native American Rights Fund |
| NCAI | National Congress of American Indians |
| NFAI | Northwestern Federation of American Indians |
| NILB | National Indian Lutheran Board |
| NTCA | National Tribal Chairmans Association |
| NWIFC | Northwest Indian Fisheries Commission |
| OEO | Office of Economic Opportunity |
| ONAP | Office of Native American Programs |
| SAIA | Survival of American Indians Association |
| STOWW | Small Tribes of Western Washington |
| VA | Veterans Administration |

CHAPTER ONE

# THE CALIFORNIA YEARS

On September 2, 1904, Angelina (Little Angel) and Christian Voreg Johnson welcomed a newborn girl into their Oakland home. In the hours after giving birth, Angelina turned her gaze from the child to the clear night sky. From its solitary bright star, she took the name for her baby girl—Morning Star. She had no way of knowing that the baby's celestial name would presage a most unusual and noteworthy life.[1]

The child would later bear the Native American name, Hussa-ud. Her Christian name, Esther Ruth, reflects her parents' faith. Although Angelina had been baptized a Roman Catholic, she and her husband were members of the Seventh-Day Adventist Church. In fact, Chris Johnson was a lay minister in the church.

As the infant grew, Angelina often took Esther to visit her family's two-story white frame house, called "The Homestead," near Hayward, California. Much of Angelina's past, however, lay to the north, near Stanwood, Washington, where she had been born in 1874, the fourth child of an Indian mother Betsey (or Betsy), who was herself the daughter of Chief Chaddus, an influential leader of the Stillaguamish Indians.[2] On November 25, 1877, Betsey married Angelina's father, Joao da Silveira, who was born in 1838 on the Vashon Grand Portugal Flores Island. When but nineteen years old, Silveira severed all ties with his family and hired on as a

Esther's mother, Angelina; the baby Esther; and father, Chris Johnson, at San Francisco's Cliff House, ca. 1904.

ship's deckhand, coming in 1860 to Stanwood (originally Centerville) in Washington Territory. He then worked in a mill at nearby Utsaladdy. Before long, his Norwegian neighbors had changed his name to Portuguese John, or John Silva. In 1882, when Angelina was eight, Betsey died and was buried east of Stanwood on a gently sloping knoll. Today an asphalt county road covers her grave. In 1892, John Silva moved to a Portuguese community near Hayward, California, with his second wife, Mary, a white woman, taking up residence in the house that Angelina would call home, even after her father's death in May of 1907.

Esther knew more of her mother's past than she did that of her father, Chris Johnson. She did know that he was born in Christiania, Norway, November 1, 1863, and, like many of his countrymen, was related to royalty. Esther was never close to her father, though she knew him to be a day laborer and an ardent church worker. At age nine, in January of 1914, she attended his funeral, where Adventist and Presbyterian ministers eulogized him as a

Left to right: John Silva's second wife, Mary; John Silva; and Esther's mother, Angelina (Silva's daughter). Silva emigrated from Portugal to the Stanwood, Washington, area in 1860, marrying the daughter of the Stillaguamish chief Chaddus.

"kind loving husband and father, a good neighbor and practical Christian." Looking at him in his casket, Esther could conjure few memories of this "kind loving . . . father," and in later life she rarely spoke of him.

As time went on, Esther and her mother visited the Hayward home ever less frequently. Instead, they more often traveled north to visit relatives in Washington State. Somehow the death of Esther's father had freed Angelina to return to her Indian roots. She shared with her daughter stories of the noble Stillaguamish, of the white men who had come to the Stillaguamish Valley, burning the Natives' houses and driving them from their lands not only by fire, but also with threats, lies, and whiskey. Angelina told Esther how the Stillaguamish had gravitated to white settlements in nearby towns such as Silvana (named for John Silva), Florence, Trafton, and Arlington. Far removed from aboriginal times, the remaining Stillaguamish now lived like Angelina and Esther in a **modern world.**

Esther and her mother, Angelina, when living in California.

Finding it difficult to raise Esther on her dressmaker's income, Angelina accepted a proposal of marriage from Oscar George Reid, a large, handsome man, a native of Canada who had immigrated to the United States in 1890. Angelina and Reid were married in September of 1915, and Esther immediately bonded with her stepfather, describing his demeanor as "touching." She loved him deeply, more so than she had ever loved her own father, and she often used his name on official documents.[3]

As a child, Esther was inquisitive and intelligent. In 1921, after graduating from an Oakland high school, she attended a private school for the next year and a half, training to become a schoolteacher. During this time she also did secretarial work for a Bay Area newspaper. In a short autobiography written years later, she summarized her school and work experience during her California years: "I attended grade ... schools," she wrote, "high schools,

Angelina and her second husband, Oscar Reid, on their wedding day, September 3, 1915. Esther was very fond of Reid, often using his last name as hers. He disappeared one day, never to return. In a fifty-year-long search, Esther made it one of her missions to learn about him and his life after he had deserted her family.

church schools, business college—and took [a nursing] course. When ready to graduate, . . . I [found I] could not stand blood. I left [and became a] newspaper reporter. I helped my mother in her dressmaking shop. . . . We ran hotel apts in 1925, [but the next year I] gave up my career to come to Wash[ington] with my mother because the relatives wanted me to help them in their Indian affairs."[4]

In high school, Esther had experienced the cruelty of racial bigotry. Before her Indian heritage was known, she was treated as one of the crowd, but once it was known, she was teased unmercifully. Her self-esteem was crushed. Pondering what it meant to be Indian, she was further deflated to learn that there was no Stillaguamish tribe as such. Her grandmother's people had ceased to exist. There seemed no one to turn to, no one to answer her questions.

Esther, a teenager, poses in Oakland, California, with her mother, a seamstress and clothes designer. A large bow accents Esther's hair, which was worn long all her life, never being cut. Note Esther's high-buttoned shoes.

Esther's next disappointment would turn her world upside down. Her stepfather suddenly deserted her and her mother. As a salesman, Oscar Reid was frequently out on the road. In September 1922, suffering a recurrence of carbuncles on the back of his neck, he was laid up for nearly three weeks in Eureka, California. On September 15 he wired Angelina twenty dollars by telegram and wrote her that he was scheduled to enter the county hospital the next day for surgery on his neck. He advised her that he expected to return to work within a few days and would send her more money at that time.

That was the last communication Angelina ever had from Reid. As time passed and her attempts to locate him proved futile, she began to fear that he had suffered a fatal accident. She wrote Oscar Swanson, coroner and public administrator of Humboldt County in Eureka, California, asking if there was any record of Reid's death. Swanson replied that he had no such record. Angelina then wrote the sheriff of Humboldt County, A. A. Ross, who replied that Oscar Reid had entered the county hospital for treatment of a carbuncle but had left no forwarding address when he departed. Returning the photos Angelina had sent, the sheriff told her that Reid had reportedly left the county. Still unsatisfied, Angelina checked with the California State Division of Motor Vehicles, which responded that Reid had not yet transferred ownership of his Ford to another person.[5] For years to come, Esther would be all but obsessed by the search for her missing stepfather and uncovering the reason for his abandonment of her and her mother.

At this time, Esther was working as a bookkeeper. Somehow she met and began dating Fletcher Valentine Carlton, a charming young man with a measure of Cherokee blood. He was a streetcar conductor, and he spent money generously on Esther. She was not so much intrigued with Carlton as with the train passes he could provide for travel to any destination. In turn, he was fascinated by her beauty. In time, Esther became pregnant. The birth certificate of the child who was delivered on April 22, 1925, carried the notation: "Mother refuses to reveal name of father of their child." Esther named the baby Margaret Ruth and gave her her own surname, Johnson.

Though he had not fathered her child, Carlton continued to pursue Esther. Angelina tried to discourage the relationship, but Carlton was persuasive. He promised Esther a free excursion ticket to Washington but only if she was his wife. Esther capitulated, and they were married on February 5, 1926, in San Francisco.[6]

In the meantime, Angelina was dealing with serious family matters. When her stepmother, Mary Silva, died December 22, 1922, Angelina expected to receive her father's property.[7] Her halfbrother was dead as were her two full brothers and a sister in Washington State. This left Angelina with two siblings, both of them adopted as children by Mary and John Silva—Frank in Washington State and Lulu, a homeless girl the couple had taken in. Lulu still lived on the Hayward homestead. Since, at the time of her stepmother's death, Angelina was settled in with Oscar Reid in their suburban Elmhurst-Oakland home, she had no immediate plans to move into the Hayward house and therefore had let Lulu live in it until the Silva estate was probated in 1925. It was then that Lulu produced a document willing the property to herself. After inquiring, Angelina concluded that Lulu had forged the signature on Mary's will. Esther agreed, recalling a family story frequently told that now took on new meaning. When John Silva was lying in his casket at the funeral home in 1907, Mary had reportedly drawn her hand across his forehead in a loving gesture. With that, a few hairs of his head had come loose and a faint streak of what Mary thought was blood had appeared under the skin where her hand had passed. It made Mary believe that her husband had been poisoned. Only now, in recalling that story, did Angelina and Esther think that Lulu may have poisoned Silva.

Seeking to prove her case, Angelina secured a number of affidavits from those who knew the family well enough to declare that Silva had intended the property to go to her instead of Lulu. Angelina also sought out a Dora Peterson, who had witnessed the signing of the deed giving Angelina the property.[8]

These developments, in addition to Angelina's desire for tribal identity, reinforced her resolve to move north. When some Stillaguamish and other Indians of the Puget Sound area submitted a claim to Congress for loss of lands and other natural resources, Angelina joined the suit. They contended that a recalcitrant Amer-

Fletcher Valentine Carlton, Esther's first husband, moved to the Arlington, Washington, area soon after Esther moved north from California with her mother in 1926. He is holding Margaret Ruth, Esther's first child, born April 22, 1925.

ican government had failed to fulfill its obligations under the Treaty of Point Elliott of 1855. Although for a time Esther was mildly interested in the claims issue, she learned of it only through her mother's contact with a Washington State attorney working for tribes of the Medicine Creek treaty (December 26, 1854), the Point Elliott treaty (January 22, 1855), and Point No Point Treaty (January 26, 1855)—and for five nontreaty tribes.[9]

Angelina urged Esther to move north with her. Though Esther was still deeply involved in trying to find her stepfather, she decided to join her mother in Washington. Weary and emotionally drained from her legal battles with Lulu, Angelina moved in with relatives in Stanwood. Esther took baby Ruth to Seattle, where she was soon joined by Carlton. However, it would not be long before Esther would leave Carlton and, taking Ruth, follow her mother to Stanwood.[10] There, Angelina's attorney wrote her from Oakland that he hoped she got enough from the expected court battle over the Hayward property that she would "not have to suffer or go hungry or have to depend upon charity from uncharitable people such as you did in this city."

Esther's transition from California to Washington would have been more difficult if her people, the Stillaguamish, had not already been largely acculturated and assimilated within the white community. Discovering that the tribe lacked an identity, just as she herself did, Esther set out to uncover her identity—and with it her Indian heritage before it faded from everyone's memory.[11]

CHAPTER TWO

# STILLAGUAMISH:
# THE LAND AND THE PEOPLE

Once settled in the Pacific Northwest, Esther was among relatives who descended from the Stillaguamish tribe and from neighboring tribes of the Coast Salish linguistic family. The Stillaguamish were tied to the river. The tribe's name comes from the Indian term, "Stoh-luk," meaning "river," and its suffix, "whampsh," meaning "people" or "tribe"—thus, "river people."[1]

It was Angelina's earlier interest in the Stillaguamish lawsuit that first attracted Esther to this scattered tribe. Attorney Arthur E. Griffin of Seattle prepared to file suit for claims of several tribes against the federal government, labeling it *Duwamish et al.* for one of the Point Elliott tribes.[2] These tribes were suing for losses that resulted from the Point Elliott treaty. A successful suit required a group effort. Esther's education and work experience made her an ideal choice to fill the nonsalaried position of secretary for the Stillaguamish.

When asked to organize a scattered people in order that they might fully participate in *Duwamish et al.*, Esther set out to make the Stillaguamish once again a viable tribe. To do that, she concluded that she not only had to assume the role of prodder but also of learner. She gleaned information from reading and from interviewing the few remaining Stillaguamish elderly. She began

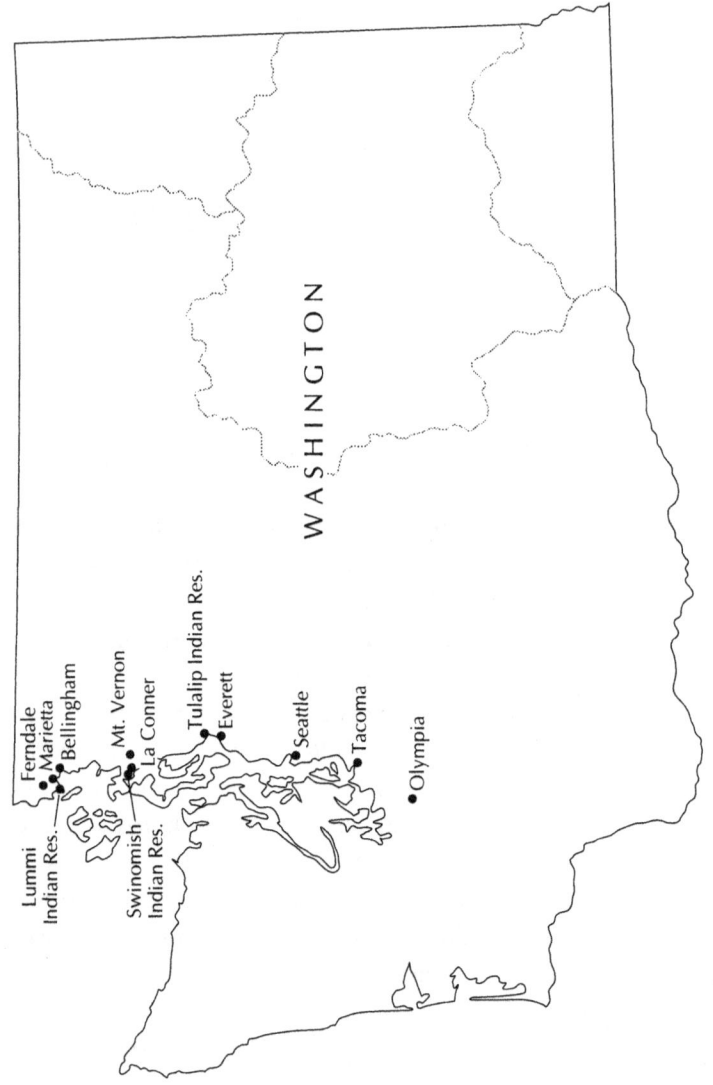

Important places (exclusive of Stillaguamish lands) with which Esther Ross was associated

to piece together a most interesting history. The Point Elliott treaty council, which had brought together tribes in the Puget Sound area to negotiate with Isaac I. Stevens, Washington territorial governor and superintendent of Indian affairs, was held near present-day Mukilteo, Washington, which natives called *Mew-kil-too*, or "good camping place."[3]

Just prior to the council, Clallam Indians from the west and combative Indians from coastal British Columbia to the north had raided Puget Sound, capturing women and children and killing their men, including Angelina's maternal grandfather, Chief Chaddus (Man of Peaceful Living) of Stillaguamish-Snoqualmie-Skagit ancestry.[4] With Chaddus's death, his people had gathered around Chief Patkanin, the influential leader of the neighboring Snoqualmie. Patkanin thus became the spokesman of the Stillaguamish, and he signed the Point Elliott treaty in their name. At the time, he led an estimated 556 of his own Snoqualmie-Snohomish and an estimated 200 to 400 Stillaguamish, many of whom had intermingled with other tribes. In a short history of her people written years later, Esther noted that through Patkanin they had "all branch[ed] down" and were now "all related."[5]

Patkanin's role in the council was not unusual since weaker, smaller groups often depended on powerful regional leaders to speak and act on their behalf when the government demanded that single chieftains represent all local Indians. Esther listened to the stories the few remaining elderly tribespeople had to tell about the Point Elliott treaty council. Susan Dorsey, wife of the self-appointed Stillaguamish chief, James "Jimmy" Dorsey, told Esther that she remembered as a thirteen-year-old Governor Stevens offering money to the assembled tribesmen in exchange for their "X" on the treaty. She remembered how, when the men failed to remove their caps at his command, Stevens passed among them and removed their hats, trying to encourage them to wave them and shout, "Hip, hip, hurrah," in imitation of the way white men celebrated such occasions. But the tribesmen knew they had little to cheer about at that council.[6]

Another elderly woman told Esther that Stevens had promised that "As long as the sun rises in the East and sets in the West, as long as the grass grows green in the spring, as long as the river flows to the sea, we will give you a bushel of gold every new moon." She also remembered that the Stillaguamish and Snohomish Indians were each promised reservations along their respective rivers.

Primarily for convenience and political control, the government lumped bands of the Stillaguamish together as a tribe, even though traditionally they had been autonomous village societies. But assigning Indians to reservations under one leader by strokes of a pen did not transform them into cohesive tribes. The tribal designation was accurate only when referring to villages of cultural similarity or when these groups coalesced during periods of crisis such as wars and natural disasters or singular events such as the signing of treaties.[7] Now Esther learned that it had been government practice to put treaty Indians on reserves bearing their tribal names. When multiple tribes were placed on a single reservation, it was named for one of the confederated tribes. Two of the four reservations established under the Point Elliott treaty by the government—the Fort Kitsap (later called Suquamish and Port Madison) and the Tulalip—were exceptions to the general rule. The other two reservations—the Lummi and Swinomish—carried the names of the principal treaty tribes. Esther's Stillaguamish had been assigned to the Tulalip, a name derived from the Indian word meaning "almost landlocked," on Tulalip Bay west of Marysville, Washington.[8]

Native groups included in the Point Elliott treaty were not removed to their reservations until its ratification by Congress. During this hiatus, confrontations between incoming whites and Indians erupted in conflict the winter of 1855–56. In the face of this conflict, temporary reservations were hurriedly set aside to separate peaceful Indians from the "hostiles." To keep peaceful Indians out of harm's way, those north of the Stillaguamish were moved to one temporary reservation, while those to the south were sent

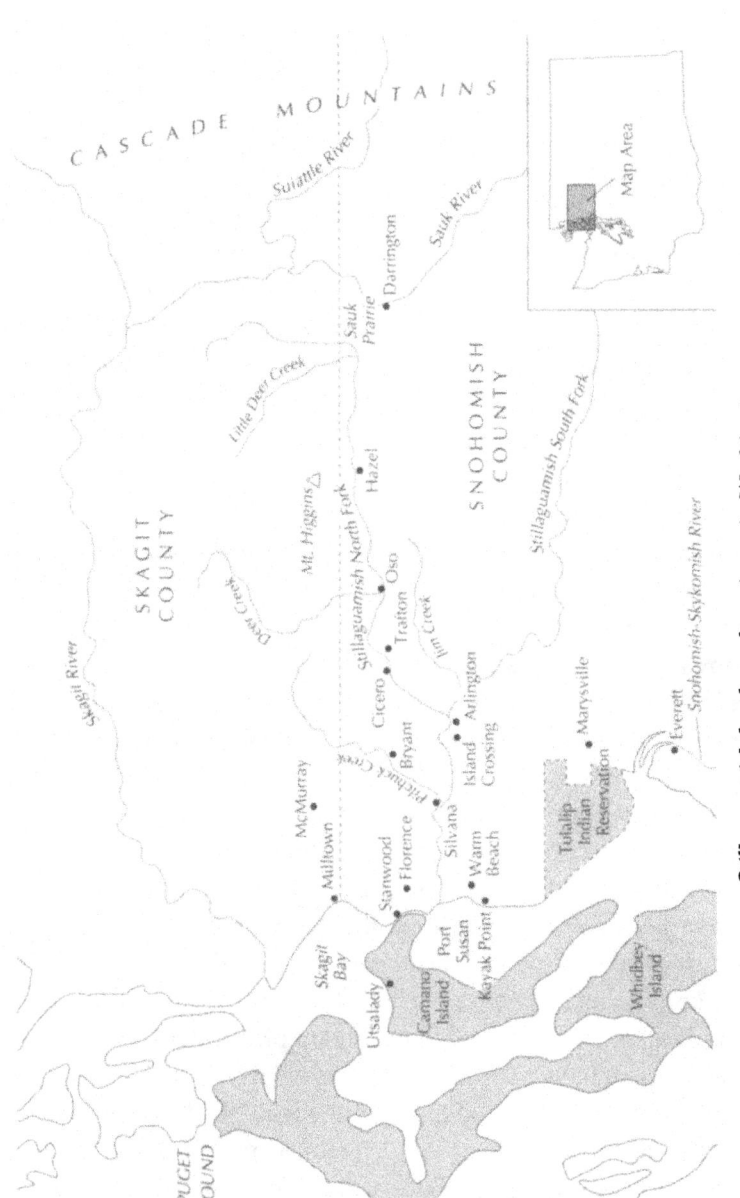

Stillaguamish lands and environs in Washington

to another. But, most likely because of their small numbers and relative isolation, the peaceful Stillaguamish escaped confinement on either of these temporary reserves.[9]

When it came time to remove Indians to permanent reservations, the Washington Superintendency of Indian Affairs took charge. Its task was difficult since no Indian group moved voluntarily. The Stillaguamish were especially adamant about staying put, as were the neighboring Snohomish, Upper Skagits, Sauk-Suiattles, and Skykomish. The few Stillaguamish who did move to the Tulalip were only too glad to return home later. They were homesick, and they feared commingling with Indians on the Tulalip since many of these reservation people were dying of diseases contracted from whites. The Stillaguamish simply wanted to avoid reservation confinement and dependence on the meager government rations. They were unfamiliar with the intensive agricultural methods used by whites in the Puyallup region; they relied instead on the cultivation of their small potato patches along the Stillaguamish River. To this day, tribal members maintain that during the conflict of 1855–56, the government promised that a separate permanent reservation would be set aside for them at the end of hostilities.[10]

As a student of Stillaguamish history, Esther learned that the base of the Pacific Northwest's coastal and riverine cultures began along waterways that penetrated the deep forests. Canoes crafted from large cedar trees provided the main transportation. They were shaped by lithic tools such as stone axes and mauls as well as animal bones and were hardened by fire. Although cultural developments are not shaped purely by physical features, their importance in Stillaguamish life cannot be overlooked. An example of this is landforms linking the tribe with neighboring Sauks, Suiattles, and Upper Skagits. Upstream, a stem of the Stillaguamish River joins its South Fork and North Fork branches near Arlington, where permanent villages of cedar slabs and planks stood. In its easterly reaches the North Fork extends to the Darrington, Washington, area, which is near the Suiattle, a tributary

Stillaguamish Indians in a dugout canoe on their namesake river.

of the Sauk. The Sauk flows into the Skagit, which flows into Puget Sound. Sauk Prairie forms a three-mile portage between the Stillaguamish and Sauk Rivers, and there the Stillaguamish, Sauks, and Suiattles gathered to socialize and share goods.

The South Fork reaches into the Cascade Mountains, and some of the villagers on this stretch identified more with Snohomish, whose major villages were along the Snohomish River, which flows into Puget Sound near Everett. Stillaguamish had their own access to higher elevations along the western slopes of the Cascade mountains in Sauk-Suiattle territory, where the men hunted bear, goats, and deer. Nonetheless, the Stillaguamish relied on salmon as a primary protein source. Occasionally they met Interior Salish speakers such as the Methows, the Wenatchees, and the Sahaptin-speaking Klickitats traveling west through the Cascade Mountain passes to trade. The lower Stillaguamish River was dotted with villages; some were large and permanent, while others up the river forks were small and temporary. At the mouth of the Stillaguamish was a permanent village of culturally unrelated Indians, the Quadsak (Kikialluses). Stillaguamish women harvested berries, bulbs to roast, and grasses and the inner lining of bark on evergreens to make clothing, mats, and baskets. Tribeswomen also harvested, prepared, and preserved food. Men sculpted canoes, pried planks from tree trunks to erect housing, and fished the waters.[11]

Commingling of riverine groups produced exogamous relationships. Women in these relationships commonly moved to the villages of their husbands, taking on the identity of their husbands' people to further mix bloodlines along the Stillaguamish and its branches. Offspring of these marriages also identified with their adopted people. These contacts developed socioeconomic ties, serving to facilitate peaceful relations among the various groups.

Near the beginning of Stillaguamish-white contact, Roman Catholic priests, called Blackrobes, visited. In 1850 the traveler-explorer Samuel Hancock, who was searching for coal deposits, visited the Stillaguamish. He found one village making the sign of the cross, evidence of previous Christian contact. At present-day Arlington he met a gathering of what he presumed to be Stillaguamish numbering some three hundred. He found some villagers along the route were wary of his visit.[12]

Scandinavian and Portuguese men, some of whom had jumped ship, were among the first non-Indians to settle in the area in the early 1860s. White settlements in the Stanwood area expanded as plots were cleared and crops planted. Settlers gradually moved farther east in the valley, harassing and intimidating Indians, pushing them from their own small plots and villages. In addition, they infected them with diseases, raising the Indian mortality rate.[13]

The elders told Esther of their many losses. Salmon catches diminished; garden patches were appropriated, forcing the Stillaguamish to beg or borrow food or perform menial tasks for white farmers for little pay. Stillaguamish males who didn't marry white women were shunned from white communities, while Stillaguamish women married to white men lived among them with their children. Their nonreservation offspring usually married whites, which gave them more employment opportunities and ownership of homesteaded farms. Some Stillaguamish were fortunate to succeed in proving up on their lands, but other, for one reason or another, lost their homesteads.

Their lands often were taken through the trade in liquor, which gave them brief euphoric respites but stripped them of their assets. Most puzzling to the dispossessed was how treaty papers could drive them from their ancestral homes. Stories of this dispossession are legion. According to one, an Indian lost his land by selling fence posts to a settler. Dependent on the sale of these posts to survive, the Indian did not realize that the settler was using these posts to enclose the Indian's property. By the time the sale was complete, the property was entirely enclosed, leaving no possible way for the Indian to reclaim it.[14] Scrounging for subsistence, the Stillaguamish slashed and cleared brush and weeded crops for white farmers on the very lands their ancestors had occupied for generations.

Stillaguamish also resented the whites' irreverent disposal of the tribe's dead. It was Stillaguamish custom to bury their dead suspended in trees or along riverbanks or to inter them in the ground. White families in the valley, however, objected to the sight of corpses and preemptorily removed and/or reburied the bodies. Esther began bending every effort to search out, mark, and secure Indian burial sites. It was too late for her to find the grave of her grandmother Betsey, but she did locate the headstones of some Indians who had intermarried with whites. Even some of these had been thrown into the Stillaguamish River after farmers removed them from their fields as they would large rocks.

Gardner Goodridge, one of a group of seven said to have been the first settlers in the Stanwood area, reportedly gave the Indians three days' notice to remove their dead "suspended in boughs of trees along the river bank."[15] After his threat to pile and burn the bodies if they weren't removed from his land, many Indians placed them in crude wooden boxes large enough to hold several bodies. Some of these were interred; others were burned.

The Stillaguamish tribal population understandably declined in the posttreaty years. Of the early inhabitants on the Stillaguamish River, by 1919 only twenty-nine remained, according to a census of nonreservation Indians by the Bureau of Indian Affairs.[16] Drastic changes occurred not only in population, but in the landscape now dotted with towns, farms, and schools. There were also changes in place-names. Glendale became Trafton, and several other towns such as Allen and Haller City merged into Arlington. In 1892 what had been Stillaguamish became Silvana. Named for Esther's grandfather John Silva, but derived from the word "sylvan," or "forested," Silvana stands today among the open farmlands the Stillaguamish Valley came to harbor.

CHAPTER THREE

# THE STILLAGUAMISH: A TRIBE REBORN

On July 1, 1926, Esther called the first Stillaguamish meeting to order at the Arlington city hall. Twenty-five people formed the embryonic Stillaguamish organization. They elected Jimmy Dorsey president, and Esther's uncle, Frank Silva, vice president. Dorsey, born in 1850, the son of the Stillaguamish chief, Que Que Kadam, had assumed the position of Stillaguamish "chief" in the late 1880s and was well known in the white community.[1] Initially elected secretary, William Robb was later demoted to "assistant secretary" since Esther performed the duties of the office in de facto fashion.

The election over, Esther introduced letters from Arthur Griffin, the attorney who had filed *Duwamish et al.*, who now cited the need to press claims against the government for land losses. Dorsey spoke in the Stillaguamish language to urge several of the elders in attendance to officially enroll as members of the tribe. S. J. Kavanaugh, president of the Northwestern Federation of American Indians, was present at the meeting to advise the group in the procedure for filing claims.[2]

At this initial meeting, the attendees passed a resolution stating that the list of enrollees be recognized as the membership "of the Stillaguamish Tribe of Indians." Then Esther closed the short meeting with the song, "God Be with You Till We Meet Again." She wasted no time sending a press release to newspapers: "This is your last chance to enroll for Compensation from the government of the U.S. You are now being notified to send in your name and addresses at once so we will know where you are. Also state whether you are Full, Quarter, Half, Eighth [Stillaguamish]."[3]

Meetings thereafter were held mostly in the Arlington city hall, but sometimes in homes of various tribal members, including that of Esther's cousin John Silva, Frank Silva's adopted son. The group's second meeting was called on July 13. Esther's minutes note that the group was called to order by "Mrs. Carlton Secty, as the Presidents were not ready to act." Again S. J. Kavanaugh was on hand. "He was glad to see our officers were elected," Esther wrote, "but we could see the results ... were not the right Kind ... [for the officers] were not prepared for the work. If they were, the Secty would not have to do all the work of starting the Meeting, etc. We should see the necessity of good officers and ... we younger ones should Co operate with these older ones, helping them if they do not understand and can not read or write."

Kavanaugh addressed the meeting: "You are going to court against the Government, you understand. You must have men at your head who can meet the Public able to speak for you who are well educated." Kavanaugh warned them that the government men would come from Washington, D.C., and they would, in Esther's words, "come around to the Stillaguamish Tribe. They will ask who are they, where do they live. What about their land. ... We should be organized in this, as where there is union there is strength. All the tribes should belong to this organization—and back it up as [it will help us] meet the government."

Among guests at the meeting were John Lyons, a leader among a neighboring Kikiallus Indian group, and Ed Percival, a Snoqualmie who interpreted the proceedings for the elderly. Esther concluded this meeting by singing "Old Flag Forever."[4]

A week later, at yet another meeting, Jimmy Dorsey, as president and as the "oldest and best informed member of the tribe," spoke about the tribal past. The thrust of the meeting was not solely to learn about the past but also to plan for the tribe's role in the claim against the government. Attorney Griffin kept the tribe informed of the progress of *Duwamish et al.* By now, sixty-six people had enrolled in the tribe, brought aboard by Esther's publicity and by the hope of receiving claims moneys.[5]

That month the U.S. government deposed Dorsey for the forthcoming suit. Adhering to protocol, Griffin sent his communications regarding the suit to Dorsey as tribal president, but it was Esther who read and interpreted for the group the legal wording of the attorney's letters. By August he was requesting final comments and suggestions prior to filing the petition in *Duwamish et al.* in the U.S. Court of Claims. The petition requested payment of $9,926,800 in Stillaguamish claims, a figure based on value of lands lost under the terms of the Point Elliott treaty. The petition also cited government failure to provide the treaty's specified annual appropriations which hadn't been paid to Stillaguamish for twenty-five years. These appropriations would have provided goods and services such as carpenters, physicians, teachers, and specialists to aid Indians in clearing their lands and building houses. The majority of the enrolled Stillaguamish undoubtedly envisioned dividing and pocketing the claims award, moneys originally intended for their ancestors. But Esther had a different purpose in pressing the suit. She needed confirmation of her Indian heritage through official recognition of the Stillaguamish tribe.[6] What formerly was cruel prejudice against her now became the basis of great pride. "I am Stillaguamish," she would one day proclaim to Roy Sampsel of the Department of the Interior.[7]

CHAPTER FOUR

# DUALITY: TRIBAL AND DOMESTIC AFFAIRS

With seemingly boundless energy, Esther kept on the go, whether afoot or on wheels, to protect and strengthen her tribal organization. This dedication to her tribe would evermore involve her in the tension of juggling work and family. Never having learned to drive, she inveigled others to chauffeur her around on her missions. Sometimes these journeys proved dangerous—such as the day Jimmy Dorsey drove her to Sultan, Washington, to attend a funeral and to discuss tribal history as they went. Angelina and two others were along on the trip. Losing power and rolling backwards downhill, Dorsey's Ford hit soft dirt on the shoulder, overturned, and came to rest on a log. No one was critically injured, though Esther would attribute frequent future stomach problems to the accident.

She continued to facilitate tribal business by introducing committees, drafting bylaws, drawing up orders of business, and recording the minutes. The bound journal of minutes of tribal meetings was visible evidence of her secretarial expertise. The journal held not only minutes, but also notes from interviews with the elders and letters from attorney Arthur Griffin.[1]

All the while, Esther continued to garner Indian enrollees, recording names on a phonetic basis. In her haste she had little time or inclination to learn the native language. But, like her, most Stillaguamish had little need of it, for almost all tribal members could speak English. Esther was a diligent researcher, tracking down information about candidates for inclusion in the tribe. Her work took her from reservations such as the Tulalip and Swinomish to county courthouses, seeking marriage and birth certificates, and to libraries where she researched local history, especially property ownerships. She also discovered an assessor's reservation map on which she marked lands the Stillaguamish had claimed. Her travel was tiring, and ironically, she had little help from her fellow tribal members who refused her any financial support.

As the July 4, 1930, celebration in Arlington neared, Esther was invited to lead her Indians in the event. At a June 3 meeting she set aside the regular agenda in order to plan their part in the day. Esther was only too happy to have her people join in the civic celebration since she believed it could serve as a forum to express the tribal goals and grievances. Shortly before the Fourth, the *Arlington Times* carried a large photo of "Princess Esther" in full native regalia, shooting a bow and arrow. Accompanying the picture were statements that under Esther's influence, tribal members were being reunited in the spirit of ancient traditions, emblems, dress, songs, and legends. These remarks also pertained to a pre-Fourth "booster" tour that paraded through surrounding towns advertising the event.[2]

Tribal neighbors such as Snoqualmie Chief Kannan, who usually attended the Stillaguamish meetings, joined Esther aboard the float in the Arlington parade. On the float Kannan staged a "war dance" with much flourishing of knives. Johnny Sam of the Sauk tribe also performed traditional dances. The float was a potpourri of Indian culture, including songs, dances, and even a "treaty cake." Postparade spectators gathered to hear a speech from attorney Arthur Griffin, who spoke to the crowd about Stillaguamish claims. Rather than being threatened, the Arlington business community welcomed the newfound Indian pride, for their claims moneys boded well for the local economy. As for Esther's role, she used the occasion to enroll members in the tribe, to plea for retaining its officers, and to publicize her quest for claims moneys. In everything she did, she carried out the theme expressed in one of the Indian banners: "Make the [American] Eagle Scream" with national pride.³

Two years later, Esther was still in control of tribal deliberations. For a meeting in March of 1932, her minutes note that "Our secretary does most of the talking for this tribe at meetings no matter how many offices it had." The other officers of record were still Jimmy Dorsey, president, and Frank Silva, vice president and treasurer. Esther, naturally, still held the office of secretary, assisted by William Robb. Wesley Patrick and Edward Goodridge were now serving as "businessmen" (later to be called councilmen). Ed Percival was the interpreter. That year, still without a constitution, tribal members decided that all officers would retain their positions for life or until they resigned.⁴

While awaiting word from Washington, D.C., regarding the decision by the court of claims in the *Duwamish* case, Esther spent time locating people of Indian blood—and attending tribal meetings. In addition to claims, meeting topics included fishing and hunting rights and the need of government provisions and services, such as schools and hospitals. She was made fully aware of the mill-grinding slowness of the bureaucratic government, when Griffin reported back to the Stillaguamish on his October 11, 1933, appearance before the court of claims. With only one hour to testify on behalf of the tribes, he came away disappointed that a decision would not be rendered "for a long time." By this time, Griffin's comments were no longer addressed to Dorsey, as had been his custom when reporting to the tribe, but directly to Esther who conveyed them to her people at regularly scheduled meetings.⁵

On June 4, 1934, the court of claims finally rendered a decision in *Duwamish et al.* It was negative.⁶ Eight months later, on February 4, 1935, a motion to set aside that decision would be denied. Griffin notified the tribe of the denial and advised them that all tribes involved in the suit should get together to appeal the case before the U.S. Supreme Court. He still hoped to reverse the decision. The necessary writ of certiorari, he said, would cost each tribal member a half-dollar.[7] A month later, Griffin urged Esther to forward immediately thirty dollars, the Stillaguamish share for filing the writ.[8] That same day, March 29, 1935, *Duwamish et al.* was docketed in the U.S. Supreme Court as No. 822.

In her juggling of tribal and family matters, Esther occasionally worked at temporary jobs. In 1928, for example, she and three-year-old Ruth moved from Seattle to Portland. A need for income, rather than a lack of interest in tribal affairs, forced that move. In Portland Esther worked part-time as a saleswoman in Lipman Wolfe and Company and in the offices of a surgeon, Joseph F. Wood, M. D. But Esther missed Angelina, and she and Ruth returned to Seattle in January 1929, when Esther was four months pregnant. She gave birth May 29 to another daughter, Marion Lavina. Ever since her move north in 1926, Esther was increasingly estranged from Carlton, and the baby's birth did nothing to repair the marriage. In 1930 the couple separated for good.

Not long thereafter, Esther met Walter Frederick Allen, a logger and fisherman whose father was of mixed Indian blood. Walter's family roots lay in the Arlington community, on upper Jim Creek, a tributary of the South Fork of the Stillaguamish. Walter was gone up to three weeks at a time, working in various logging camps, but he faithfully handed over his paycheck every payday, and Angelina approved of the relationship.

Esther visited Walter in the logging camps on the weekends he could not come home. On March 21, 1931, she bore him a son—Frank Ellsworth.[9] With Walter away at work, she was now caring for three small children. Then it was back to work again in a nontribal role as a cleaning lady in hospitals and homes. One such job took her into nearby Everett to the home of Peter Jackson, a building contractor, and his wife, Marie, the parents of Henry Jackson, who, first as a representative and later a senator, would become politically important to Esther's cause.

Esther still had to handle her ties with Fletcher Carlton. She sought an apportioned payment of his veteran's compensation,

Walter Allen, Esther's second husband, with Cap at the Allen family homestead on upper Jim Creek in Snohomish County.

owed him for a minor disability. She sought the compensation not only for herself but also for daughters Ruth and Marion. In January of 1931 the Veterans Administration had threatened to discontinue payments unless Esther answered its inquiries and furnished more detailed information about her family. In 1932 Esther was in court with attorney Arthur Griffin over her separation from Carlton. She testified truthfully and soon heard from R. L. Popwell of the Seattle VA office that "information has been received in this office to the effect that in a hearing in court in Everett, Washington . . . you admitted the above-named veteran Fletcher V. Carlton is not the father of Margret Ruth Carlton." Esther was requested to inform the VA at her earliest convenience if that was so.[10] At the time, although not legally divorced, Esther had no qualms about collecting monthly support for Frank, who was registered on his birth certificate as Frank Ellsworth Carlton. And she dragged her feet in responding to more questions when, following a nationwide review of VA benefits for the disabled, the Seattle office notified her in June 1933 that it appeared Carlton would no longer be eligible for benefits. However, after a final review it was determined that in accordance with updated public laws, Carlton would be entitled to "less than $18.00 for himself." The same notice advised Esther that "on the account of yourself and three minor children," the amount of $9.75 monthly would be discontinued. In a later revision of Carlton's veteran's benefits, beginning June 1, 1944, Esther would receive an apportioned share of $4.48 for Marion, his only biological and legal heir, until December 14, 1945, when benefits would be increased to $17.25 monthly until she turned eighteen in 1947.[11]

An interloculatory divorce decree for Esther and Carlton was issued April 17, 1933. On April 27, 1934, the final divorce decree was granted in King County, Washington. With the dissolution of the marriage, Esther wanted to change Frank's last name to Allen. As it turned out, he would never obtain a corrected birth certificate, but he did use the name Allen on documents when entering school and when obtaining a Social Security card.

Even after the divorce Esther remained bitter, claiming Carlton had said he would pay for the divorce when, in fact, he failed to do so.[12] She raised fears in her children by telling them that Carlton would kidnap them and carry them off. Indeed, the children had little contact with him. Ruth only vaguely remembered him and Marion claimed never to have seen him until she had a child of her own.[13]

Through all of this—and likely because of it—Esther's health was deteriorating. She had stomach problems, which caused her to be careful in her choice of foods. She found some relief in eating soft foods. Although she joined others at mealtimes, she became a culinary isolationist. She blamed her stomach ailment on the earlier car accident; a doctor diagnosed it as gallbladder trouble. She also had problems with her teeth. They became infected and required surgery. The infection also affected her auditory nerves. Stress and continuing health problems combined to send her to the hospital twice in 1934.

On August 23, 1935, Walter Allen and Esther Carlton were married in Bellingham's First Presbyterian Church. On returning to her family, Esther intermittently tramped and hitchhiked between East Stanwood and the Allen homestead on Jim Creek to check on her sister-in-law Agnes Allen, debilitated by diabetes, cancer, and near-blindness. Carrying Frank in a backpack until he was old enough to walk, she left the girls with Angelina and other relatives near Stanwood. She was inured to traveling afoot since she had done so much of it when interviewing Indians.[14] That all changed after an injury one day when Walter was driving through the Everett streets in his five-ton White truck. White trucks were open at the sides of the cab except for small half-doors. The half-door on the passenger side flew open as Walter turned a corner. Esther spilled to the street on her head. The accident left her with intermittent headaches and back pain the rest of her life.

Because Esther so frequently left her children in the care of others—or sometimes alone—she was reported to state officials for child abuse and neglect. The state sent, in Frank's words, some "old ladies" to the house to take him and his siblings away. They succeeded in taking Ruth and Frank, but not Marion. A very determined little girl, she kept crawling under the bed from one side to the other while the women tried to run her down and drag her out. Years later, Frank remembered being taken to a place and put in a darkened room with a bed and many toys. Shortly thereafter, Esther retrieved the children with help from Seventh-Day Adventists who intervened for her whenever she sought their help.[15]

CHAPTER FIVE

# THE NOMADIC YEARS

Motoring south in 1939 in search of work, the Allen family stopped in Oregon, where the children labored in the strawberry fields and harvested other crops. Esther worked sporadically at this time, and the family moved from one place to another in second-hand cars and pickup trucks that held the few worldly goods they had. Soon it was on to California where Esther sought to confront Lulu Silva over her ownership of the family homestead and to continue the search for her missing stepfather, Oscar Reid.

Their first stop was the Hayward homestead. Lulu was prepared for the visit and had notified the sheriff, who was there to escort the Allen family to the police station. Meeting defeat in that respect, and finding no clues to Reid's whereabouts, Esther temporarily gave up, and the family returned to Washington in 1940. On October 5, 1941, Angelina died. As if to carry memories of her mother and Reid, Esther removed the plain wedding band Reid had given Angelina and placed it on her own finger. After the burial in the Stanwood cemetery she cleaned out her mother's house.

The family now took up an almost itinerant life, moving first to Mount Vernon and then a few miles east to Clear Lake, where Esther enrolled ten-year-old Frank in a public school and the girls—sixteen-year-old Ruth and twelve-year-old Marion—in a Seventh-Day Adventist school in Mount Vernon. In early 1942,

The truck that carried the Allen family to California in early 1942.

Walter quit his job with the Maywood Logging Company. He and Esther gathered up the children, their few belongings, and the Stillaguamish tribal records and once again headed for California—this time aboard an old Reo truck with a tarp-covered bed that sheltered the three children and the family's possessions. They also made room for their springer spaniel Mickey, after he had chased the truck down the road. Recalling that period, Esther later wrote: "I was silenced [in] a world to my self. Walter knew it and he warned the children to be careful what they say. It was hard to speak to my family. I was lost. Mother was the last of our board of directors in our tribe. . . . Was I to carry on alone?"[1]

In California, the Allens joined thousands of wartime Americans on the move. Restrictions on food and gasoline made for difficult traveling. Reaching Richmond, Walter hired on as a mechanic in the shipyards. In his spare time he pieced together some rough lumber to build a one-room shack and, with Frank's help, dug a hole for a privy. He also bought a cookstove. Esther had to carry water not only for drinking, cooking, and cleaning, but also for the children's baths on Friday nights—using the same water she had used for washing their clothes, which she hung outside to dry on a line. She again put the children in school and kept house during a very uncomfortable nine-month stay.

During this time, Esther continued her search for Oscar Reid. At a large quadrennial Adventist convention she put out an announcement on the speaker system asking Reid to come forth for a message. A response never came. Years later Esther would learn that her stepfather had indeed been at that convention but was absent from the hall when she called for him.

The war intensified, and the government froze workers in critical defense jobs. Unaware of how long the war and the freeze might last, Walter, following his pattern of short-term employment, decided to take off with his family, telling his foreman he was leaving for Kansas to take a job as a mechanic. When his foreman asked his reason for leaving, the disillusioned Walter snapped, "What did I do all night? I turned one plank over and went to sleep on it." Would the family move to Kansas or would they head for Walter's relatives in Alaska? Walter broke straws from a broom. If Esther drew the short one, then it would be Kansas; if the long, then Alaska. Esther drew the long straw, and the family began the drive north.

It was late fall of 1942 when they reached Seattle, where Walter sold the truck. Boarding a ship for Alaska, the family arrived in Ketchikan and took up residence on a twenty-six-foot powerboat, *Tuna*. Here the family would spend the winter. Coming aboard besides the family of five was Mickey, the spaniel, and a mother cat who would bless their household with five kittens. On the *Tuna* Esther stored the tribal records under one of the bunks, placing them in a plastic bag to keep them from getting wet. Walter found a job fishing. The family made weekly purchases of boxes of bread and gallons of milk to feed the kids and soothe Esther's queasy stomach. Before summer 1943 arrived, the family moved to a house in Ketchikan. Walter sold the *Tuna* and bought a larger powerboat after receiving a contract to carry the mail.

When fall arrived, the children attended school sporadically in town. Frank at least felt at ease there with his Indian classmates. Esther kept busy, visiting Metlakatla Indians, learning of their problems and offering them advice. During this time, Henry Jackson, now a congressman from Washington, visited her while on a

Left to right: Esther's younger daughter, Marion; husband Walter; and older daughter, Ruth, at the waterfront near Ketchikan, Alaska, by their boat, *Tuna*. Along with son Frank, the five lived on the twenty-six-foot boat through the winter of 1942–43.

wartime junket. He informed her of a legislative plan that would establish an Indian claims commission to enable Indians to press the government with their claims without going to Congress for permission. The commission would also enable the Stillaguamish to present their claim without joining other tribes. Jackson was enthusiastic and urged her to reactivate the tribe. Years later, she would write: "Henry Jackson saw me and he said you get back there to Everett, your tribe wasn't recognized at [the Tulalip] meeting. . . . There were no representatives." Esther heeded Jackson's advice. Leaving Walter to complete his contract to carry the mail and daughter Ruth to finish one more year of school, she took Marion and Frank and her tribal records home to Seattle.[2]

By March 1944, Esther was back among the Stillaguamish. Calling a meeting of the group on March 17, she told the members of Jackson's proposal for Indian claims. She also discussed the upcoming election of officers.[3] Esther's renewed efforts in tribal affairs again competed with concerns for her family. In Everett she placed Marion in an Adventist school for a time but soon withdrew her to enroll her in a public school across from a busy Everett freeway, the same school where she had enrolled Frank. For Marion, the move to the larger school was a nightmare. From Everett, Esther and the children moved to the Allen homestead on Jim Creek, where the children were bused to the Darrington school.[4]

Before the end of the school term, Walter returned from Ketchikan, but family life was still unstable. Marion resented her parents' itinerations. "They were [always] ready to take off and run," she later recalled. Having attended school only three months, she was forced to repeat the eighth grade. She was now fifteen years old. "I couldn't see straight," she said. "Mother was gone, I don't know what she was doing. I don't know where she went. She [just] wasn't home."[5]

With the same energy she had exerted in prewar days, Esther established a rigid schedule of visiting the sixty-some tribal members. She was discouraged to discover that their eagerness to receive award moneys outweighed their zeal to prepare for it. In 1945 as America celebrated its successful overseas crusade, Esther continued her own, cajoling members to become active and attend meetings to help achieve her goals. To hold her grasp on her people and retain her leadership, she knew she had to hold tribal elections.

With the death of Jimmy Dorsey and of her Uncle Frank, Esther hoped to assume the title of chief, though that was not a traditional tribal status for women. It was assumed that Dorsey's chiefly mantle would fall to her cousin John Silva. It was now apparent that during her Alaskan interlude Esther had lost much of her grip on tribal affairs for now Kathleen "Kate" Martin, sister of the influential twenty-five-year-old Llewellyn "Lew" Goodridge, contested her for tribal control. Esther's minutes reveal her discomfort at this turn of affairs. In the fall of 1945, she noted the members' general disinterest in tribal meetings. Certain members, Esther wrote, could not care less who led their tribe.[6]

While spending the winter in Concrete in the upper Skagit Valley where Walter worked, Esther sought to affirm her leadership. In the minutes for the October 1, 1945, meeting, she noted that from the start she had led the tribe and moreover that she intended to "hold on until we get what we ask for." Chiefly title or not, she let everyone know she was still in control.[7]

On August 13, 1946, Esther's doggedness and tenacity began to pay off. Congress established the Indian Claims Commission, allowing tribes in the United States to submit claims for previous injustices. Esther sent out notices for a meeting to be held on September 1, 1946, in Mount Vernon to elect officers. It was decided to separate the title of chief and president and elect a person to each post. Problems of leadership, aggravated by differing personalities, came to the surface. One faction, led by Lew Goodridge, preferred John Silva as chief. Goodridge urged his people to attend the meeting. About a fourth of the sixty-nine enrolled members, mostly his supporters, showed up, and Silva was elected chief. Goodridge was elected president, and Esther secretary. Though her official title was secretary, she continued to conduct the meetings as she always had; she had no intention of yielding the reins.[8]

A week later, another meeting was held "for final agreement of officers." Wesley Patrick was elected subchief; Edward Goodridge, vice president; and Kathleen Martin, treasurer. If Esther had hoped enough of her supporters could change the outcome of the election, it didn't happen. At a late October meeting, only five people attended.[9]

Replying to Esther's letter concerning the situation, attorney Arthur Griffin wrote her, "I do not think you should worry about the party being elected Chief not to your liking. If he is not satisfactory you can probably get the one you prefer at your next meeting and in the meantime it is not likely anything will come up for action of importance and that you can not vote down by your friends in the tribe. It would make hard feelings to put him out and he has his friends." Griffin reminded Esther that no provision in the new law denied tribes party to *Duwamish et al.* the right to bring new grievances before the claims commission.[10]

Disappointed with the election results, Esther decided simply not to participate in tribal affairs. Gathering up her papers, she left with her children to follow Walter from one logging camp to another. The family moved down the Washington coast to Moclips, Aberdeen, and Pacific Beach. Next they moved on to Springfield, Oregon, where Esther and the children found summer work. That fall Esther put Frank and Marion in school. However, it was difficult keeping Frank there. Even after a session with the principal, he was tardy. He chronically skipped school to mow lawns for ninety cents an hour or shovel sawdust in basement bins for furnace use. At age sixteen he had advanced no further than the sixth grade. When he finally dropped out altogether, Walter, who had envisioned an education and a better life for him, was disappointed.

After harvesting crops in Oregon that fall of 1947, Esther gave in again to an urge to move to California to look for her stepfather. Since the family's possessions filled their 1938 Graham Paige, Esther and Marion took the bus to California, while Walter and Frank headed down U.S. Highway 101 in the second-hand car. Arriving in Los Angeles, where they were to meet, Esther and Marion took up the vigil, but as the days slipped by there was no sign of Walter and Frank. During the wait, Esther sought work in the Loma Linda Adventist Hospital and continued her search for Reid. But she grew increasingly anxious about her missing husband and son, fearing they had suffered an accident.[11]

After more than three weeks of looking and waiting, Esther thought it best to return home. Hitchhiking north, she and Marion caught a ride with a trucker heading to Washington. At Coquille, Oregon, the driver wheeled off Highway 101 for a rest stop. Alighting from the cab, Marion walked across the street, only to see the back side of a familiar figure looking into a shop window. It was Frank! The shop was next door to the police station where Frank continually checked in to see if the authorities had made contact with Esther and Marion. It seems that Frank and Walter had been held up by car trouble. There was no replacement part in town to repair the Graham Paige's motor, and while waiting for the part to come in, Walter and Frank found work in order to pay for it. With the rig finally squared away, the Allens decided to abandon the California plan and continue north. One of the first stops was Springfield, where they visited Frank's old school. When he went to his locker to clean it out, Frank discovered that someone had taken everything, including a yewwood bow and arrow he had made.[12]

The family spent the next year in various places in Oregon, where Walter hopped from job to job until his employment and life were cut short.[13] On November 18, 1948, he was seriously injured on the job when a heavy rock fell on his head. Rushed to the hospital, he clung to life for twelve days but died on November 30.[14] Esther had him buried on the Tulalip Reservation.

Following Walter's death, Esther was contacted by insurance company representatives who wanted her to sign a settlement agreement. Refusing, she sought the services of a Tillamook attorney, Warren McMinimee. She remained in Tillamook for a while, though she occasionally visited the Tulalip. It was there that she met Walter's first cousin, Bill Dunbar, a "shade tree" attorney who lived on the reservation. They soon became close, and Dunbar moved to Netarts, near Tillamook. He and Esther went to work in

Hebo, while Frank worked at Rockaway. Despite her new relationship with Dunbar, Esther grew ever closer to Frank. In the meantime, Marion, who was now eighteen, met the dashing young Edgar Fitchen. With her mother's approval, Marion married Fitchen. All this while, Ruth was living in Seattle, though once, between Seattle jobs, she worked briefly in the Tillamook hospital's business office.

Since each of the girls was over eighteen, only Frank was still a minor and eligible for Walter Allen's death benefits. McMinimee had these moneys put into a trust account, giving Esther only very limited access to it. According to Ed Fitchen, her son-in-law, "Money was just a thing to [Esther]. . . . She could never handle [it]."[15]

Frank, whom Esther called "Frankie," continued living with his mother even after Dunbar moved in with her. Esther and Frank had a symbiotic relationship. Since the 1930s, she had slowly been losing her hearing because of infected teeth and mastoiditis. Frank now served as her ears. For her part, Esther interpreted the literate world for her son, who had many learning problems. Compensating for these problems, Frank's autistic-like ability enabled him to recall events in minute detail long after the fact. And when Esther was without a driver, he willingly drove her to her various destinations. Although he failed three times to pass the Oregon driver's exam, he gained a Washington license during a visit to that state.

During this time the family held on to Walter's stately Graham Paige, which Fitchen taught Frank to drive. Frank desperately wanted the title to the car, but because it needed a new engine, Esther had him and Fitchen take it to Portland, where they unloaded it on some unsuspecting buyer.[16]

Esther received the first installment of Walter's death benefits on March 1, 1949. Cashing a nine-hundred-dollar check that McMinimee intended for the payment of bills, Esther went on a shopping spree at Penney's and other stores. She also wrote four checks totaling $918.85 for furniture from the Fisher Brothers store in Tillamook. In Portland she paid $610.10 for a fur coat from the

Esther Ross in her fur coat, purchased at the Arctic Fur Company in Portland, Oregon, with funds awarded her from the accidental death benefits of her late husband, Walter Allen.

Arctic Fur Company. Then, after buying Frank an accordion to compensate for his not getting the Graham Paige, she took off for a brief visit to Arizona.

Over the ensuing years, as though she had put his tragic death behind her, Esther seldom mentioned Walter. Whenever she did mention him, she reiterated her contention that he was a good man who had kept his marriage vow never to drink again. In a brief memoir, she wrote that she "was very happy with Walter. . . . Every thing [I would] want to do he agreed till death took him," she noted. Reminiscing about her Oregon years, Esther wrote, "[When] Walter met with [the] accident that took his life, here was another blow to me. We were in Tillamook Oregon. . . . I was so lonesome. No matter [that] the insurance paid $13,000 had no bearing to me. I was again in a world to myself. The hospital put me to work. There it was nightmare to me. I moved back to be by tribe members but [was] unable to throw off the sadness."[17]

CHAPTER SIX

# CLAIMS: LAND LOSSES AND FAMILY LOSSES

It was midsummer of 1950 when Esther received the urgent call to come north. John Silva and Kathleen Martin needed her assistance in meeting with representatives of the Indian Claims Commission and with the commissioner of Indian affairs, D. S. Meyer, who was coming to Seattle to talk to tribes wanting to file claims.

In Esther's absence the tribe had met no more than two times, attendance was minimal, and business sparse. Now events required meetings with substance. And Martin felt unable to carry the load. During Esther's absence, the tribe had elected Martin secretary and elected Silva chairman, a post that combined the positions of chief and president.

Esther eagerly agreed to come to Seattle to represent the tribe. Ed Fitchen and Silva drove to Oregon to bring her back. Uncomfortable with her diminished hearing, Esther rented a hearing aid for the occasion. Not only was the hearing aid a great help, its on and off button proved very useful, allowing her to tune into and out of discussion as she pleased.[1]

After the Seattle meeting, Commissioner Meyer met with regional tribal leaders in La Conner. At this time fifteen tribes of the Western Washington Agency had taken steps to have their claims investigated. The Stillaguamish was one of ten tribes that had not initiated any action. What should have been a high-profile meeting was poorly attended. At its conclusion, Meyer returned to D.C., promising answers to lingering questions.

Developments just prior to the meeting with the commissioner help explain the urgent call for Esther's help. On August 12 Martin had gone to the BIA's Western Washington Agency in Everett to talk with Acting Supt. F. A. Gross. She asked him for a copy of the list of tribal members. He complied, stating,

> If the Stillaguamish tribe wish to have me call a meeting, a group of them ought to get together in the near future and discuss the idea of filing claims against the Government and if they decide to file claims, they should let me know and request the Superintendent to issue a notice calling a general council of the Stillaguamish tribe at some central point where the majority or a good percentage of the members could meet. . . . Also, if the Stillaguamish Indians have any attorneys they would like to have present at the meeting, a notice could be sent to any of the attorneys suggested. The attorneys could give their own version of the claims commission act, etc., in some respect better than the Superintendent.[2]

A tribal meeting was called for September 10, 1950, at the home of Ruth Goodridge in Arlington. Vice president Gus Smith presided in Silva's absence. Members discussed hiring an attorney. A week later they received a letter from Gross in which he enclosed a copy of a field memorandum for dealing with attorney contracts having to do with Indian claims. Gross cautioned the tribe that August 13, 1951, would be the filing deadline for initiating claims against the government. The Stillaguamish had eleven months to employ an attorney and have the contract approved.[3]

Though Kathleen Martin was officially the secretary, once Esther was back on the scene, she took minutes of every meeting she attended, adding these to her personal collection of papers.

Each of these documents concluded with "Esther Allen, Stillaguamish Tribe Secty."

Although no longer an elected officer, Esther continued to spend time on tribal claims and enrollments. Seeking answers from various sources, almost to the point of annoyance, she targeted a host of people, including Bureau of Indian Affairs officials and leaders of neighboring Indian groups. In seeking to establish the intertribal boundaries that had pertained before whites had settled on their lands, she discovered variation between the findings of some anthropologists and those of her own Native sources. She also began serious inquiry into Stillaguamish ethnohistoric identity. On September 21, 1950, she requested the territorial backgrounds of her tribe from the Smithsonian Institution's Bureau of American Ethnology (BAE). Her BAE contract replied that "In fact, we have been unable to find anything at all except for the brief statement which appeared in our *Handbook of American Indians*, . . . [that] the Stillaquamish [sic] were a branch of, or closely related to, Snohomish." Even as late as 1941, according to the BAE, there were no references to the Stillaguamish in George P. Murdock's *Ethnographic Bibliography of North America*.[4]

Esther did not wait for the council to hire an attorney for the tribe. At the Tulalip tribal meeting on November 12 she asked Supt. Raymond H. Bitney, who by now had replaced Gross, to recommend attorneys. He advised her that the selection would have to be proposed by a tribal committee organized for that purpose.[5]

A December 13 council meeting was devoted to defining territorial boundary lines of surrounding tribes as well as those of the Stillaguamish. Upper Skagit chairman Charlie Boome gave input in the discussion, and Esther outlined what she believed to be aboriginal Stillaguamish lands. Of eleven members present, only four held council seats. John Silva, seeking to undermine Esther's leadership, said he had received a letter announcing that any meeting not called by him was illegal, but when asked to read the letter, he was unable to find it. Esther had a report and papers in hand but was not called upon to read any of them. She pointed out that those in attendance at this meeting had not attended previous meetings.[6]

Esther's problems persisted. Calling a December 16 meeting, she asked the chair, John Silva, if she could speak for ten minutes. She was refused. The question of the secretary's position was the basis of contention. Kathleen Martin claimed that Esther's long absence—and her own interim election to the post—made her the secretary, but Esther believed that once she'd been called back to represent the tribe at the claims commission meeting, she had automatically been reinstated.[7] Both Martin and Esther kept notes of meetings. However, because of the tribe's dependence on Esther, she superseded Martin when it came to making decisions and arranging meetings.

It was John Silva himself who called a council meeting the next day, December 17. This time it was he who was angry. He was unhappy with Esther's resumption of authority. He noted that Esther's hearing loss diminished her effectiveness and called for her resignation. The motion was made and passed. At that point Silva appointed Alvin Anderson secretary. Anderson's first minutes note, "The Chairman refused to accept any minutes of any meeting that had been held without his authorization."[8]

But Esther was not to be deterred. She held numerous informal discussions with other nonreservation tribes, including the Snohomish, Upper Skagit, Sauk-Suiattle, Skykomish, and Snoqualmie, all with claims for land in approximation to Stillaguamish territory. Such meetings would take up much of the next year. Esther hoped to coordinate claims among these tribes so as to forestall any later confrontations before the commission over tribal land ownership. This time the tribal representatives depended heavily on published anthropological reports. And each tribe agreed to support the others' petitions before the claims commission. From her meetings with these landless tribal leaders, Esther produced a large, detailed folding map of the area. It was to be used in settling the boundaries. It was difficult to establish exact locations because of missing markers. But once they were established, Esther wanted them labeled on the map in no uncertain terms. She borrowed a lipstick and with it sketched the Stillaguamish boundary lines on what became known as the "lipstick map."[9]

Esther may have reached agreement with other tribes, but she found no such agreement on matters within her own family. Marion had finally met Carlton. She and Ruth had visited him in a veterans' rest home where he was being cared for after suffering heart trouble. It gave Marion a chance to introduce her infant son, Lloyd, to his grandfather.[10] With Esther and Frank once again residents of Washington, Dunbar decided to follow suit. Since Marion and Ed Fitchen were now separated and in the process of divorcing, Esther and Dunbar moved in with Fitchen, sharing a rented place in nearby Snohomish. Frank got a job, rented an apartment in Everett, and bought a used Chevrolet pickup. Following Carlton's death on November 12, 1951, Marion attended his funeral, though her mother did not. Marion resented her mother's continuing friendship with Fitchen, her ex-husband, and her relationship with her mother grew ever more strained. She blamed her mother for paying scant attention to her in her childhood, and she flared when Esther admonished her after she had left Fitchen, "You gotta be careful now, you're a divorced woman." "I looked at my mother [then living with Bill Dunbar]," Marion said, "and told her to clean out her own back yard before start[ing] on mine." "Oh, yeah, Mommie was no saint," Marion concluded. "But anyway she did a lot for the tribe."[11]

More troublesome family problems emerged when Dunbar's son Ernest, or "Sparky," started for Darrington in Frank's pickup, a 1942 Ford V8 that had replaced the Chevy. With Sparky at the wheel, Frank in the middle, and Esther on Dunbar's lap, they never reached their destination. Crossing the Cicero bridge over the Stillaguamish River, the pickup collided with a county road grader stopped on the bridge. Esther was thrown against the windshield and smashed her jaw, losing all but eight teeth. A Marysville dentist pulled the remaining teeth without benefit of anesthesia. Most people were unaware of her edentulous condition and those few who did know attributed her peculiar eating habits to it.¹²

At a time when Indians were forbidden to purchase alcoholic beverages, Frank, who was never challenged for his Indianness, bought beer and wine to sell to an Indian crew cutting cedar-shake bolts and cutting and hauling lumber for an Arlington mill. Although a teetotaler herself, Esther also sold spirits to the crew and gave the money to Frank to buy gasoline. Despite her Adventist upbringing, she bought a card that allowed her to purchase liquor. She used it to supply Bill Dunbar—and a new friend, Arnold Ross, a beer drinker to whom Frank had introduced her. By now she was breaking off relations with Dunbar, who didn't want to get married, and was turning her attention to Ross, a fifty-year-old Lummi. Believing he could provide her security and believing his promise that he would stop drinking, Esther married Ross on July 11, 1953, at the home of her relative, E. Cornelius Qualley, in Carnation. She was now forty-six years old. During the ceremony, performed by E. N. Sargeant, an Adventist minister, Ruth stood up for her mother and signed the marriage certificate as a witness. Frank gave the newlyweds a pickup for a wedding present.¹³

Having found a semblance of security in her personal life, Esther returned her attention to tribal affairs. Warren J. Gilbert of the Gilbert and Bannister law firm in Mount Vernon was one of three attorneys who had been hired by the Stillaguamish to represent them before the claims commission. The others included Frederick W. Post and Malcolm S. McLeod. According to the BIA-approved contract, the tribe was to pay the lawyers 10 percent of any award they might win.¹⁴ Some question arose as to whether the Stillaguamish could join the petition before the claims commission. There'd been a fear that any petition from a tribe who'd been a party to any previous unsuccessful suit against the federal government, as in *Duwamish et al.*, would be res judicata for the same claim. Since the commission had decided that the Lummi were not in a res judicata position, the same decision would have

At the July 11, 1953, wedding of Esther and Arnold Ross. Left to right: Cornelius Qually; Arnold; E. N. Sargeant, Adventist minister; Esther; and her daughter Ruth.

to be allowed for the Stillaguamish. Gilbert had so informed Alvin Anderson, acting tribal secretary, on April 16, 1952. Esther was now eager to sign up any person with but a small quantum of blood. Gilbert advised the tribe to enroll "down to one-sixteenth." This blood quantum was lower than that required from any other tribe for membership.

Gilbert also advised the Stillaguamish to employ the services of a historian and an anthropologist, warning that it was urgent "that we do this so that we can proceed with determining boundaries and values of land and all the various factors involved in our action"[15] The Stillaguamish petition before the claims commission was docket No. 207. In preparing for her testimony, anthropologist Sally Snyder drew from Jimmy Dorsey's deposition given March 4, 1927, in *Duwamish et al*. Both Snyder and Carroll L. Riley, the government's ethnologist, deposed Silva on June 12, 1952. He stated that tribal membership then stood at fifty. His testimony was followed by Esther's. She talked of the time she'd spent with the tribe as secretary since 1926. She said she had recorded "the full history of all our tribal rights and tribal relationships, and our ancestors names and things like that." She had gleaned this history, she said, from her great-grandfather, great-grandmother, and her grandfather and grandmother, all leaders of a once-powerful tribe. Attorneys present to cross-examine Silva and Esther saw little relevancy in Esther's remarks since they were pertinent only to the history of the tribe since the Point Elliott treaty. "Miss Allen's testimony, considered as a whole, . . . applied to the claimed area during a period of time many years after the Point Elliott Treaty of 1855," the report noted.[16]

The commission took more stock in anthropologist Snyder's testimony that a sizable portion of the land Esther claimed for the Stillaguamish was what anthropologists termed "nonexclusive land"—a "no-man's-land" consisting of areas and strips used by the Upper Skagits, the Sauk-Suiattles, the Snohomish, and others.

Besides working within the system, Esther continued working on her own. Among other things, she consulted with an assistant professor of anthropology, Wayne Suttles, at the University of British Columbia. Suttles advised her that the Stillaguamish could "make a convincing argument for all of the territory drained by the Stillaguamish River, including both forks and the smaller streams that flow into them," adding that "before you can make your claim to the east shore of Port Susan convincing, we will have to clear up the question of the relationship of the Stillaguamish Tribe with some people reported as living there (at Warm Beach) called 'Kwadkzakbiwh'"—known today as the Kikiallus.[17]

Since Esther was, in effect, performing all the duties of secretary, she wanted to have official tribal sanction. Toward this end, she met first with Acting Superintendent Gross at the Everett agency and then with Supt. Ray Bitney. She reminded these men that "our best leaders are gone" and explained how she had sought to reorganize the tribe. In a follow-up letter, she told them that tribal matters were at such an impasse that even John Silva's wife, a nonmember, had run tribal affairs. Aggravating the situation was discord between those with more Stillaguamish blood and those with less.[18]

When Esther heard back from Bitney, he told her that his superiors in the Portland Area Office of the BIA had informed him that Stillaguamish who did not wish to be assessed could not be barred from membership. Nor could they be dropped from tribal rolls for nonpayment of dues.[19]

Esther went back to Bitney, complaining of the conflict within the Stillaguamish secretariat. The next day Bitney wrote Silva about his encounter with Esther and asked him to call a meeting of the tribal council to pass a resolution to determine whether or not Esther was the secretary. "I would suggest that you hold a meeting of the Stillaguamish Tribal Council at the earliest possible moment and have them pass a resolution to the effect that Mrs. Esther Allen either is or is not the Tribal Secretary for the Stillaguamish Tribe," Bitney wrote, adding "[Y]ou should also include the position of Treasurer with the Secretary and insist that whoever is the Secretary-Treasurer should be bonded and make reports to the Tribe as to the condition of the tribal treasury, as I have been receiving some remarks in regard to the disposal of money collected by members of the Stillaguamish Tribe for the purpose of furthering the interests of the Stillaguamish Tribe." Bitney also wanted the tribe to produce a copy of its constitution and bylaws. This troubling lack of a constitution dated back to 1934, since the passing of the Indian Reorganization Act. That act called for tribes to reorganize and function under a constitution as approved by the BIA. It also required the establishment of a democratic process with elected officers, reversing the previous paternalistic government control over Indian tribes.[20] Esther always claimed that her health problems at the time the act became law were the only reason the Stillaguamish had not organized under the IRA.

Following Bitney's advice, tribal members met on January 10, 1953, to nominate candidates for secretary and treasurer. Kathleen

Martin was the only nomination. Undeterred, Esther drafted the major portion of a constitution, assisted by her daughter Ruth. This document set the blood quantum for membership at one-sixteenth. The constitution was presented to the council, and it was approved. A copy was sent to the agency for its approval.[21]

Family problems resurfaced soon after Esther married Ross. Seven-year-old Joan, the eldest of four children of Ross's Yakama daughter Margaret, reported her mother to authorities. She claimed her mother was either drunk or drugged most of the time. Three-year-old Donald, Suzie, two, and infant Dorothy, were virtually motherless—and fatherless, with their father, Walter Baker, in jail.[22] On learning that the children had been placed in foster homes, Esther and Arnold hurried to Yakima to get custody of the children. In March of 1955 the Rosses gained custody of all four children. Baker was unsuccessful in his attempt to get them back; in fact, he was arrested for his threats to take them. For the support of the children, Esther began to collect welfare money and funds from agencies on the Yakama Reservation as well as on the Colville since Baker was from that reservation.[23]

Joan was assigned to tending the house and children during the eleven years they would spend with Esther and their grandfather, whose disability would soon render him unable to work. During her infrequent periods at home, Esther helped care for Dorothy but left the disciplining of the children to Arnold, who systematically punished Joan on behalf of the other children since Esther held her responsible for their care.[24]

Esther used some creativity in raising the children. For instance, she once went to the *Everett Daily Herald* seeking help in providing for the first Christmas she had them. A headline in the *Herald's* December 23, 1955, issue read, "4 Youngsters Find Proof Santa Exists." Thanks to the story and the warm hearts of *Herald* readers, at least a hundred dollars was donated, along with the bundle of toys deposited for them at the Fireside Tavern. Astounded by the dolls she received, Joan could not understand this caring public, which also provided the children with packages of clothing, can-

Esther and Arnold on Esther's fifty-second birthday, September 2, 1956.

dies, and toys. The children had spent the previous Christmas in juvenile detention for foster care, but now they had "their first real Christmas."[25]

Esther enrolled the children in Adventist and in public schools wherever they lived and she made certain that funds for their care arrived on time. She taught Joan to sew, even taking her to church sewing bees. At Joan's initial menstruation in 1962, having given her no previous orientation, Esther curtly remarked, "That's OK," but, recalled Joan, "She did give me some fresh sheets and washed me up."[26]

When Joan was still a young child, Arnold let her drive his many cars. Small and scrawny, she could barely see over the dashboard. In her first trip of any distance, she chauffeured Esther home from the Swinomish area, a frightening experience for the child but no more so than later when she would have to drive the family across the Cascade Mountains to the Yakama. During

Arnold's abusive periods, Esther hustled the children into the car, and with Joan at the wheel, the group drove around until his alcoholic storm blew over. Before Joan was sixteen, Arnold had introduced her to beer. But he also took her fishing and taught her to use a chain saw. "I wish you were a boy," he told her more than once. "I wish you were a boy."[27]

Sometime during the 1960s, the children began thinking that life with their real mother, Margaret, might not have been all that bad. Consequently, at a 1966 Halloween party in Bellingham's Adventist Church, the younger ones hatched a plot, including a false claim of molestation by Arnold. Turning themselves over to the police, they asked to be returned to Margaret, who over the years had sought their return. During their absence she had given birth to four other children. Thanks to the deception on the part of the four living with Rosses, they returned to the Yakama Reservation where they were put in foster homes.

Esther had few social acquaintances—that is, until she met Margaret Greene. Their meeting on New Year's Day, 1964, was an auspicious event in Esther Ross's life, for it brought her her first true friend. And from that friendship came a common crusade for Margaret and Esther. They were joined in the mission of achieving viability for their respective tribes—Esther's Stillaguamish and Greene's Samish.[28]

At a meeting in October of 1964, the Stillaguamish passed a resolution asking the BIA to protect the tribe's fishing rights on the basis that they were treaty-granted to be protected in the same manner in which the BIA protected Indian allotments on and off reservations. That the Stillaguamish did not rely on fishing for sustenance nor as a commercial enterprise did not prevent Esther from making fishing rights a major issue during what had become a long lull in the claims case.

Esther focused on the Puyallup-Nisqually fish-ins, arguing that tribal members be able to fish by Indian rules and seasons. She badgered state fisheries personnel over these rights. She also badgered the BIA for written confirmation showing state fisheries employees that her people were entitled to these rights.

By 1965 the claims commission, having moved through the finding-of-fact phase, set out to render an opinion in the case, with the Indians' attorney Fredrick Post pitted against the government's attorneys, first Craig A. Decker and then Ramsey Clark. The commission believed the Stillaguamish to be an identifiable group of American Indians within the meaning of the August 13, 1946, Indian Claims Commission Act and recognized their aboriginal title to lands claimed, but for a greatly reduced area. The Stillaguamish were credited with only 58,600 aboriginal acres, half of what Esther had determined it to be. To her dying day she would blame the decreased acreage on Frederick Post for encouraging tribal acceptance of the ruling and anthropologist Sally Snyder for her damning testimony.[29]

Referencing the boundaries outlined on her lipstick map, Esther accused Snyder, Carroll L. Riley, the government's anthropologist, and Post of labeling a substantial amount of the claimed acreage a "no-man's-land" because of its multiple use—by the Upper Skagits, Sauk-Suiattle, and Stillaguamish. The commissioners accepted the anthropologists' contention that large acreages were intertribal. Beyond what the Stillaguamish claimed as their area drained by the Stillaguamish River were lands at its mouth occupied by Kikialluses at contact with whites. In making a final petitioners' draft, Post excluded sixteen thousand acres of what Snyder told him was Kikiallus land.[30] As for the contended area, the commissioners on February 26, 1965, called for calculating its acreage as determined by the anthropologists and not as indicated on Esther's map. To settle it, the commissioners offered the Stillaguamish $64,460 for the 58,600 acres, far short of the tribe's expected compensation.[31] The compensatory value was set at $48,570 after $15,890 was allowed for services provided in the immediate posttreaty era. The total received as amended amounted to $1.10 an acre.

On March 31, 1965, Post, on behalf of the tribe, discussed a compromise settlement. On April 8, J. Edward Williams, on behalf of the government, wrote Post, outlining a basis for settlement. This was presented to the tribe at a meeting on July 24, 1965. In Silva's absence, Esther reluctantly considered the offer. She wanted an additional seventy dollars an acre for logging that dated back to the 1860s. But the tribe was anxious to settle for whatever amount they could get, and the members passed a resolution to accept the government offer of $48,570. To Esther's way of thinking, it was like money purchasing "yesterday's whiskey," but she grudgingly signed the resolution to settle the Stillaguamish claim for 58,600 acres. Post then advised the government the tribe would accept the settlement.[32]

Eight months after the government's offer was accepted, Assistant Attorney General Edwin L. Weisl, Jr., advised the Stillaguamish that the offer to settle the tribe's claim was subject to stated conditions—that nothing could preclude offsets for expenditures for services to the tribe prior to the 1855 treaty or subsequent to June 30, 1951.[33] That only increased Esther's bitterness over the low award. She blamed the government more than tribal members. She and Frank cooked up a means to protest what she considered an outright injustice. A letter with Frank's signature was mailed to Pres. Lyndon Johnson, explaining that as an 1855 treaty tribe, the Stillaguamish people were being paid $1.10 an acre for their land. Frank asked Johnson to sell him an acre of his property in Texas for $1.25. He enclosed a money order for that amount. The letter was referred to the BIA for response. On March 17, 1966, Acting Commissioner J. L. Norwood returned the money order, advising Frank that "The President and his family love their home in Texas and do not wish to part with it."[34]

The Stillaguamish were asked to accept terms of the settlement by appropriate resolution approved by the secretary of the interior. However, Interior would not approve the resolution without another meeting to discuss the new conditions imposed by the Justice Department. Thus, the tribe met on September 10, 1966, in

Arlington and voted once more to accept $48,570 and the sanctions. Led by Silva and Kathleen Martin Johnson (now remarried), the members adopted a rewritten confirmation of acceptance. Silva and Johnson signed the resolution.[35]

A year previously, Esther had objected that the settlement did not account for interest on the amount offered from the time the 1855 treaty was ratified until the present. Frederick Post had discouraged her from filing this objection with the commission, stating that previous appeals on that point by Nooksack and Muckleshoot Indians had failed. At the same time, tribal members had asked the tribal operations officer of the BIA's Portland Area Office, Vincent Little, for certificates of entitlement for use in filing for public domain allotments with the Bureau of Land Management under the Dawes Indian Severalty Act of 1887. The Stillaguamish, as nonreservation Indians, had no proof of bloodlines from precontact times. As "canoe Indians," unlike "reservation Indians," they were allowed to take patents along their river, but in the end they were unable to keep their land and cemetery plots from going for taxes.

The claims case to her mind still unresolved, Esther now took up again the cause she hoped would have a better outcome—fishing rights for her people.

CHAPTER SEVEN

# FISH WARS: THE COURTS AND THE RIVERS

The loss of fish resources in stream, river, sound, and ocean devastated Indians of the Pacific Northwest. Many complained that the federal government had failed to live up to provisions of treaties that allowed them to fish in their "usual and accustomed" places. In posttreaty years white entrepreneurs appropriated traditional fisheries with giant wheels and large nets, processing their catches in local canneries to satisfy increasing demands for fish. Sportfishers also moved in to reap the harvests, leaving Indians by the mid-twentieth century with roughly 5 percent of the harvest.[1]

Officials of the Washington State Departments of Fisheries and Game looked the other way rather than challenge the disproportionate numbers of fish caught by non-Indians. When in 1963, the Department of Fisheries filed suit to prevent traditional Indian net fishing, the Washington State Supreme Court ruled that the state had the right to prohibit Indians from using nets. Such restrictions intensified the continuing conflict between Indians and the state and introduced Esther to demonstrations called "fish-ins." Leading these demonstrations protesting police action was Robert Satiacum, described by one reporter as a "self-styled" chief of the Puyallup Indians. Bob Satiacum and Esther became close friends. "[Bob] was just like a brother [to me]," Frank said. "He and his wife let my mother and me stay overnight. And they gave us gas and they gave us food, and Satiacum told my mother what she should do, how she should do it, and when she should do it."[2] Esther took her cue from Satiacum and his wife, Susan, as to how to oppose government regulation of Indian fishing.

Violent confrontations erupting on the Puyallup and Nisqually Rivers pitted net-fishing Indians against game department law enforcement officials. Injuries were sustained on both sides. In a hail of rock-throwing at officials confiscating boats and gear, one young Indian woman was killed. Arrested on August 26, 1965, for net fishing, Satiacum was given a sixty-day jail sentence.[3] Susan Satiacum, Janet McCloud, founder of the Survival of American Indians Association (SAIA), and Esther Ross planned and led an October 26, 1965, march on Seattle's federal courthouse. Esther carried a banner bearing the words "Stillaguamish Indian Tribe of Western Washington." So he could join the protest, Frank phoned his boss at the Seaboard Lumber Company on Harbor Island, requesting sick leave because of a sprained ankle. Joining his mother and about twenty-five placard-carrying Indians, some in Native regalia, he was in front of the demonstrators, surrounded by signs reading, "Show Some Justice Honor Our Treaty"; "Has Uncle Sam Forgotten the Papooses?"; and "Save Our Salmon."[4]

The next day Frank's boss found a photo in the *Seattle Post-Intelligencer* of Frank marching with the demonstrators. There being no indication of an injured ankle, Frank was fired. It was hardly the reaction he and Esther had wanted from their demonstration.[5]

At several fish-ins in December 1966, Esther met the Tuscarora Indian, Mad Bear (Wallace Anderson) of Niagara Falls, New York, a legal spokesman for the Six Nation Iroquois Confederacy of New York and Canada. He urged Esther to trash the Stillaguamish constitution and name a tribal chief. Esther, however, was aware that a Stillaguamish chief was traditionally weak, except in crisis times.

In that same month, in Arlington's Pioneer Hall, Snohomish, Lummi, and Yakama Indians joined the Stillaguamish in a ceremony in which Mad Bear presented them a red-ribboned, certified

Frank Allen called in sick so he could demonstrate with his mother when they joined Susan Satiacum, Janet McCloud, and others to march on the federal courthouse in Seattle, October 26, 1965. The demonstrators were protesting police brutality against the Indian fish-ins and the arrest of Bob Satiacum. *Reprinted courtesy of the* Seattle Post-Intelligencer. *Photograph by Tom Brownell.*

copy of the Point Elliott treaty. The *Arlington Times* reported that Esther received the copy, "her voice trembling with emotion, as she pleaded to continue the fight to regain her Tribe's treaty rights and preservation of ancient burial grounds." As part of the ceremony, Joe Washington, a Lummi, told of his tribe's attempts to return to its traditional songs and dances by restoring one of the last longhouses for winter dances.[6]

Esther used Mad Bear's presentation to point out the absence of the superintendent of the Western Washington Indian Agency in Everett. Mad Bear had other concerns, telling Esther that comedian Dick Gregory's appearance in November to assist protesting Indians had been a "bad mistake" since his arrest and trial revealed important differences between problems of blacks and Indians.

Mad Bear believed that Indians should not join up with blacks and, moreover, that while Indians owned and occupied their lands, blacks had no such territorial pedigree because their ancestors were enslaved. Ignoring his warnings, Survival of American Indians Association activists Bob Satiacum, Hank Adams, Janet McCloud, and Ramona Bennett would welcome Gregory when he returned to Tacoma to serve jail time.

In a temporary break from the fish-ins, Esther called a tribal meeting for Sunday, February 5, in Seattle where she was now living. She was determined to increase the tribe's aboriginal acreage. Rather than focus the blame for her people's unjust award on the government or Sally Snyder, she now zeroed in on attorney Frederick Post, and she wanted him present at the meeting.[7] She wanted him to hear her side of the issue. Beyond that, she also hoped to be elected secretary at this meeting.

In preparing for the meeting, Esther typed up and circulated an announcement with the word ATTENTION sprawled across the page five times, in uppercase letters and underlined. At this Sunday morning meeting Esther regained her title as tribal secretary without opposition. John Silva retained his position as chair and Gus Smith was elected vice chair. Council members Donna Soholt, Frank Allen, Carol Mayberry, and Colleen Swanson were reelected. Esther's rival, Kathleen Martin Johnson, did not attend.[8]

Frederick Post arrived late, after many of the officers had left. Esther wasted no time in telling him that the information in his files about Stillaguamish land holdings had been supplied by an anthropologist, not by older Indians. A Kikiallus Indian who was at the meeting backed her by stating that his people claimed no part of the Stanwood vicinity, which Post and anthropologists had designated Kikiallus territory. Esther then advised Post of the tribe's decision to investigate on its own and asked him to delay the claims case. He agreed to go along—but with one provision: The investigation must take no longer than a few weeks. Not surprisingly, this investigation was Esther's idea, not the tribe's. In her minutes of the meeting she wrote: "We have had several disputes with Mr.

Post until he has given the book of the [claims commission] findings to Esther Ross. . . . We have been in the dark about reports and findings that was made by the government and . . . by the anthropologists, . . . all done without any of our tribe being present. And remarks we see written seem unfair."[9]

Seeking more help from the government, Esther began asking Indian Commissioner Robert Bennett, who had replaced the acting commissioner J. L. Norwood, to come to Seattle to discuss fishing rights with the Stillaguamish and other tribes. He had sympathized with Esther on that issue the previous fall when he had met her, Frank, and John Silva at a "New Horizons" Indian conference in Spokane. Now, on February 21, 1967, he offered his regrets that commitments prevented him from coming to Seattle: "I am well aware of the problems Indian people are having with fishing rights in the State of Washington and it is hoped that the Department of Justice will soon bring a suit against the State of Washington . . . so that the problem may be finally resolved." She urged her state legislator, Rep. Henry Backstrom of Arlington, to put in a bill to negate the claim award as it was. Backstrom replied that it was too late.

That prompted a new aggressiveness from Esther. "We want to regain our cemeterys and without court costs," she wrote. "Instead of the white man [running] the fish hatcheries in our tribal territory. Why cant our Indian people have that job. If we cant have a say in our territory about our fishing let us stop all sports fishing of the white man in our Stillaguamish River."[10] She carried her cause to the state capital at Olympia, where she joined Janet McCloud and twenty-five Indians from other tribes in what was to be a peaceful protest before the Washington state senate. The demonstrators wanted to call attention to the ruling of the U.S. Supreme Court, which had upheld the state supreme court's decision that Indians could fish off reservations but only with adherence to state regulations. They also intended to protest another recent decision of the U.S. Supreme Court that the state had the right to administer regulations for conservation of fish resources.[11]

When the group in full Indian regalia reached the senate gallery on Monday, February 6, the sergeant-at-arms, Charles Johnson, denied them entry, ostensibly because their signs were offensive. One of the signs read, "Ho Chi Min Beware of U.S. Treaties." Another sign carried a swastika above the printed words "Washington State."[12]

When told they could enter the senate gallery, but without their signs, the protesters nevertheless carried the signs in and seated themselves. Ordered to leave, they refused. Two Thurston County sheriff's deputies removed McCloud and four other women from the room. "Those people were the rudest I've met in my 29 years here—and I'm all for Indians," Sergeant-at-Arms Johnson said. The next day, the *Daily Olympian* carried the headline, "On the Capitol Warpath." Esther Ross was quoted as saying she had come expecting to talk directly to the legislature. "The tribe charges they have never been given their reservation and the land they were promised under the Point Elliott Treaty," the article continued. "They now demand that the State remove its fish hatchery from the North Fork of the Stillaguamish River since tribal members aren't allowed to fish on what they claim is their native ground."[13]

CHAPTER EIGHT

# ESTHER MEETS THE REBEL GENERAL

Esther Ross was now fully engaged in the Stillaguamish cause. Along with John Silva, she attended meetings of several Indian organizations. She took increased interest in the Survival of American Indians Association and in other groups such as the Intertribal Council of Western Washington Indians (ICWW), which was made up of the leaders of Washington tribes. The members of the ICWW would just as soon Esther would lose interest in their business, for she was constantly presenting them with problems outside the scope of their mission. Nevertheless, the Lummi Juanita Jefferson, a council member, made sure Esther was notified of meetings. "I always sent Esther a notice," Jefferson said, "and she usually showed up."[1] Esther also worked with the Community Action Project Director's Association and with a similar group at the University of Utah. Both groups were established to derail the proposed termination of relations of reservation Indians with the federal government.

In early 1967, Esther met with Craig Carpenter, a part-Indian activist from Cedarville, California, who introduced her to Herbert C. Holdridge, a retired U.S. brigadier general. Carpenter, a printer, visited the Pacific Northwest and often helped Esther photocopy various documents. Among these was a 1928 booklet by Nels Bruseth, who wrote of Stillaguamish history and culture. The publication proved invaluable to Esther, not only because she learned much from it, but because she was able to share its information with others.²

At about this time General Holdridge was in the Pacific Northwest to recruit Indians to his organization, Constitutional Government of the United States. Working from his headquarters in Wells, Nevada, Holdridge had conscripted many Paiutes, Utes, and Shoshones in a "rebellion" against what he considered the evil conscription of the U.S. military for service in the Vietnam War. Adopting a Mohawk name meaning "Bringing the Message," he called himself "Chief Magistrate and Defender of the Constitution and Commander in Chief of the Armed Services of the United States." Since under the Constitution the president of the United States was commander-in-chief of the armed forces, Holdridge proclaimed himself a candidate for that office. His intention was to oust those in the government who were fostering the war in Vietnam.

Esther was attracted to the general's antigovernment message. She felt he was acting as an Indian spokesman in advancing his grand plan to save the country from its wars and other ills. It was a time when the Vietnam War was the centerpiece of protests stretching across America. And Holdridge fanned the flames. In December 1966 he revealed his plan for establishing a "supreme court" within his organization, and he warned that should he and his supporters fail, a "fateful hour of prophetic destruction" could strip Indians of their sovereignty and trust funds. This proclamation was co-signed by eight Indian chiefs of his executive council.³

Holdridge was particularly forceful in condemning the conscription of Paitue and Shoshone Indians and began a campaign against the government, from Pres. Lyndon Johnson on down through the Departments of War and the Interior to secretary Lorraine Peterson of the Selective Service office in Elko, Nevada. Holdridge was a prolific letter writer, sending messages to various people in government and private institutions. Sometimes these letters were signed by any number of Indians whom he

Retired Gen. Herbert G. Holdridge, who mobilized Indians during the Vietnam War to resist going into the military. He wrote copious articles and letters urging Indians to abandon the government and its leadership. He set up his own court to convict Pres. Lyndon Johnson, his cabinet, and other political and military leaders for various crimes. *Courtesy of the Toledo (Ohio) Blade.*

called "chiefs," a title Holdridge bestowed on his supportive Indian males.[4]

In February 1967, at about the same time Esther was marching on the state house in Olympia, Holdridge was planning a massive protest of the U.S. participation in the Vietnam War. He wanted especially to target the conscription of Indians. His plan was to purchase a large portion of the Nevada desert and turn it into a sovereign nation for Indians. Addressing an essay to "The United Press International The Associated Press and the Seditious Press Generally," he wrote, "For 400 years you have rubbed salt into the wounds of your two implacable, traditional enemies—the Indians and the Negroes—whose racial purposes differ in detail, but whose relentless enmity turns acid with years as you pile injustices upon injustices."[5]

Holdridge decided to constitute a court as his protest format. He set himself as judge, jury, and prosecutor for a public trial in the "Supreme Court of the Constitutional Government of the United States" to try all people who were involved in carrying out the Vietnam War. He sent out a release, which was at the same time an invitation to Indians and friends of Indians to attend the trial scheduled for March 11 and 12, 1967, in Wells. Written on two pages of legal-sized paper, it was a summons to members of the "outlaw government" to appear in court "to answer Charges of Kidnapping, Unlawful Arrest and Imprisonment; Murder; and Treason. Should any fail to appear, their trials will proceed nevertheless, 'In Absentia!'" Names listed included those of Lyndon B. Johnson, Earl Warren, Richard Helms, Cardinal James Spellman, J. Edgar Hoover, and various senators, generals, and BIA personnel.[6]

Esther was interested enough in the trial to attend, especially after Holdridge offered to pay for hers and Frank's lodging and for that of any other members of the tribe who might attend. He was encouraged that she would come to the court hearing, and he sent her some information on what he was trying to accomplish. He also wrote that he was discussing the issues daily with four Shoshone chiefs, that the decisions were not his alone:

> Mad Bear would tell you how I have fought side by side with the Indians for ten years, and how dangerous and expensive it has been to me in every way. . . . The time for surrender to the White man has gone by, and this is the time selected by the Great Spirit (as we fully are convinced), to

restore the Indians as stated in the prophecies . . . we expect a strong demonstration here at a level of public trial of the criminals on the issue of unconstitutional draft. . . . I have been in touch with Chiefs of the Six Nations of the Iroquois, and am quite sure that they will send someone to speak officially for them here. . . . A young woman whom I have just met, who had been travelling all over the country to learn about the Indians and to help them, and who has powerful Extra Sensory Perception (spiritual "medicine",) had told the Chiefs here that a few days ago, on her way here, the spirit powerful Grand Council of Indians, told her to tell us that they will be present at our meeting with strong help.[7]

Esther and Frank rounded up John Silva to drive them to Nevada. Shirley Oman, who went in place of her father, Gus Smith, joined them. They stayed in the Allon Hotel in Wells. Holdridge anticipated that the hearing, set to begin at 10 a.m. on March 11, would last two days. In fact, it lasted only one day. It took place in the lobby of the Allon Hotel. Reports were that a hundred Indians attended, but the number was actually less. The judgment of Holdridge's court was "Guilty as Charged, Individually and Collectively." The sentence handed down was "Under the Law of the Great Spirit: 'live by the sword, and perish by the sword'—'live by fire, and perish by fire' (napalm), and Sentence of the Court is <u>Death By Fire</u>!"[8]

Holdridge later wrote a summary and analysis of the trial and sent a copy to Esther. In it he wrote,

> In my personal opinion as an Historian, the Trial will be established historically as the greatest single event in Indian History since the coming of the White man, marking the end of the era of Indian retreat, and the beginning of a new era of Indian Restoration. . . . The concept of Indian Common Law, which arose through a comment by Janet McCloud, enlarged upon by the Wells Chiefs, must displace English

Common law which is not part of the US Code, for this Constitutional (Indian) Government of the United States. This government was originally inspired by the Six Nations of the Iroquois Confederacy. Now that the lawful rights of Indians over their "Original Territory" have been proclaimed, the force of Indian Common Law must follow logically. . . . The names of many in attendance would be recognized by many Indians throughout the country, the list too long to be repeated in this brief report. Janet McCloud was not able to come, but was represented by members of her family, and by officers of the Stillaguamish group in Washington.[9]

Esther had come up against a new vocabulary and new issues. She could understand that the federal government needed reining in, and she could support Holdridge's efforts to some extent. But hearing his harsh words and colorful epithets—"the great whore and mother of harlots of Rome" (Pope Paul VI and all archbishops, bishops, and priests); the "world ego-maniac and murderer" (Lyndon B. Johnson) and his wife, "Ladybird MacBeth Johnson"; the "seditious cabinet"; and the general (Curtis LeMay) who had "the appearance of a fat toad crawled out of the bowels of the earth"—these she found extreme.[10] Despite any reservations she may have had, Esther returned from Nevada imbued with new resolve to bypass government red tape and recoup the losses suffered by her tribe and others. Under the title of "Report on Stillaguamish," she wrote:

> The time has come for a decision for each of us. The time has come for action for each of us. Over the years we have been held down by war, by those who have taken advantage of us. We have had to give up our homes, our lands—not because we wanted to but because we had no choice.
> The history taught in the schools was written by our oppressors. The history books say the Indians were savages because the Europeans had to justify their oppression of the

Indians. In our territory the white men were forceful with our Indian people.

Grandfathers should we pick up our rifles again?

My people I would like to ask you a question. "Why are we fighting the white mans war?"

"Why was our grandsons urged, demanded to go into foreign countries to fight?"

You might answer, "To contain Communist aggression and keep world peace." Yes it is quite true, but why are we fighting in foreign country or fighting for what was once ours and to protect what is no longer ours, now?

Once free to roam this peaceful territory [we are] now confined to only a lot.

That is what my people should be fighting for nonviolently. Against internal corruptions and unethical utilization of white business man and many more unsolved problems.

Haphazardly young Stillaguamish men joined Uncle Sams imperialistic society to find themselves in limbo somewheres in the midst of mosquito infested fox holes.[11]

Frank returned not only sharing his mother's opinions, but with something else of great importance to him—the title of "chief," bestowed by Holdridge on him and on John Silva. Esther furthered Frank's new self-image by immediately ordering eagle feathers from the Washington State Department of Game. Frank himself had a friend fashion an attractive Plains-type headdress.[12]

In early April, just weeks after the "court hearing" in Nevada, Esther invited the general to Seattle to meet with Stillaguamish and other Indians. Holdridge replied that he was ready to fly out to talk with interested Indians, though "The thought occurs to me of need—perhaps—for reasonable caution in case Gov. Evans tries to mess around in our business. I don't think he will, for if the gang in Washington can find nothing wrong with our legal positions, neither could he, and the issue becomes too hot anyway. But when you meet me at the airport, take a look around and bring along Frank Allen. We might get some fun out of this situation [if] they try to get tough."[13]

If Holdridge and Esther hoped for a colorful confrontation in Seattle they were to be disappointed. Not only did few attend the meeting, there was no press coverage. The meeting probably stirred up little excitement because the general was not well known. In a letter written upon his return to Nevada, Holdridge cited John Silva's difficulty in accepting his views. Of Silva, Holdridge wrote Esther, "[Y]ou can tell him for me that if he takes the attitude that our fight is wrong, then, he should not be a chairman, and should be removed. . . . He acts like a BIA man." Holdridge had already scolded Esther herself for paying more attention to Washington, D.C., politicians than to him. He complained that lack of Indian unity would seriously hamper his grand plans.[14]

At the twelfth annual state Indian conference, held on November 1, 1967, in Everett, Esther was the only one attending in Indian attire. The *Everett Herald* published a photo of her as she talked with Washington's governor Dan Evans. In his address to the conference, Evans vowed that the state would respect Indian treaty rights. Always skeptical of such promises, Esther told Frank that the governor's words were spoken at the very time he was "telling us that his state troopers were ordered to make arrests on the Puyallup River." Others at the meeting found little comfort in the words of Thor Tollefson of the State Department of Fisheries, who, in speaking to the delegates, admitted that "whatever solution we come up with isn't going to be acceptable to the extremes on either side." Despite her exasperation at the failure of the state to solve the Indians' fishing problem, Esther realized that the responsibility also rested with her own people, remarking that "The treaties guaranteed to us the right of self-government and we wish no encroachment on the sacred right. We all accept our responsibility that we must be responsible or our rights will disappear or be taken away by Congress."[15]

In the spring of 1968 the state was still fumbling with the fishing problem. Dick Gregory's return was followed by the state supreme

Esther and Gov. Daniel Evans depicted in a cartoon in the *Everett Herald*, November 10, 1967. The cartoonist clearly shows Esther's disgust with failed government promises, a constant theme of hers. *Reprinted courtesy of the* Everett (Wash.) Herald.

court's decision upholding Gregory's 1966 conviction for illegal net fishing. Unlike Mad Bear, Esther had supported Gregory's 1966 visit, and she now enlisted the help of General Holdridge, who supported both blacks and Indians. In a letter to Governor Evans, Holdridge wrote, "I am in receipt of a letter from one of the chiefs—a member of this [Holdridge's] council—that during the 'fish-in' . . . the Negro actor, Dick Gregory, was tried and sentenced to 90 days in jail by one of your seditious State judges, whereas white Actor Marlo[n] Brando who participated in fishing . . . was not confined. . . . I shall bring your racial prejudices to the attention of Negro leaders," Holdridge warned Evans.[16]

Gregory was jailed June 7, 1968. He fasted and was released after forty days of his ninety-day sentence.[17] Brando's attorney Malcolm McLeod admitted to the actor's preferential treatment when he had first been jailed in 1964 for illegal net fishing in the Puyallup River. McLeod had prearranged for state lawmen to arrest Brando and Bob Satiacum. McLeod then went to prosecutor John G. McCutcheon and told him it was all a publicity stunt benefiting the Indians. He asked McCutcheon to release Brando, which he did, "on a technicality."

Now Holdridge charged Evans with the "deterioration of justice in the State of Washington under your executive powers. . . . I call upon you to verify the legal facts in this case," Holdridge challenged the governor, "and furnish complete and accurate information thereon, without delay. In connection with our lawful duties you should remember that I have full authority to swear in a 'posse cimitatus' [sic] of Indians or white or negroes, or all combined."[18]

CHAPTER NINE

# THE POOR PEOPLE'S CAMPAIGN

Esther preached that her tribe's failure to regain its fishing rights for sustenance and revenue had left them in a hopeless situation. Throughout May and June of 1968, she joined what was called the "Poor People's Campaign." Frank, his stepdaughter Barbara, his daughter Lois, and his son David accompanied Esther and a group from the Pacific Northwest on a three-thousand-mile journey to Washington, D.C., to air their grievances against the government.[1] The campaign was the brainchild of Rev. Ralph Abernathy, leader of the Southern Christian Leadership Conference, who planned to bring blacks together in a nonviolent demonstration in the capital to keep alive the spirit, memory, and dream of Martin Luther King, Jr. Abernathy invited other minorities to participate in the campaign.

Esther, now sixty-three, and Frank, now thirty-seven, were among an Indian and black delegation from the Pacific Northwest led by Florestine "Flo" Ware, a well-known Seattle activist. The fifty-person group was co-led by Hank Adams, who was identified as an Assiniboine Sioux living at Frank's Landing near the mouth of the Nisqually River. The entire caravan was composed of twenty-six busloads from Washington, Oregon, Montana, the Dakotas, and Alaska. The group was fed and housed in churches along the way.

Esther and son Frank prepare to go to Washington, D.C., on the 1968 Poor People's Campaign.

When their buses reached Minneapolis–St. Paul on Tuesday, May 21, the *Minneapolis Tribune* carried an account reading, "Indian Chief, on Poor Campaign, Says 'Renters Fail Landlords.'" It was a reference to Frank's allusion to Indians as landlords and non-Indians as renters on their lands. Frank was flattered to be noted as "chief"—and he certainly enjoyed the supper served him and fellow travelers in the basement of the Hennepin Avenue Methodist Church. About 125 Twin Cities church members provided a good audience for his tales of his people's problems. In response, the members pitched in to give the entourage an average of about a dollar per donor. The *St. Paul Pioneer Press* noted that the buses were expected to stop at Madison, Wisconsin, and Toledo, Ohio.

Two days later, on May 23, Frank and Esther were pictured in the *Toledo Blade* mapping the last leg of their journey with Nisqually campaign leader Al Bridges, who claimed to have been jailed eight times for disobeying Washington state fishing regulations. Other members of his family, he said, had endured similar arrests. Hank Adams cited government violation of treaty rights. Blacks in the group advocated better housing and less job discrimination.

Arriving in the capital, Adams escorted his group to quarters in the basement of a church at Sixth and K Streets. Blacks and Indians were housed separately. According to Frank, the Reverend Abernathy arranged for Esther to be served her special soft foods. But it was evidently difficult for her hosts to get anything but eggs, and she quipped that capital residents did not seem to know the benefits of milk, mashed potatoes, and other basic foods.

Through the remainder of May and into June, other campaigners poured into Washington. Late arrivers, including many more blacks, swelled the crowd to three thousand, many of them camped on the fifteen acres of Capitol grounds dubbed "Resurrection City." Small groups of white hippies sprang up among the blacks and a few Hispanics. Groups arriving daily invaded government offices.

On one march in the city Esther cornered a Forest Service official in his office to plead that the land of the Stillaguamish be freed of roads, trails, creeks, and helicopters. She was given a low-key welcome at her congressman's office. However, Henry Jackson, now a senator, had his aides respond quickly to her request for milk and canned soft drinks. Still, the senator did little to accommodate her pleas for hunting and fishing rights for her people.

On May 31 a contingent of sixty Indians made their way to the claims commission offices where they were welcomed by Chairman John T. Vance, who wore a Poor People's Campaign button. The visit lasted for more than two hours while various Indians aired their grievances.[2] On June 1 the *Washington Post* carried a picture of Frank and Vance after Frank made the same land purchase offer to the commissioner as he had to President Johnson two years earlier. Despite the reiteration of the offer, "$1 an Acre for LBJ Ranch," there were still no takers.[3]

Abernathy organized a group, including Esther and Frank, to tour Arlington National Cemetery. There Esther purchased a wreath which, with the help of a Marine guard, she laid on the grave of

John Kennedy.[4] In early June Esther, Frank, and John Silva also visited the offices of the BIA, where they met with Acting Commissioner Theodore W. Taylor. When asked why the Stillaguamish still could not fish in their own river, Taylor advised Esther that as party to the Point Elliot treaty, the tribe should indeed have the right to fish the river. If the state challenged that right, he added, the Stillaguamish had only to prove that, in words of the treaty, they were fishing at their "usual and accustomed" places. To Esther's prodding, he told her merely that the Indians would have to assert the right themselves; the BIA would not ensure it. Two days after Esther's visit, Taylor sent her a letter summarizing their conversation: "While the Federal Government has not undertaken litigation to obtain declaratory judgements spelling out Indian fishing rights, the Dept. of Justice had provided legal representation for Indians who were arrested and prosecuted by state authorities while exercising their treaty rights."[5]

Next, Esther, Frank, and the other Indians turned their attention to the Supreme Court building. Protesting the Court's upholding of Washington State's fishing regulations, the group was stopped by police a few blocks from the building. Federal law decreed that political placards, such as the banner Esther and Frank were carrying, could be taken no closer than two blocks from the Court building. Confiscating the signs and posters, the police put them in the bed of a pickup, assuring the carriers that they could retrieve them after they had passed the building. Galled by such restriction, Esther retrieved her banner from the pickup, folded it over her left forearm, and walked by the police unchallenged. (She later explained that, had the banner been taken from her again, she would not have tried to retrieve it since the police would probably have "just dumped it somewhere.") In front of the Court building Esther brazenly unfolded her banner, which read, "Stillaguamish Indian Tribe of Western Washington." Only fifteen Indians, including her and Hank Adams, of about thirty people were allowed into the Court chambers. They expected to talk with one or more justices, but as it turned out, they were permitted to speak only with the clerk of the Court. Meanwhile, outside the Supreme Court building, Indian women shouted, "Earl Warren, you better come down now."[6]

Word of Robert Kennedy's death on June 5 broke up the campaign as hordes of mourning marchers streamed out of the capital. Hank Adams expressed the loss of one of the campaigners' heroes: "Nothing more for us here. We will go home."

Soon after Frank and his mother returned from Washington, D.C., the *Seattle Post-Intelligencer* reported on the journey of the mother-and-son team. That "fiery-eyed Indian crusader with a weathered face," the *P-I* said, had uttered "A War Cry along the Stillaguamish."[7]

CHAPTER TEN

# WAR CRY ALONG THE STILLY

In the fall of 1968, Esther and Frank were in Olympia, asking the state to recognize treaty-promised fishing rights. Esther planned meetings with Senator Jackson, Governor Evans, and federal and state officials to discuss Stillaguamish concerns.

On September 10, the *Everett Herald* reported that angry Indians patrolling the Stillaguamish had chased off sportfishers. Esther told fisheries personnel that until her people's rights were observed, the tribe would police a wide area extending from the Tulalip Reservation to Milltown; from Deer Creek to Mount Higgins to the borders of Darrington; and from Harlow Pass to the northeastern corner of the Tulalip Reservation. Esther said that if her people could not rightfully fish in the defined area, she would prohibit all non-Indians from fishing. At one point, an official reportedly told her, "Go ahead, you'd make a good cop."[1]

A tribal resolution, dated September 9, read: "If non Indians are found fishing we will arrest and pick up the gear. There will be no fishing by non Indians after Sept. 10, 1968, until further notice." Shortly after the resolution was issued, Frank was appointed tribal patrolman. On each door of his Buick Skylark was printed, "Fisheries Patrol" and "Stillaguamish Tribe Arlington 652-7452." To help carry out his threat to stop outsiders from fishing the Stillaguamish, Frank rounded up several hippies. His alternative would have been to try gathering fishermen of other tribes for a Puyallup-Nisqually–style fish-in. However, unlike these tribes that fished commercially at their "owned" sites along their rivers, the Stillaguamish had no such fishing rights at designated family sites since few of them fished at all.[2]

Responding to the Stillaguamish policing of their river, Lee Strickland of the state fisheries department in Seattle warned that "Anyone who molests the fishermen in this manner will be dealt with according to law."[3] Frank would later assert that with the help of John Silva and the hippies he had chased thirty fishermen off the river. These left without complaint—until one person reported the incident to the authorities. After Frank ordered a Louis Gusman to leave and threatened to confiscate his gear, Gusman walked straight up the riverbank and on to Arlington to report the incident. The next day, aided by Snohomish County wildlife agent Bill Hermes, Strickland arrested Frank. He was jailed, then released on bond. He was ordered to present himself on October 11 in the Cascade district court in Arlington. Appearing on that day, with Donald Horowitz as his counsel, Frank won the case on a technicality. The press he was getting reinforced his image as chief. A *Herald* reporter identified him by his name tag, "Chief Allen."[4] Having had enough of Frank's flaunting of the title, tribal member Marie Antoinette MacCurdy of Everett claimed that her father, Gus Smith of Oso, was the real Stillaguamish chief, having succeeded to the position after Jimmy Dorsey's death.

The fishing rights controversy did not completely overshadow the Stillaguamish land claim before the commission. Esther was still trying to forestall acceptance of the $48,570 award. She was convinced that insufficient time had been given to consideration of the land holdings she believed to have been the tribe's at the time of the Point Elliott treaty. Nor did she give up the attempt to seek interest on any award.

Tribal census counts still fluctuated, and attendance at meetings was poor. Conflicts remained among elderly members who were of mixed Upper Skagit and Sauk-Suiattle blood. Conflict also arose involving those who were part-white and part-Indian. When they appeared at meetings, Esther referred to them as "stay-away whites." Many of them, especially those of one-sixteenth and less blood quantum, wanted to settle the claim. But, if the award was divided, instead of having membership in a cohesive, federally recognized tribe, each enrolled Stillaguamish would realize only about six hundred dollars after attorney fees were paid.

By now, Esther had progressively less contact with Herbert Holdridge, although she was still on his mailing list and hence received his letter of November 8, 1968, reflecting on the national election held earlier that week: "The election still uncertain: 'Tricky Dick' Nixon, puppet of the 'Dirty Dollar,' tricked us again. Final 'election' by the electoral college may still select 'trickster' HHH; or 'Big Bomber' Wallace; or accomplice Edward Kennedy—all on the 'Dirty Dollar' team. Blundering seditionist LBJ, by exposing President Thieu as a trickster and puppet of the Vatican, betraying his people, carries disaster to Vietnam to betray US troops deeper into the mud of the Mekong Delta, to face the forces of South Vietnam now united against us, and united with North Vietnam."[5]

For Christmas that year Esther sent greetings to Holdridge and his wife, Dorothy. Shortly thereafter, she learned that the general had been "very sick with the Hong Kong flu." Despite the illness, however, he remained as upbeat and positive as ever—and as recriminatory. Since it was just prior to the presidential inauguration, he wrote, "the Great Spirit will never permit [Richard Nixon] to take office, for he is a very evil man . . . [one who] has already involved us in a war between the Zionists and the Arab Nations." What was needed, Holdridge said, was "to get that gang of scoundrels out of Washington, with our own Indian government going in to clean things up."[6]

Esther spent time and energy during the next year hunting for ways to upset the agreement the tribe had made to accept the claims commission award. This drove a wedge even further between her and Frederick Post. The attorney arranged a meeting with Kathleen Johnson—Esther's rival—for December 28, 1969, to be held in her trailer outside Arlington. He had her send out notices to the membership notifying them of the meeting.[7] Not surprisingly, Esther was not on Johnson's mailing list. But John Silva called her and ended up driving her and Frank to the meeting. Entering the trailer, Esther faced fifteen people whom she later identified as "whites." Post arrived soon after. Laying his hat, coat, and briefcase on the table, he asked, "How many want to settle?" Hands flew up. Among those saying yes was Silva who, placing his hat on his cane, raised it and waved it above his head. Esther later characterized Silva as "the kind of guy who would sell off the tribe for a can of Copenhagen." When Post asked how many were opposed to settling, Esther's and Frank's hands went up. That was it, sixteen to two. Post then walked over to Silva with a prepared resolution for him to sign.[8] In part it read:

> It is hereby resolved by the Stillaguamish Tribe of Indians that the prior resolutions to [accept a] compromise [in settling] its case for the net sum of $48,570.00 [are in effect] and the Tribe's attorney, Frederick W. Post, is hereby authorized to consummate said compromise and settlement by entering into a stipulation with the United States Department of Justice for a judgment in favor of the Tribe against the United States for the net sum of $48,570.00.[9]

After signing the resolution to accept the award, Post handed it to Esther. She refused to sign. He then handed it to Johnson who signed "Kathleen R. Johnson" above the typed word "Secretary." Since members were to be notified of the action, Post put the final sting on Esther by handing Johnson $5.35 to send out notices of the signing. And he immediately sent the resolution to Washington, D.C.[10]

The tug of war between Johnson and Esther would continue, revolving mostly around tribal correspondence. Esther adamantly expressed her right to incoming letters, even though Johnson was secretary. Esther carried her quarrel with Johnson to Supt. George Felshaw of the Everett agency, requesting immediate receipt of all letters sent to Johnson from attorneys Warren Gilbert, Frederick Post, and Malcolm McLeod, since she needed them to check certain records. "I know if I write her she will ignore me so am asking for you to get same for me," Esther wrote Felshaw.[11]

Unlike the neatly typed letters she received from Felshaw and others at the BIA, Esther's letters were written in longhand. In order to convert them to more official-looking documents, Esther called on people such as a Samish friend, Ken Hansen, who was living in Seattle at the time, and other "volunteers" to type them for her.

With the prospect of receiving an award of government money, tribal members showed increased opposition to Esther's autocratic manner. They wanted to snatch back some control of the affairs of the tribe. As 1970 progressed, Esther became aware of their feelings. They charged her with using for herself money she collected to get Indian burial grounds turned over to the tribe. Accusations were exchanged. Esther committed her fears to her diary: "Last month Gus Smith's children and Kathleen Johnson got together with Paul Harveys Sauk Suiattle family at Gus Smith's daughter, Marie's [place] and they tried to get resolutions to put John Silva incompt [sic] and Esther Ross and Frank Allen out of office not to represent them any more."[12]

Esther was still rankled over the meeting wherein the tribe had voted to accept the settlement. She decided to fight the vote as illegal—Johnson had signed as secretary and no quorum was present. This would be her strategy. In a January 3, 1970, letter to the claims commission, she listed the reasons the vote was illegal. She even managed to persuade Silva to sign it. It read in part that as chief he questioned the validity of the resolution because of the lack of a quorum and because a person who wasn't the elected secretary signed off the resolution as secretary.

Within two weeks Esther received a reply from the commission acknowledging receipt of her letter, but advising her that the commission had signed the "Stipulation for Entry of Final Judgement" on January 8, awarding the Stillaguamish $48,570.[13] Undeterred, she pushed on. But to get the judgment overturned would require travel, which was becoming more difficult for her each year. Not only did she fear traveling by plane, she was limited by her deteriorating health and lack of money. On January 24, she solicited help from Hank Adams for one-way plane fare to Washington, D.C. Truck dealer Antone Neyens, she told Adams, would contribute enough for the return fare. Esther traveled to Frank's Landing to pick up $150 from the SAIA, then back up to Everson, Washington, where Neyens, an officer in the Lynden Assembly of God Church, was able to present her with a check for $125 from church funds.[14]

Esther put her faith in Frank to climb the bureaucratic ladder of the claims commission back in the nation's capital. While Frank was on his way, she prepared another letter, repeating her objections to the commission's acceptance of the December 28, 1969, resolution, executed without full authority of the general membership. She and Silva signed the letter, and she sent it to the commission chair, Jerome K. Kuykendall. She informed the commissioner that a copy of the letter had been sent to the commissioner of Indian affairs. A copy was also sent to the Small Tribes of Western Washington (STOWW), Sen. Henry Jackson, and the National Congress of American Indians (NCAI).[15]

Back in D.C., Frank missed any chance to use his powers of persuasion on the commissioner, but he met with BIA officials on January 30 to discuss the judgment. Moneys awarded by the commission would have to be paid out on a per capita basis, the officials told him. In order to keep the money as a tribal asset, there had to be an official governmental structure such as those established under the 1934 Indian Reorganization Act. In addition, he was told, the Stillaguamish still lacked a tribally owned land base to qualify them for a reservation to put in trust status. They remained an unrecognized tribe.[16]

Changing planes in Chicago on his flight home, Frank arranged for a layover so he could take a bus about 150 miles east to Swanton, Ohio, for a social call on the Holdridges. He found them living in a trailer, the general broken in finances but not in spirit.

Arriving home, Frank gave Esther an overly optimistic report. The tribe could organize, he told her, under the IRA. But that notion was disputed in a letter the acting associate commissioner of Indian affairs sent Frank. There had been some misunderstanding on the issue, he wrote: "The Stillaguamish Indians have no reservation, and are scattered throughout western Washington. The Stillaguamish Tribe . . . is no longer a recognized tribe, and the Stillaguamish Indians living today can be considered only as individual descendants of members of the aboriginal tribe." The Stillaguamish could "not organize themselves into a tribal entity which can be recognized by this [BIA] Department for any purpose." This seemed to close the door to securing a land base in order to get federal recognition.[17]

Still Esther sought to waylay any per capita disbursement of claims moneys. If the tribe received a lump sum, it could buy land to put in trust to achieve federal recognition. Or if it were a recognized tribe, the Stillaguamish could get the claims award in a lump sum. In seeking federally funded services similar to those received by recognized tribes, Esther proposed forming a cluster of tribal homes in the Arlington area. If claims moneys were paid on a per capita basis, she feared that members would abandon any motive for coming together as a viable tribe.

The Everett agency turned a deaf ear to Esther's complaints. Deciding to sue Frederick Post for his position on the claims award, she consulted other attorneys, but none of them would take her case, including Malcolm McLeod, who talked her out of it. Nonetheless, she did not give up. She petitioned the Indian Claims Commission to revoke Post's authority to represent the tribe. "We did not realize that attorneys are not to be involved in conflicts of interests," she asserted. "In point of fact, we have been led around by the nose and misled as to our interests." When she received no response to the petition mailed in February, she followed up with another letter to the commission in October. In it she conceded that the commission's position was probably not changeable.[18]

CHAPTER ELEVEN

# LEGACY OF THE DEAD, LAND BASE FOR THE LIVING

Esther had not forgotten the quest she'd begun in 1966 for tribal ownership of Indian burial sites along the Stillaguamish North Fork, especially near Trafton, Oso, and Hazel. She saw "destruction and desecration of the [sites] as a symbol of the white man's attempt to erase the proud Stillaguamish people from the nation's history just as the Secretary of the Interior has refused to let them take their rightful place among the nation's Indian tribes."[1] She sought to acquire these plots and put them in trust status. However, she faced a tangle of property owners that mimicked the bush and brambles she battled to find the sites.

Esther's search for the burial plots took her to courthouses to study maps and records. She also visited Charlie Smith, a white man considered a friend of Indians and a former Snohomish County commissioner. She talked with elders such as Wesley Patrick and Gus Smith. Charlie Smith pointed out to Esther cemeteries at Trafton and Hazel that he had prevented from being plowed up and desecrated. He had lived in Trafton since 1903 and had access to county records, so he was able to provide Esther with useful information. He knew the names of Indians buried there and knew their families as well. Esther not only took notes on the remarks of Smith and others, she also recorded them on tape.[2]

A weary Esther trudges the shores of the Stillaguamish River hunting for Stillaguamish burial sites.

Whites not only desecrated the graves of Indian dead, their government did not allow survivors of the deceased to take up patents on lands along their river. "The Indians did not understand the white man's laws which allowed much of the land (including cemetery plots) to go for taxes," one local newspaper reported.[3]

Esther scouted the length of both forks of the Stillaguamish, struggling through difficult terrain looking for signs of the twenty-nine five-acre burial grounds she'd been told of. Many Indians, not wishing grave sites to be disturbed, had left them unmarked and allowed them to be overgrown with vegetation. Esther found three sites along the North Fork, including one untended at Hazel. She found another at Trafton further down the main Stillaguamish, closer to its mouth, where Stillaguamish sites were especially hard to find. She found a third at Oso, in between the other two.

After whites came to the Puget Sound area, Indians began to bury their dead, sometimes marking the plots with monuments, some of which Esther found overgrown with vegetation. One white man, however, owned land with a small, picket-enclosed Indian burial plot that he maintained east of Stanwood.[4] Another burial ground lay on a farmer's land near Milltown along a road running south to Stanwood. Esther discovered that this site had been stripped of topsoil to build a dike against flooding from a tributary of the south fork of the Skagit River. Human bone fragments had been kicked around like pinecones. Esther learned that the Milltown farmer kept a skull before giving a gunnysack of bones to anthropologists at the University of Washington. Frank Falk, who lived near the Milltown cemetery and was raised among Indians, gave Esther a few bones that had already been exposed to the elements. Elders told Esther that, as had happened in other places in the Pacific Northwest, many of the dead were said to have died from smallpox carried in infected army blankets given to Indians as welfare tokens by the whites.

Esther's requests for ownership of Indian burial grounds began in earnest once she received some agency help. In March of 1967, she asked agency officials to identify owners of the sites, most of which she had located on maps. The next step would be to acquire them so they could be put in trust status. Tribal operations officer Vincent Little at the Portland Area Office searched for what records he could find. Everett agency Supt. George Felshaw told her that only through congressional action could such lands be parceled out and set aside for trust status. She believed Congress had failed its responsibility to set aside these lands. She also believed that Felshaw was not as attentive to her efforts to retrieve the sites as he was to her other causes. In spite of this, he was the one agency superintendent Esther respected. He listened to what she had to say, and, when her legs were bothering her, he often walked out to street level to visit with her as she sat in the car.

In the summer of 1968, Esther petitioned Sen. Henry Jackson, who sent her concerns on to the BIA. Assessing the situation for the senator, the BIA suggested an onsite inspection of the cemeteries.[5] That inspection was arranged for July 19, when Esther was just home from the Poor People's Campaign. The new agency realty officer, Steven "Bud" Lozar, was fresh on the job. Esther took advantage of his newness to unburden herself. Lozar would soon become adjusted to Esther's long-winded conversations, and like everyone else he used tactics to limit the time of her office visits. He also became aware of her penchant for storing up information about her tribe. He found this more than helpful. Because the Stillaguamish were not a recognized tribe, Lozar had few records on them at the agency, and he often referred people in search of Stillaguamish information to "Esther's agency."[6]

On July 19 the inspection entourage—Esther, Bud Lozar, John Silva, and others—traveled to Trafton to view the Indian burial site there. The group included Lee Atkins, who was listed as owning the five-acre plot on which there was a fenced sixty-by-sixty-foot burial plot. Atkins had deeded the plot to his daughter and son-in-law, Edward Zeine, a short time previously. However, the Zeines now decided to offer the burial plot to the tribe as a gift. Esther was not satisfied; she wanted the entire five acres. The agency saw no justification for that. Further investigation showed that the Zeines did not own the land under question. A Robert M. Talbot owned it. Being "very cool" toward the group, Talbot offered it to the tribe for seventy-five thousand dollars.[7]

The agency's criminal investigator, John W. Bushman, reported to the BIA's area office in Portland on the July 19 field trip: "Mrs. Ross contends that the Bureau of Indian Affairs did not give the necessary protection to the Indian people by allowing the non-Indian to obtain the tract at Trafton containing the cemetery."[8]

Another field trip was planned. The party setting out for Trafton on October 8 included Esther, Frank, Kathleen Johnson, and Charlie Smith. The group aimed to locate a site on the right bank of the Stillaguamish near Trafton. After fighting heavy undergrowth, they were about to give up the search when they met a neighbor who led them to the burial site. There they found three grave markers. Now it appeared that the burial was on a piece of land purchased by three Mount Vernon doctors. The doctors had the 131 acres surveyed, and a month later, one of those doctors, Richard Hoag, joined Esther; Bud Lozar; Jimmy Dorsey's grandson, sixty-five-year-old Wesley Patrick; John Silva, struggling along with his cane; and Charlie Smith, who had once owned property nearby. An *Everett Herald* reporter described the party's soggy stomp through quagmires, bushes, and brambles. Esther wanted the party to know that they were searching for the graves of her relatives as well as those of Jimmy Dorsey's family.[9]

Esther stumbled onto some moss-covered stones. Lozar's main concern had been to clear the brush to establish boundaries. As it turned out the property lay inside the boundary line of land formerly owned by Robert M. Talbot. Later his ex-wife had owned it and sold it to Masao Fuji of Seattle. When contacted by Lozar, Fuji said he was unaware of the cemetery but could not respond to offers to sell until learning more about it.

Lozar did not find such outings pleasurable. A decade later he would have a different outlook. Complimenting Esther for her accomplishments, he would write:

> Throughout your long struggle many humorous things have occurred which helped you keep you spirits active.... Many sad things happened that would discourage a normal person.... However, Esther, you are not one of the normal persons, you are an extraordinary person and this is why you pushed on.
>
> I remember when I had to name you the Superintendent of the Stilly because you [led] me through thorn bushes, up

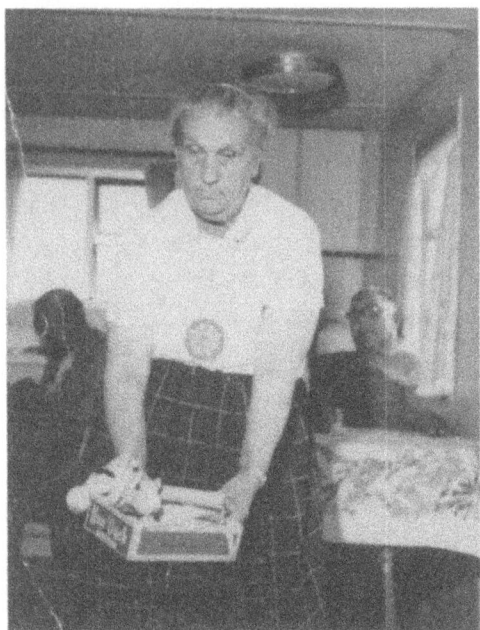

Esther holds a cigar box containing bones of Stillaguamish dead. She displayed them at the Washington state capital in Olympia and in the nation's capital.

and down hills, in my good suit, on a grave yard hunt and also maintained, in your home a complete file of the Stillaguamish tribe.[10]

The next year, Esther took her fight to Gov. Dan Evans's office. She brought with her a Van Dyck cigar box full of the small bones Frank Falk had given her. Tossing them on the governor's desk, she asked him where his grandparents were buried. "I want to go dig them up," she blurted.[11]

Esther also took her bones in a shopping bag to Washington, D.C., where she displayed them in congressional offices and meeting rooms. Photojournalist George Ortez remembered her coming to an NCAI meeting in the capital, toting her bag, saying something about her ancestors' bones. Ortez quickly saw a news story in the making. But as time passed, Ortez grew jaded. "We listened to this thing over again and again," he said. "She would start complaining about their neglecting to settle the dispute . . . so she could bury her bones."[12]

After having been transferred to the Indian agency at Hoquiam, Washington, Bud Lozar remembered Esther and Frank coming to his home at four o'clock in the morning to talk about cemeteries. "We lost our cemeteries and . . . we want our land back," Esther told a reporter for the *Seattle Times*. Of that land she once declaimed, "White men either took our land or paid off ignorant old Indians with a horse or a bottle of whiskey."[13]

Searching for another means of acquiring property for a land base, Esther sought to obtain a vacant public school building in Oso. One day in March of 1970, she, Frank, Hank Adams, and several other Indians met with the Arlington school district board, which administered the property. She told board members that since the Stillaguamish had received little money and since there was now "little hope" of their ever acquiring land and a building, she hoped the district would give her tribe the Oso school property. She envisioned using the old school building for classes in handicrafts, mechanics, cabinetry, and canoe building as well as a place for the seventy-five remaining Stillaguamish to gather for meetings and practice traditional dances. Adams, the activist with the SAIA, reinforced Esther's request by assuring the board that he was well aware of the plight of the Stillaguamish and the legitimacy of their needs. However, board chairman Erland Elefson turned down the request, stating that, since the school was abandoned, the land on which it stood must revert to the original owner.[14]

Undeterred by this setback, Esther continued searching for a land base. Her next target was Gus Smith, tribal elder and owner of four contiguous lots in Oso. In early summer of 1970, he willed the lots to the tribe, but his seven children, especially Marie MacCurdy, opposed the gift since they felt they had been promised the lots as their inheritance. Because his children were also to be beneficiaries of his holdings on the Port Madison Indian Reservation, however, and because they were careless in taking care of his property, Gus Smith offered his four Oso lots to the tribe. His daughter had failed to pay the taxes for him on a fifth lot in Oso where the house of her deceased mother had burned down, and

Smith lost the property. He no longer wanted to leave the lots to Marie and her siblings.[15]

The unexpected death of Gus Smith on July 25, 1970, less than two months after he had signed his will, left Esther hoping the tribe now owned the land. But hopes slowly drained as months, then years slid by without the lots becoming the Stillaguamish Reservation. It would be October 1973, before attorney Charles R. Carey, representing Earl E. Allen, administrator of Smith's estate, would admit the will for probate in the county. He submitted with it two resolutions signed by Esther Ross as "Alternate Chairman and Secretary" for the tribe. They were dated September 22 and 29, 1972. These resolutions requested the BIA to legally arrange for transfer of Smith's four lots to the United States in trust for the Stillaguamish. Carey cautioned that he could not tell from evidence presented that the tribe would be eligible to have lots accepted as trust land.[16]

CHAPTER TWELVE

# ORGANIZATION, DISORGANIZATION, AND MILITANCY

For years Esther Ross had moved around the Pacific Northwest. In late 1969, when she turned sixty-five, she and Arnold pulled a trailer to a wooded hillside he owned on Cagey Road on the Lummi Reservation. It would appear she might find a measure of permanence. Barely months later, however, Esther and Arnold decided to move from their trailer to a new house. On May 20, 1970, they signed for a loan, securing BIA approval, for a Home Improvement Agreement (HIA) with the government. Later in the year they moved into their new three-room frame house whose one-room kitchen–eating space–sitting room occupied half the house. There were also two bedrooms, a hall, and a bathroom. Esther rented a post office box in nearby Bellingham.

During this time, Ross's favorite granddaughter, Dorothy, who had lived with Esther and Arnold when she was a child, occasionally came over from the Yakama for short visits. Many times these visits meant she was in trouble, such as the time Esther had to arrange an abortion for her. But sometimes she came only to take Arnold fishing. The fishing expeditions meant consuming quantities of beer, of course, but Esther had by now decided that she could not change Arnold's behavior. As she accepted her illnesses, she also accepted his physical abuse. For several years she did not reveal that during one of his alcoholic bouts, Arnold had pummeled her with his cane, breaking her left hip. He had mistakenly believed she was in bed with another man. She was, in fact, in bed with her grandchild. He was reasonably social most of the time, but not during alcoholic bouts. It was Esther's practice on the Sabbath to have him drive her to Bellingham's Adventist Church. While she sought spiritual solace inside the church, he sat in his car in the parking lot, drinking beer.[1]

About this time, the ailing John Silva resigned as chairman of the tribe, and the mantle of leadership fell on Esther's shoulders. She was, in effect, appointed the new chair. She was therefore the incumbent at the next tribal election. There was, however, a growing movement among some council officials to challenge her leadership. But outside forces demanded a strong leader, and Esther knew it. Governor Evans had urged the state in the fall of 1967 to develop a program in Indian affairs, and Indian Commissioner Robert Bennett had told the Indians not to "sit back and wait for . . . [programs] to be developed for you. . . . [D]irection . . . will depend on your local leadership." Now there was discussion of establishing a statewide Indian organization to form a united front for the state's sixteen thousand Indians.[2]

Through the '60s and '70s Esther seemed to have been more successful in dealing with individuals of other organizations than she was in dealing with her own tribespeople. A notable exception to her success with other groups was the National Tribal Chairmans Association (NTCA), which was under leadership of Robert Jim, a Yakama who opposed recognition for smaller tribes. Offsetting the position of the NTCA was the new force, STOWW—Small Tribes of Western Washington—which was organized and incorporated in 1969. STOWW received funding from the Office of Economic Opportunity (OEO). In 1964 Pres. Lyndon Johnson had launched a vigorous war on poverty with a program administered by the OEO as part of the government's Comprehensive Manpower Program. The following year money was funneled to states for each to run its own programs for minorities and the poor.[3]

The deputy director of the OEO for the state of Washington headed the Governor's Indian Advisory Committee (GIAC). A black man, he dispensed most of the money to black groups. William R. "Bill" Jeffries, a Cherokee-Sioux, was hired in 1968 as an intern in the governor's office; it was he who discovered that none of the funding was reaching "smaller Indian tribes," tribes defined by Esther as tribes without land, tribes owning no land in trust status, and unrecognized tribes. Western Washington had more than its share of these small tribes because the area was rich in natural resources, providing subsistence for many tribes in pre-contact times. However, tribes with large populations and funds—like the Colville, Nez Perce, and Navajo—had more political clout and influence.

In July 1969 Governor Evans changed that by naming Jeffries as coordinator of the GIAC. A combination of individuals and ideas now began to change the entire picture for the state's Indians. Jeffries extended financial assistance to Roy George, an ambitious Nooksack who had recognized that Indians were getting too little of the poverty-program pie. He and Ted George, a Clallam, and Frank Wright, a Puyallup, began organizing the small tribes into STOWW. Charles "Chuck" McEvers of the American Friends Service Committee in Seattle helped the group. The Friends at that time was working with others to produce a manuscript titled *Uncommon Controversy*, published in 1970. The publication was intended to set the stage for an upcoming court case over Indian fishing treaty rights, later called the Boldt case.[4]

McEvers and his group provided the impetus for Roy George to organize STOWW. Jeffries made sure the group received OEO funding. STOWW became an effective advocate for various tribes. The organization was soon drawing money for all sorts of programs from many sources.[5]

To empower the GIAC, Jeffries changed its status from that of a committee to that of a council, believing as he did that committees were token organizations without power. Thereafter, the deputy director of the state OEO was unable to regain control of GIAC because now Jeffries was reporting to the national, instead of the state, office. And for 1970 Jeffries was able to earmark $125,000 in funds for STOWW.[6]

Under Esther's leadership the Stillaguamish council passed a resolution on January 4, 1970, to join STOWW's member tribes in an effort not to only solidify Stillaguamish tribal organization and programs, but also to receive federal funds now channeled through STOWW. The leaders of STOWW treated Esther in the same way other organizations did. They tolerated her. "Esther was one tough lady. You could never keep her quiet. Her facts were not always right," said Leota George, who attended almost all STOWW meetings for years with her husband, Roy.[7] Chuck McEvers, who was named executive director of STOWW in April 1970, quickly became acquainted with Esther. He found she would not take no for an answer. She was relatively unschooled but totally dedicated, he said. "[Esther] was an embarrassment [to leaders of large tribes] and they kind of wished she'd go away," McEvers said, adding, "STOWW [too] had to deal with lack of acceptance among the larger, more influential, [and] more generally recognized tribes in western Washington."[8]

As help from STOWW increased, so did Esther's interest in the organization. Her friend Catherine Troeh, a Chinook, said Esther and Frank "were faithfully present for every STOWW meeting." There she greeted old friends. "She was always well dressed and clean, but very deaf," Troeh remembered.[9]

Esther juggled her schedule according to available transportation. Either Frank chauffered her or she hitched rides up and down the Puget Sound corridor. Usually these trips took her from her home out from Bellingham to Sumner, headquarters for STOWW. When she traveled, she generally placed grandson David, now almost twelve, for the day with friends or acquaintances, and occasionally with Ruth in Seattle. Some days were given to taking Arnold to the doctor or hospital. She often visited Hank Adams at Frank's Landing or traveled to Everett to talk to Al Cooper of the Snohomish.

This compulsive attendance at meetings of various organizations caused her no end of frustration and weariness, which came through in her personal notes. For example, after the March 21,

1970, STOWW meeting, she wrote, "there are some statements made by certain officers . . . at this meeting that I was ready to Blow My Top." On her trips, she and Frank often stayed overnight at friends' homes in the Puget Sound area. Arnold no longer chauffered Esther other than to church, if he was physically able, or on errands into Bellingham. His health was deteriorating rapidly. But Frank would always be at the ready to chauffeur his mother. Money for gas, food, and lodging came from friends who were aware of the work she was doing for the tribe. Sometimes when Esther and Frank were caught late in Seattle with little money and no place to spend the night, they would go to the city's all-night theater, the Green Parrot. There, between the sounds of gunfire from some B-Western movie, they would nod off. Even if they had the money, they would not stay in motels because Esther didn't like them.[10]

Esther's travels brought her in contact with other Indian activists who wanted to preserve fishing rights for their people. She read everything she could about protests and closely monitored the intensified "fish wars" waged by Puyallup-Nisquallys. She was aware that the state was challenging their growing militancy by giving law enforcement officers riot training. She also kept abreast of Indian activism across the nation. The American Indian Movement (AIM) was at the center of this unrest. AIM members demanded treaty rights, sovereignty of their lands, and compensation for their losses. In 1969 militants occupied Alcatraz Island in San Francisco Bay, claiming rights to properties of this former federal prison that once held Indians the government regarded as "contentious." On the East Coast, a planned March 1970 occupation of Ellis Island was foiled when the militants' launch developed engine trouble off the New Jersey coast. In the West, Indian militants and their allies were more successful in occupying the eleven-hundred-acre Fort Lawton near Seattle.

Fort Lawton was of special interest to Esther, for when the United States decided to release the land that composed the complex, she believed she might have a vested interest in the property.

Walter Allen's grandfather, Solomon Allen, she believed had owned land there before donating it to the government for use as a fort. She hoped that with its release she, as Allen's widow, and Frank might be entitled to some proceeds from the sale. When the land was offered to the city of Seattle, the Indians objected, basing their claim not only on grounds of aboriginal possession but on grounds that the government had declared it surplus. (In 1865, the second session of the Thirty-eighth Congress had given Indians the right to surplus military property.) Esther and Frank would blame Bernie Whitebear, one of the activists who had launched the Fort Lawton demonstrations, for their not having profited from the released land, claiming that he persuaded them to abandon claim to it with assurance that their claim would be reopened when Indians finally possessed the land.[11]

Esther knew that were she to obtain her share of the property she had to retain legal counsel. She contacted Herbert Holdridge for help. In a letter signed by Frank she included information on the Fort Lawton property, her intentions to sue, and pertinent press clippings. Frank included pictures of Esther, John Silva, and himself. In his reply, Holdridge wrote, "I am a good lawyer—believe me—and am working for the Indians 'for free,' not against them, so I tell you the law! I would never agree to go into a white man's court. In the first place I don't know of a single case the Indians have ever won in the white man's courts." He reminded Esther that those courts had no lawful jurisdiction over Indian treaties. "Make him come into your courts, before your Chiefs," he wrote, and he encouraged Esther to "go all the way! Don't throw away your . . . case!" adding, "I will never accept any decision of any official whose source . . . violates their treaties, and will overrule them all, and still restore Indian lands, as I have promised to do."[12]

It was at this juncture that Esther dropped all correspondence with Holdridge. She also dropped her plans to sue.

The attempt to take over the Fort Lawton property became a national media event that lasted more than a month. Bob Satiacum and Bernie Whitebear led eight Indian picketers who camped outside the main gate. Calling themselves the United American Indian Fort Lawton Occupational Force, they attempted to storm the grounds but were confronted by military police as they were scaling the bluff to set up a tipi. At the main gate others sang and beat drums. A proclamation declaring that an Indian university and cultural center would be developed at the fort was read. About seventy-two demonstrators were arrested and held briefly at the fort's stockade. In addition to Satiacum and Whitebear, others arrested included Ramona Bennett of the SAIA; Leonard Peltier of AIM; Grace Thorpe, Jim Thorpe's daughter; and others from in and out of the area. Actress Jane Fonda was among those held briefly at the Fort Lewis army base near Tacoma. One Yakama claimed that he and seven others who were jailed were beaten when they refused to leave their cells.[13]

Frank drove demonstrators to and from the fort, carrying sandwiches and potato chips for them. For a time it looked like the demonstrators would gain nothing for their efforts. However, when Seattle accepted the land from the United States, the city gave sixteen acres on the north side of the fort to the Indians. On it they eventually built and managed a complex called Daybreak Star. Bernie Whitebear became its executive director. One of its promotional bulletins read:

> United Indians of All Tribes Foundation,
> Daybreak Star Indian Cultural-Educational Center
> Discovery Park, Seattle, Washington 98199

Below the sign was a greeting in Chinook jargon: "Klahowya!!! Welcome to the Indian Art Mart at the beautiful Daybreak Star Art and Cultural Center."[14]

Bill Jeffries brought the GIAC and the Indian Affairs Task Force together late in 1969 to evaluate Indian conditions on the reservations and the legal status of Indian claims. The two groups released a report in the spring of 1971.[15] This study was so successful that a second task force was organized in 1972 to deal with problems of landless and urban Indians. Esther was one of seventeen members of this group. Following a series of meetings sponsored by a committee of the Human Affairs Council, the report of the task force, *The People Speak: Will You Listen?*, was published in 1973.[16]

Esther was ever an active participant in GIAC, though she would always spin her own agenda. "She was a bother," Robert Comenout, a committee member, admitted. Bill Jeffries remembers the day Esther asked if she might have a few minutes of the committee's time before adjourning for lunch. When Jeffries called on her, she took out her cigar box and spilled the Milltown bones on the table. She was determined to keep alive her hopes of locating and acquiring Indian burial grounds, even though that wasn't a committee goal. Jeffries even accepted her repeated invitations to join her in looking for cemeteries along the Stillaguamish River.[17]

CHAPTER THIRTEEN

# Mrs. Ross Goes to Washington—Again

Esther was in Washington, D.C., in November 1972 when Indian activists arrived at the end of what they called their "Trail of Broken Treaties." After wending their way to the capital from the West, they took over offices of the BIA, smashing furniture, destroying records, and appropriating artifacts. Among the protesters were Janet McCloud and Hank Adams, who found BIA records for Margaret Greene's Samish. Esther couldn't join them in protest because her swollen legs confined her at times to her wheelchair and walker. She was not even a part of the "Trail"; she had come instead on Stillaguamish business: She hoped to force the government to put the Gus Smith lots in trust as her people's land base.

When Esther alighted from the bus, her wheelchair in tow, Margaret Greene was there. "I met with Esther," Margaret recalled, "I was free. She asked me to help her. I wheeled her. It was hard for her to get around."[1]

Whenever Esther arrived in Washington, D.C., she drew as much attention as if she were some foreign dignitary come to seek funds for his or her country. Whether in recessed conference rooms along halls of the Capitol Building or in legislative offices and suites, she made herself at home and her wants known. Word of her arrival soon got around through buzzwords like "Oh God, here comes Esther Ross."[2] Venting her feelings, she sought her objectives by zeroing in on a person and demanding that she be given what she wanted. Her target had little choice other than to plan a rebuttal or wriggle away from her verbal grasp. Of her demeanor, Linda Dombrowski, a leader of STOWW recalled: "Anybody else goes to Washington and the Congressional people or the Bureau or whatever, they know you'll be going home and they have to put up with you, and are polite to you. But Esther, they couldn't get rid of her. She would just sit there.... She was really a good activist. She got the job done. We are sitting here with anthropologists and attorneys and all this good stuff and here is Esther with little or no resources, her commitment and her tenacity refuses to go away."[3]

While in the capital Esther would visit the National Archives and the Smithsonian Institution. Sam Stanley, a specialist in Tlingit culture in the Smithsonian's Department of the Study of Man, remembered her coming in with Frank and sometimes two or three others in tow. Stanley responded by ferreting out information she requested—though he had the sense that Esther was not precisely sure exactly what information she wanted or how to go about finding it. "She could do her share of talking," Stanley said.[4]

Among Esther's most helpful contacts in the capital was Charles "Chuck" Trimble, executive director of the NCAI and a frequent visitor to Washington State. Trimble remembered being "impressed by stories I had heard of Esther's persistence in seeking support [for the] Stillaguamishes' reinstatement. I introduced myself and promised her that before I left NCAI she would have her wish. She told me in essence that she had heard that line before but she would wait and see. That was a challenge to me, and grabbed me to her cause."[5]

Esther frequently sought financial help from NCAI. Trimble recalled that "we didn't have an awful lot of money. [We were] always strapped for funds." Nevertheless, the organization usually came up with what Esther needed. On one occasion Lucy Friedlander Covington, a Colville, obtained funds from NCAI to pay for Esther's fare home from Washington, D.C. Linda Dom-

Charles "Chuck" Trimble, executive director of the National Congress of American Indians, displays a "welcome" cake given him when he visited the Stillaguamish tribal council at the Island Crossing office. Trimble was a favorite of Esther's. On the reverse of this photograph she wrote, "A smile that will never be forgotten." Attorney Alan Stay, Stillaguamish counsel, is seated at the left.

browski remembered other times when Esther was unable to obtain money for the trip home and she would sit silently in the BIA office "for days and finally the staff would take up a collection and send her home." That she had no official standing with the bureau did not keep her from the use of its offices in the capital or in the state of Washington. The BIA's tribal operations officer back at the Everett agency, William "Bill" Arthur Black, remembered that BIA officials in D.C. made certain Esther got from the hotel to wherever she had to go. He also remembered the "many times Esther took her Social Security check and . . . [bought] a one-way ticket to Washington, D.C., and she didn't have a dime in her pocket, just her ticket, and she'd fly back there and she'd go right after the commissioner and she'd put them [in the BIA] through the grinder." BIA Solicitor Scott Keep kept Black apprised of her progress through the labyrinthine bureau offices in the capital.[6]

Esther attended three levels of meetings. At the highest level, at least from the standpoint of public awareness, were those in the Washington, D.C., offices of the BIA, Congress, and organizations such as the National American Indian Association and the National Congress of American Indians.[7] At the middle level were meetings in regional BIA offices such as those in Everett and Portland and with regional groups such as the Washington State Indian Conference and STOWW. On the local level were the Stillaguamish tribal meetings and those of other tribes. These meetings of other tribes were of great importance to Esther; they gave her the opportunity not to only apprise her allies of Stillaguamish happenings but also to learn from them as well. Whatever the level of meeting, Esther spoke in a voice that was usually high pitched, strident, and cracking. She never retreated from a verbal confrontation. And Frank was always there, sitting beside her in the front row of each meeting.

Esther was amply aware the tribe needed more-permanent offices than her home and her car. In January 1973 she rented a small building, once the County Realty office, for tribal headquarters. She paid the hundred-dollar-a-month rent out of her monthly salary from the OEO—her title was "Community Aide"—for four hundred dollars. With the balance of her check, she bought office supplies and paid for the maintenance of the office, which was located on 1.9 acres at Island Crossing, three miles west of Arlington. Any money left over went for the household. Driving to the office required about a sixty-mile commute from her home on the Lummi Reservation.[8]

Esther still met with the Governor's Indian Advisory Council to discuss treaty fishing rights as interpreted by the state. She also continued membership in the Survival of American Indians Association, which Hank Adams now led, and regularly attended meetings of the Portland-based ATNI. Ramona Bennett of the SAIA observed that she "would just kinda be everywhere. If she had been paid by the mile, she would have died very wealthy indeed."[9]

Ramona Bennett was among the few people with whom Esther was comfortable discussing things of a personal nature. With Ramona she talked about her early California years, years she otherwise rarely discussed. Esther told Bennett of her encounters with Greg Duchene and Forrest Gerard of the Interior Department and with Chuck Trimble, "her special favorite person," and with prominent Indians and of their responses to her. In Washington, D.C., "When someone [a congressman or bureaucrat] didn't want to be seen, [Esther] managed to head them off in their path and do a perfect ambush. She would always share [those stories] with me," Bennett said. One of her frequent targets was Sen. Henry Jackson. Esther would sneak up on him when he least expected it. "He could be saying to someone, 'That damned Esther Ross is . . . waiting for me in my office, and so I'm coming over [to your place].' And there she'd be [right at his elbow]." She would ignore the rules and camp out all night at the office door of the person she wanted to see, said Jack Kidder, a Snohomish Indian who once found himself in Washington, D.C. when Esther was there.[10]

Mel Tonasket, former chairman of the Colville Confederated Tribes, recalled Esther's standoffish behavior, especially at mealtimes. Of her sojourns in the capital, he recalled her as "quite a lady," remembering her as "traveling all over . . . on a shoe string." "She never seemed to have money," Tonasket continued. "And when she'd go there the BIA or somebody would come up with money [to get her home] and somehow they'd get her a room." He confessed that "the rest of us were kinda spoiled. Here I come from a large tribe, with a lot of resources and always recognized and here she was with a dream and a mission and traveled really poor."[11]

Tulalip tribal leader Wayne Williams described Esther's attendance record at meetings as "probably better than anyone else['s]." She had "complete and absolute dedication" to her causes, he said. Williams observed that "she hammered on [her own agenda] in [every] meeting I was in." Recalling an ATNI luncheon meeting he attended in Seattle one day, Williams described a room prepared with small tables for six to eight people. Esther sat at a table with a couple of others. As the room filled, members took their places at other tables. Williams, the last to arrive, was left with no choice of table other than Esther's. There was no small talk with Esther; she was all business as she ate her bread and drank her milk.[12]

On the home front, a new granddaughter, Sandra Martine, joined the household in June of 1972. She was Frank's child by an intermittent relationship with Gloria Fay Grant, a Musqueam Indian from near Vancouver, B.C. The relationship was formalized with the exchange of marriage vows before a justice of the peace on November 9, 1972, in Bellingham.

Frank's marriage to Grant didn't last. Her addiction to alcohol caused problems, and she returned to Canada, leaving Sandra behind. The baby joined her half-brother David, who had moved into Esther's household under similar circumstances when his mother, Mary, failed to appear in court for custody hearings. Though David remained at home with Frank, Lois had married young and was out on her own.[13]

CHAPTER FOURTEEN

# HALF THE SALMON: THE BOLDT CASE

Any introduction to Esther could become a significant meeting. Through Hank Adams, Esther met attorney David Getches of Boulder, Colorado, when both were in Puyallup in 1969. She was interested in the fish-ins, and he was studying Indian law and the federal government's preparation of a suit against Washington State to end confrontation between Indian and non-Indian commercial and sportfishers. Getches was there to represent two of the challenged tribes.[1] He took an immediate interest in Esther as head of a nonrecognized tribe and intensely concerned for its welfare.

Getches had begun his career in California working for Legal Services. He moved to Washington State briefly, then left Legal Services to help organize what became a well-funded Native American Rights Fund (NARF), which was based in Boulder. The group was organized to help Indian activists merge Indian people into mainstream America by helping them fight their legal battles with the government.[2]

Esther, sitting in on Survival of American Indians Association strategy meetings, had by now become deeply involved in tribal fishing issues. Despite escalating violence and many arrests, the Indians continued fishing with nets at their traditional sites. On August 8, 1969, the Washington Departments of Fisheries and Game petitioned the state superior court to further clarify the state's regulatory authority over fishing, as laid out by the U.S. Supreme Court in 1968. Indian fishing cases had alternated between the two supreme courts, giving rise to various rulings on river closures to Indian net fishing without satisfactory solution for Indians or whites. The Puyallup-Nisquallys continued clashing with state officials over conservation regulations that banned net fishing. Compared with Puyallup-Nisqually catches, other Washington tribes took fewer fish for personal and commercial purposes. The only exception were the Yakamas, whose primary operations were on the Columbia, where they used nets to harvest large numbers of salmon.[3]

A suit contesting the state's control of Indian fishing rights was filed by the federal government on behalf of seven tribes on September 18, 1970. It was scheduled to be tried in Tacoma's Western Washington U.S. District Court. The case was assigned to Senior District Judge George Hugo Boldt, whom some attorneys characterized as pompous. Nevertheless, he was a friend of Indians—and of the government's lead attorney, George Dysart, assistant solicitor for the Department of the Interior's Portland office, who was representing the Puyallups and Nisquallys in the suit.[4]

Back in the area as counsel to the Muckleshoot and Skokomish tribes, David Getches met with Esther at the Legal Services offices in Seattle to discuss her situation. He defied the image of the lawyer as a distinguished-looking man, slightly aged, in handsome gray suit and tie, face neatly shaven. Instead, he presented himself as a young, bearded man in casual clothing. From the first, he found Esther "fairly outspoken and insistent." Like everyone else in her line of fire, he could not escape her indictments of the government for injustices perpetuated against her Stillaguamish in particular and against all Indians in general. With her, he noted, "the curve went steeper . . . in terms of being insistent and a hard-driving task master, in terms of having her will projected and reflected in the work of the attorneys that were working for her. . . . She was telling me [the Indians] had been treated unfairly by the government historically and if we wanted to represent her we

Esther joins attorney David Getches for dinner. He represented the Stillaguamish in the Boldt case after he had won the tribe's right to intervene in that case, decided in 1974. He then led Esther through two years of rigorous negotiations with the Department of the Interior to win federal recognition for the tribe.

had to understand—internalize her feelings about the situations." Getches listened to Esther's grievances, became convinced that her people had the legal right to share in provisions of the Point Elliott treaty, and agreed to represent Esther as special counsel should he succeed in adding her as an intervening plaintiff in the upcoming fishing rights case. He agreed to argue for Stillaguamish inclusion as a plaintiff tribe, despite its nonrecognition by the government.[5]

It would be three years before the case would come to trial. Principals in the pretrial period included people from various agencies and organizations presenting exhaustive information in fisheries management, biology, anthropology, history, and other fields of technical expertise, augmented by a battery of statistical and visual information. Agreed-upon facts were settled so the case could be resolved as quickly as possible.

Esther kept up on the pretrial proceedings, and whenever Getches was in the area he would bring her up to date on the progress of the case. When he was in Tacoma in court Esther would attend the hearings, hoping her tribe would get in on the case. But at a March 1971 meeting of STOWW, Guy McMinds, head of the economic development program's Fishing Advisory Committee, told her that there was so much disagreement among the Stillaguamish in terms of getting fishing rights restored that, unless they united, STOWW would not support their intervention on the Boldt case. Esther admitted there was tension.[6]

In pretrial hearings, Getches argued that the state should use its police powers to regulate Indian fishing only when basic fish resources were suffering, and then, if necessary, use force to regulate non-Indian fishing to ensure Indians their fair share of the catches. Evidence presented in the hearings revealed that a century and a half of tribal self-regulation had been effective with tribes. At treaty times, they would simply agree to barter with neighboring and distant tribes. Getches pressed for restriction of non-Indian commercial fishing, arguing that various court decisions declared Indian fishing a "reserve right," meaning the right to meet present and future needs. Going beyond the government contention, he pointed out that now, with pollution threatening rivers and streams and possibly adversely affecting fish numbers, Indians should have first choice at all times to meet their needs. Furthermore, he and other attorneys for the tribes set out to show that the Department of Game was more interested in providing steelhead for sportfishers than in preserving fish populations for Indians.

Actions may beg the question, Why didn't more tribes intervene? They could have, except that only representatives of tribes signing treaties with Governor Stevens in 1854–55 were brought together to meet with government representatives. George Dysart, the lead prosecuting attorney, explained that the government planned to have at least one tribe on the case from each of the

Stevens treaties concluded in western Washington. Once it was determined what treaty rights would be upheld, then such a decision would apply to any recognized tribe party to these treaties. The other tribes could join as posttrial intervenors, which was economically feasible. Thus Dysart asked that tribes admitted to the case as intervenors be kept to a minimum.

Getches and Dysart succeeded in persuading the court to add the Stillaguamish to the case, but by trial time it became increasingly difficult for other tribes to be included as plaintiffs, whether they were recognized or not. Political maneuverings increased near the end of the pretrial period. A case in point involved Margaret Greene and the Samish. A student at Evergreen State College near Olympia at the time and more and more active in Samish affairs, Greene requested inclusion of her unrecognized tribe as a plaintiff in the case, and she occasionally attended hearings. In many ways, her struggles on her tribe's behalf paralleled those of Esther. Like Esther, she worked with Getches. It wasn't until 1972, however, that Greene found time to sit in on pretrial meetings. Failing then to get in on the case, she felt betrayed by what she believed to be the politics of the STOWW Fishing Advisory Committee.[7] Greene also believed her Legal Services attorneys were inept and inexperienced.

Eventually Judge Boldt decided to allow three nonrecognized tribes to intervene in the case—the Stillaguamish, the Sauk-Suiattle, and the Upper Skagit.[8] These three tribes thus joined the four recognized tribes—the Squaxins, the Lummis, the Yakamas, and the Quinaults—as pretrial intervenors.[9] Actually, Boldt allowed the Sauk-Suiattle and Upper Skagit to intervene during pretrial maneuvers, knowing the two tribes were close to being federally recognized. Getches believed that Judge Boldt permitted the Stillaguamish on the case only because of his interest in the tribe and in Esther. Dysart favored allowing the tribe to be a plaintiff and that also helped in Boldt's favorable decision. Another factor could well have been Getches's passionate representation of the Stillaguamish. That the Stillaguamish without any acknowledged treaty rights were allowed to join would have far-reaching consequences.

Trial date was set for Monday, August 27, 1973. Esther's deposition was scheduled on June 28, two months prior to the opening of the trial in Tacoma's federal building. Her deposition was taken in the presence of Washington State's assistant attorney general, Earl R. McGimpsey; George D. Dysart, assistant regional solicitor for the Department of the Interior; and attorneys Michael Taylor and David Getches. McGimpsey led off. No sooner had he asked her his first question—whether or not the Stillaguamish were federally recognized—than she blasted him with a litany of the tribe's ills.

When asked if there were fishers among the Stillaguamish, Esther replied, "Not today. We were told that we could not fish. We did protest because we thought it was time to wake up the sportsmen and wake up the State when the Stillaguamish was still alive." When asked when the Stillaguamish had begun their protest, she replied, "In 1968." She reiterated that her tribe wished only to restore its fishing rights for food, that there were no commercial fishers among the Stillaguamish, and, further, that only about a half-dozen tribespeople cared to fish. Pressed by McGimpsey, she admitted that she could not name any specific Stillaguamish fishers, explaining that her son fished whenever he could. Queried as to whether she fished, she replied, "I could if I was allowed to, but I am not paying no big fine for the State," qualifying her response that she would fish for food were she allowed.

When asked if the Stillaguamish held traditional ceremonies, she gave another extended answer, admitting the tribe participated only in ceremonials of other tribes since it had no longhouse in which to hold its own ceremonies. She did say she participated in white-sponsored Fourth of July celebrations. Quickly taking the offensive, she cited a hearing her tribe attended to obtain the four lots Gus Smith had willed the tribe. Of these, she said, the tribe was unable to get them into trust status, since it was not federally recognized—nor was it known on which plots it had to pay taxes. McGimpsey received far more information than he had requested. And he found it impossible to hold Esther to specific answers to his questions.

Next up was Getches, who tried to get Esther to clarify some of her answers. When she asked if she could question Dysart, since he was "the main gentleman," Getches reminded her that she could not ask the questions when she herself was being deposed. Getches wanted to know if any branch of the government had ever denied the Stillaguamish party status in the Point Elliott treaty. She either evaded or misunderstood the question, replying, "I give you [the answer] by [my] authority." "I want to know from [Dysart]," she continued, "why we have come here and there. I have [given] statements . . . all over the State of Washington and in Washington, D.C., and Missoula, Montana, and back in Minnesota [while on the Poor People's Campaign]. All over everybody knows that the Stillaguamish is a tribe. There was over 200 [on] the upper [fork of the Stillaguamish] and 200 on the lower [fork] when the Indians began to wake up to know who was who." When Getches asked if the government differentiated between treaty tribes and those it recognized, Esther replied that she believed that only reservation tribes were recognized.

Getches then yielded to Dysart, who resumed questioning. He asked about the tribe's membership and her role as secretary and chair. What about enrolling members? What about blood quantums? She explained that the one-sixteenth blood quantum was established so children of elders could become tribal members. Dysart continued questioning Esther about tribal council elections, asking if officers had fixed terms. To that, she replied that she had turned minutes of meetings and enrollment papers over to the BIA, which had lost them. To Dysart's question as to how she was elected tribal chair, she replied, "By the members." "Was it the entire membership?" Dysart asked. "A quorum," she replied.

When asked what the tribe would do if they were allowed to fish, she stated that she, Frank Allen, Llewellyn Goodridge, and

Wesley Patrick served on a fisheries committee to determine what to do if allowed under the Boldt decision to fish under certain regulations. Concluding her deposition, she said, "There is no use making a fish regulation now . . . [since] we don't know what we are going to do. We never had any regulations before, we just went out and fished." Neither Dysart nor Getches had any more questions.[10]

In a letter of August 11, 1973, Hank Adams and other SAIA officials requested Judge Boldt to delay the trial. SAIA members had learned of correspondence with the U.S. attorney general that no pretrial agreements had been reached on how annual fish harvests could be apportioned. Thus, the government case would not "represent the rights and legitimate interests of the affected tribes," unless they believed there was determination for apportioning salmon catches. In such case, it would be a repetition of a 1969 case tried in the U.S. district court in Oregon. This case began when Sohappy family members, who were Yakamas, sued Anthony Smith and the Oregon State Fish Commission in *Sohappy v Smith*, soon after which the government intervened and added the case to *United States v Oregon*. Judge Robert C. Belloni had then ruled that Indians fishing in the usual and accustomed places were entitled to (an undefined) "fair and equitable" share of all fish from a given run. At that time the federal government had determined that Indians were catching some 5 percent of the runs.[11]

Soon after Esther's deposition, Ramona Bennett also asked for a delay in the trial. She had just replaced Robert Satiacum as Puyallup chair after a bitter contest. Having had no prior visibility in the trial, she asked for a delay, but as he had with the SAIA request, Judge Boldt refused to move back the August 27 opening of the case.[12]

When Tacoma's federal courthouse opened at 8 a.m. on Monday, August 27, Esther and Frank were waiting at the doors—as they would be most mornings during the trial. At 9:30, Judge George Boldt brought down his gavel to open the trial. The opening day addressed the preliminaries required for the proceedings. At midweek the court reviewed the percentage of annual catches the Indians should be entitled to, a critical issue with the Puyallup-Nisquallys. The government attorney advised the court that Indians were entitled to 50 percent of the fish harvests, a quota that contrasted sharply with the 5 percent of salmon and steelhead catches they were receiving. Testifying for the defense, state fisheries director Thor Tollefson maintained that any limit to percentages should be the province of the court. Game department attorney Joseph Larry Coniff suggested that the Department of Fisheries donate salmon to Indians to compensate them for their "fair share" of steelhead. But Tollefson opposed this suggestion. A third option proposed would have the Indians regulate their own fishing in the interest of conservation. J. E. Lasater, chief of the State Department of Fisheries management, turned his thumbs down on this option, testifying that Yakama tribal officers had failed to bring before tribal courts many instances of their own people violating their own regulations. Yakama special counsel James Hovis reported the Yakamas' annual catches as 8 percent.[13]

The first week of the court session ended with an order to resume on the following Monday, even though it was Labor Day. The delay gave Esther the weekend to spend at home on the Lummi. Though most others from up that way stayed overnight in Tacoma on Monday through Thursday rather than driving back home every evening, Esther and Frank believed it more economical to buy a tank of gas for their daily round trip, except for the occasional nights they stayed with Ramona Bennett.

Waiting close behind Esther for court to open on Monday, September 3, was the Yakama Robert Jim, who good-naturedly chided her, "Sister, are you sure you went home last night?"[14] The second week in court opened with more discussion of harvest percentages. Lasater defined the Indian position as "open-ended ... that would go on and on with the tribes wanting more and more" and argued that a specific number of fish allocated to a specific tribe on a specific river would dangerously reduce already poor salmon runs in bad years. The best means, Lasater maintained, was for the court to make a "fair-share" percentage, so that in bad years both Indians and non-Indians would have a reduced number. He wanted Fisheries to be able to set seasons, locations, and types of gear and, in poor harvest years, to apply restrictions on Indian fishing as a last resort since their treaties gave them priority over sport and non-Indian commercial fishermen. Because the Oregon circuit court had ruled that Indians were entitled to "a fair and equitable share," Lasater argued that it should be the court's decision to specify the amount.

Anthropologist Barbara Lane testified that at the time of the treaties, fishing was vital to the Indians for their subsistence. She countered written statements of evidence by the state's witness, Dr. Carroll Riley. Lane offered lengthy testimony on the Indian and white concepts of land ownership and other aspects of their respective cultures. Riley reminded the court that Indians such as the Stillaguamish did not fish for subsistence, as they had in earlier times. He contended that acculturation within the white community had changed all that. He further contended that treaties should be reinterpreted every generation or two in light of the progressive acculturation of Indians into white society.[15]

When asked point-blank if Barbara Lane's testimony was acceptable, Riley testified that it was formulated long after the fact. "We are asking these people to give us an opinion as to what the situation in western Washington was in 1855. I do not believe one can rely totally on any of these documents," Riley said. Already irritated with Riley's testimony, Judge Boldt had asked him earlier in the day to answer questions with a flat yes or no. Now Boldt told him, "If you continue to appear to persist to dodge answers to questions of this kind it will bear heavily on my assessment of your veracity."[16]

On Monday, September 10, with the opening of the third week of the trial, Indian witnesses began their testimony. Cal Peters, a Squaxin, led off. Others included the soft-spoken, hard-of-hearing, sixty-three-year-old Lena Smith, granddaughter of Chief Jimmy Dorsey and, other than Esther, the only Stillaguamish to testify. Smith testified that when she was younger, fish had been plentiful in the Stillaguamish River. When she was about six or seven years old, she said, families subsisted on fish until "the fish commissioner" stopped Indians from fishing. She recalled going to the river to fetch water only to find so many salmon that the slime residue of their passage forced her to fetch water from a smaller stream.[17]

Then it was Esther's turn on the stand. David Getches led her through a review of Stillaguamish River history. She testified that the whites "that live in that area in the years past, threw their cattle, threw their chickens [into the river where Stillaguamish fished], anything that was dead, if they didn't want it, they threw it in the river, their stoves they threw in. It went on in the early days." When Getches asked if dead animals and trash had made it more difficult for the fish to survive, Esther replied, looking at Boldt, "I feel, your Honor, and the attorneys who are listening here that we Stillaguamish descendants of the treaty should not be ignored by the State of Washington at no time," adding, "Why, we went to Mr. Tollefson [state fisheries director], Bob Satiacum was in that office, Malcolm [McLeod, the tribal attorney,] was in that office, my other former Chairman [John Silva] was there, my son was there, I was there [when] Malcolm asked Tollefson, 'Is there any way that you can let these people fish for their food?' He [McLeod] asked him in ten different ways, and he said no. It was at the time we needed the food and we weren't allowed to fish."

Esther told the court that sportsmen were allowed to fish the Stillaguamish River when Indians could not. Attempting to establish that the Stillaguamish were a viable tribe, Getches guided Esther carefully through testimony to the fact that the Stillaguamish had had tribal continuity since 1926. In response to Earl McGimpsey's cross-examination, Esther irrelevantly replied that her husband, a Lummi, had fished the Nooksack River where Indians of its namesake tribe fished, but he could no longer fish there after suffering his third stroke, forcing him to sell his boat. Esther told how Arnold Ross had regretted that sale since "he could have gave it to me and my son to get out and fish." She explained that now he had to buy fish for up to forty dollars from Lummi Indians.

Following this revelation, Judge Boldt asked her, "Before he was sick, did he fish?" "Right," Esther responded. McGimpsey followed with a line of questioning attempting to show that the Stillaguamish wanted fish for food and not for trade. Esther replied that she and Frank would fish off "the first boat we can get ahold of." When McGimpsey asked, "Do any of your members live on the Tulalip Reservation?" she responded, "The what?" McGimpsey repeated the question. "I don't get you," she replied. It was Boldt, not McGimpsey, who interpreted for her the question: "Are there any Stillaguamish Tribe members that now live at the Tulalip on the reservation?" She replied, "There is."

McGimpsey asked if any Stillaguamish fished with the Tulalip. Esther responded, "Well, you know, for our Stillaguamish rolls..." Before she could finish her statement, Boldt interjected, "Do you know?" "I'll answer that this way," she replied. "On the Stillaguamish roll living on the aboriginal area all these years, there are some that still have Stillaguamish blood that live on the Tulalip, they aren't on the rolls, but he [name not given] wouldn't be really fishing yet, he has a little arthritis in his kneecaps." When asked if the federal government recognized the Stillaguamish as a treaty tribe, she answered, "I guess they are going to. I don't know just how they stand on it." Getches came to her rescue, clarifying for the court the government's continuing nonrecognition of the tribe. In the matter of fishing identification cards, Esther explained that the tribe had not been issued any but had instead issued its own membership cards. McGimpsey asked: "Am I correct in understanding that the federal government or the BIA has never issued to you an Indian fishing card?" Boldt, with a penchant for direct answers, interjected, "Have you ever had a fishing card from the federal government?" Esther responded, "I just told him no, just a little bit ago."

When it came time for Esther to testify whether or not the Stillaguamish were organized under any law such as a voluntary organization, she appeared vague, stumbling, not understanding the context of the word "organization." Again Boldt rescued her from her semantic predicament, asking, "Is your tribe organized in a legal way with legal papers and all that, just like other organizations of that kind in this State, do you know?" She responded:

> I don't class myself or my tribe members as State people. [We] are still under federal. We are still wards of the government. We have not received any money from the government. That bucket of gold never came to our members. Neither did the government put down a stamp and give us a trust land. I want to explain something now, Judge, that you don't know, Your Honor. From Milltown was our fishing, drying of fish, berries. It finally ended in that area that the State put a dike, and the high waters come. Our Indian bodies were laying all over. . . . There a yellow house sits back just about a mile back and all around there underneath the house, under the barn and one side is our Indian bodies. That man told me he had skulls in his house. When that tide came up, why, them people, University people took bags of that bones to the University.

Esther was now primed to run away with her testimony. But Getches interrupted her, seizing upon the chance to enter the tribal constitution and bylaws as exhibits. Conceding, McGimpsey broke in, "I will drop this, your Honor," and he offered exhibits from the depositions of Esther and Lena Smith. To this concession Boldt replied, "All right, the [depositions] are admitted. That is all, Mrs. Ross, for today." But Esther was not ready to yield the witness stand. Having no good stopping place and wishing to have the last word, she answered in homiletical fashion:

> I want to tell you. Something should go down in the record. From Milltown up to McMurray on up to Little Creek, up to the northern part there of the Darrington on over to the Stillaguamish watershed, to Granite Falls on down to the northeast and northwest of the Tulalip Reservation on through to [Warm] Beach to Stanwood was our territory. I want to also

say that my territory went over halfway to Camano [Island], on down to Wilsillati [Utsaladdy].... We went for clam digging in that [area], but in 1926, John Lyons came to me from Kikialis [sic] Tribe from Swinomish. He said, "Don't you dare say that you went any further than Stanwood," so it went that way in the Court of Claims. We lost that other area just to give those people [in] that area, but it is still on record with me.

Boldt replied, "I am sure it always will be. That is all, Mrs. Ross. You are free now to go whenever you wish and stay as long as you like." And the court was recessed until the next morning.[18]

Several Skokomish and Bill Frank, Jr., a Nisqually, also testified. When asked when Nisquallys had been free to net-fish, Frank replied, "You could fish when you weren't in jail or going to court." Testifying as to when Nisqually festivals were held, he said, "The end of winter would be a good time, if you weren't in jail." As to what percentages of catches represented a fair share, members' responses varied. Bill Frank thought that for his people it should be 100 percent of salmon and steelhead up the Nisqually. On the other hand, the Skokomish Joseph Andrew replied that a court-designated percentage would be acceptable.[19]

On Tuesday, September 11, Benjamin Rubin Wright, Puyallup treasurer, testifying on behalf of his tribe, replied that for a fair-share quota he also would trust the word of the court. The following day, leaders of six tribes testified; all agreed to a court-set fair-share percentage. McGimpsey conceded. It was okay with him, he said, if the court set the percentages.[20]

During the remainder of the week, employees of the Departments of Fisheries and Game attempted to contradict the statements of the government's witnesses. Fisheries offered to make up the difference in fish quotas with salmon for steelhead. The next Monday, September 17, steelhead club representatives testified that they would be dismayed if the state allowed net fishing for steelhead off reservation sections of state streams.[21]

Getches was more than satisfied with Esther's performance in court. She was impressive, he thought, and she "spoke up with an authoritarian air. She'd look right at the judge and shake her finger at him. And telling him how it was in the old days and about the old people fishing. We got the judge to let us put the elders on to testify not only about what they remember but . . . also to testify about what they heard from their elders, their parents, grandparents and in some cases that reached back and touched the actual signing of the treaty." Getches observed that Judge Boldt indeed took great interest in testimony of elderly Indians. Captivated by Esther's recitation of early events, Boldt leaned over the bench in some instances to ask leading questions of her. Much of her affinity for her people, as Getches attested, had come through researching their past. Yet the vicariousness of that experience lessened none of her excitement over it. According to Getches, it was clear that Esther had made an impression on the judge. "That was important to our case," he said, noting that if there was any reason for Judge Boldt to recognize the treaty rights of this unrecognized tribe, it would be "because of Esther's testimony along with the fine historical work that had been done by Barbara Lane."[22]

After three and a half weeks and the testimony of forty-nine witnesses, Judge Boldt said he would rule on the case by the end of the year. His decision, he said, would be "at least a beginning" toward resolving "the grievous problem that has plagued the people of this area for a great many years."[23]

CHAPTER FIFTEEN

# THE BOLDT COURT: THE FALLOUT

In early 1974 Esther's main drive was to get a piece of land put in trust status so that the tribe could have a reservation land base, a requirement for achieving recognition. She had first had her eye on the Gus Smith lots, but when that went nowhere, she considered buying land with the tribe's claims commission judgment money.[1]

Taking up more and more responsibility for the tribe, Esther spent less and less time with her family. In their busy rounds Esther and Frank left the Lummi house early in the morning and returned late at night to catch some sleep in what Arnold came to call their "flop house." Esther spent little time with him, except when taking him to the clinic or the hospital. His infirmities and inability to get about intensified his loneliness—which was relieved every time his granddaughter Dorothy, now almost twenty years old, rode the bus from the Yakama to spend time with him. In January 1973 Dorothy had tried to reenter the Chemawa Indian School near Salem, Oregon. However, she had been denied admission on the basis of her previous attitude and behavior. Rebuffed, she considered entering a program to obtain a GED and learn a trade or applying for the Job Corps. But Arnold, wanting her near him, talked her out of those ideas. Esther was uncomfortable with Dorothy in the house. Like his mother, Frank was not enamored of Dorothy. On the other hand, Arnold wasn't fond of Frank and considered willing his property instead to Dorothy.[2] Relationships in the household were strained.

During the Boldt trial, Esther at times had to take Arnold to the hospital in Bellingham, to Dr. Arthur B. Watts's office, or the Veterans Administration hospital. He was even hospitalized with heart trouble a few days during the trial. Now seventy years old, he was also suffering from the effects of mini-strokes, liver trouble, and prostate cancer. Recalling these hectic days during the Boldt case Esther would later write, "I was in fish court [in] Tacoma and he in and out of the hospital. Dr. said for me to do my tribe work—don't let him get frustrated [with the tribal business]."[3]

On January 16, 1974, Dorothy came over from the Yakama to drive Arnold to the Everett agency to make out his will. In the absence of notary Earl Allen, assistants Sharon A. Redthunder and Inez MacNamara wrote up the will in which Arnold left his entire estate to "Dorothy Baker," it being his intent "to leave nothing to my wife, Esther, and my daughter, Margaret." The contents of the will were not disclosed to Esther.

That same month Esther wrote Secretary of the Interior Rogers C. B. Morton, advising him of the four lots Gus Smith had willed the tribe but which were now held up in probate. She also told Morton about the Indian cemeteries of "five acres each" holding about 150 bodies. Until the tribe was recognized, she explained, she could not stop non-Indian property owners from obliterating the graves by building structures over them. In late January she again wrote Morton: "I need [federal recognition] for my Tribe by return mail." In this letter she gave him a brief history of the case: "Somewhere along these years were papers made in Washington, D.C. for late James Darsey [sic] . . . to be our chief and that our tribe was Federally Recognized. But after the chief's house burned and he died no trace of his papers were found by his family." She informed Morton that she had appointed Dorsey's grandson Wesley Patrick as tribal chief. Dorsey's other grandson was Gus Smith. She told Morton of her plans to seek federal funds to build

Left to right: Stillaguamish tribal chairman John Silva, Esther, tribal elder Toddy Smith, and her son Gus Smith of Oso, Washington. Esther got Gus to will his Oso home to the tribe.

an eleven-unit motel on the tribal office's 1.9-acre piece of property, which she planned to purchase with $45,000 from the government. Citing the problem of having to pay taxes on nontrust land, she concluded her letter, "Every where I go is Taxland."[4]

Nearly five months following adjudication of the Boldt case, the judge rendered his decision. On February 12, 1974, he confirmed the right of the Stillaguamish to fish. The decision would not go without a challenge in the U.S. Supreme Court. Although pleasing to Esther and tribal fishers, the Boldt decision rocked non-Indians in the Pacific Northwest. It allocated treaty Indians half the annual salmon harvests, while requiring tribes to fish within their own aboriginal boundaries.[5]

Legal Services attorney Alan C. Stay, though not deeply involved in the Boldt case, noticed that in pretrial maneuverings there had been few intertribal challenges between the so-called have and have-not tribes. However, once the trial began, smaller tribes feared they would come up with empty nets or with no nets at all. The politics of the STOWW advisory committee on fishing became more pronounced with its representation of competing tribes. The Indian–federal government victory over the state in the Boldt case now intensified intertribal rivalries. Stillaguamish consultant Rod Sayegusa observed that "the unrecognized non-reservation tribes, wanting to be so recognized and formerly [pre-Boldt] equal with Esther in the realm of little influence, now feared the balance of fairness betrayed them." In other words, the smaller tribes wanted what Esther had achieved.[6]

Esther and Frank had high hopes for tribal fishing—as did attorney Malcolm McLeod. He told his client Robert Satiacum, who was well versed in fishing matters since he purchased fish from individual Puyallup-Nisquallys and sold these catches at a nice profit, to find a boat and tackle for Frank. Satiacum's brother loaned Frank a boat and fishing gear. Since the Puyallup-Nisquallys had long-standing designated family-owned fishing sites on their rivers, Satiacum sent Frank and Frank's son David to the mouth of the Puyallup to try their luck. They made a few catches and sales, but within a week the two had turned in their gear.[7]

Energized by the Boldt decision, Esther hurried to establish rules and regulations for Stillaguamish fishing. Following his appointment as fisheries patrol officer, Frank announced in newspapers in Washington and Oregon that the Stillaguamish River would be closed to fishing. "[W]e are going to establish our own law and order for fishing and show the community and state that we can regulate and control our own fishing," he proclaimed. The sportfishers' response to this pronouncement was immediate. Seven hundred people gathered on March 5, 1974, on the steps of Tacoma's federal courthouse. To their leader's blaring bullhorn shouts of "Are we going to fish the Stillaguamish?" angry protesters shouted their affirmative responses. Intimidated, Frank recanted in an article published the next day. The Stillaguamish would not prohibit fishing, he said, until "our tribal constitution and bylaws are complete." That is, the declaration would not go into effect until the Stillaguamish were federally recognized.[8]

To establish the tribe's fishing ordinance, Esther called a meeting for March 12. Only seven members attended, but they adopted a resolution that read, in part, "No person shall operate or control more than one fishing location at a time."[9] Esther sought to return to fishing practices that resembled the aboriginal practices. During the Boldt proceedings, she was set on restructuring the Stillaguamish as fishing people like the Puyallups and Nisquallys. She looked to STOWW for support. Seventeen members of STOWW met March 16 to sign a resolution, stating that because the Stillaguamish were participants in STOWW and used STOWW minigrant programs and those of the OEO, the organization supported the tribal ordinance adopted on March 12 "that the Stillaguamish Tribe is fully capable of regulating their tribal affairs, to include their treaty fishing rights."[10]

The Boldt decision established for Esther a new playing field and new ground rules. Where formerly others had patronized her, they now recognized her potential as a viable political-economic force, and by the same token, a threat to federally recognized tribes contending with her for federal funds.

Six tribes would intervene in the case before the U.S. Supreme Court concurred on July 2, 1979, with the Boldt ruling, allowing them to share in the 50 percent salmon and steelhead harvests. Despite the fact that the Stillaguamish still were not a recognized tribe, Esther was now a serious contender in the scramble for federal moneys and other resources. Opposition to recognition for nonrecognized tribes in general was spearheaded by the National Tribal Chairmans Association. But her greatest opposition came from the already recognized Lummi and Tulalip tribes. The Tulalips feared that Stillaguamish recognition would dilute their own federal appropriations. They claimed that, following the ratification of the Point Elliott treaty, the Stillaguamish were supposed to have moved to the Tulalip Reservation. Had they moved, the Tulalips would have received a greater annual share of federal revenues. The lack of Stillaguamish status, they said, might cause them to "eat at the Tulalip table."[11]

Even though the Tulalips clashed with Esther on fishing matters, she had good relationships with some Tulalip individuals. One of those was Bernie Gobin, who eventually became a tribal board member and director of the tribe's fisheries. Earlier, Esther had spent time with Gobin's grandmother, Nancy Jones, who lived near him. During many winters in the 1950s, Esther and Bill Dunbar had stayed with Jones. Later, when Frank or Arnold drove Esther to visit Gobin, she would give him the standard treatment—instead of getting out of her car, she would signal him to come out to meet her. "We were not political enemies," he remembered, "but we were on opposite sides of the fence." Esther called him "Old Busy Body." Whether they met on the Tulalip or elsewhere, their conversations centered mostly around Indian history. A symbol of their friendship was Gobin's colorful bolo, a Tulalip whale beaded into the design. Knowing Esther admired it, he took it off one day and handed it to her.[12]

Termination of the Boldt case did not end Esther's relationship with attorney David Getches. Soon after the trial, Getches talked with Esther about how to go about getting recognition.[13] He advised her to seek immediately the secretary of the interior's approval of the Stillaguamish "structure of organization," required for formal recognition of her tribe. Asking Getches to take on the case for her, Esther gave him an arsenal of information. Her longtime penchant for gathering clippings and mailings and for hoarding tribal and BIA notes and reports helped Getches. He spent one full day in Esther's house examining the boxes of materials she had squirreled away. These documents, with odd and sundry other bits of information, enabled him to develop a chronological history for the petition and exhibits that would be more persuasive and impressive than oral or written petitions. The resulting evidence of a half-century of Stillaguamish contact with the federal government was contained in an inch-and-a-half-thick petition for recognition, dated April 5, 1974, and sent to the secretary of the interior.[14]

On May 11, 1974, while Esther was engrossed in the drive for recognition, Arnold Ross died. When Esther heard about the disposition of Arnold's estate, she was shocked. Despite their twenty-year marriage, he had disinherited her, leaving several pieces of Lummi property to his granddaughter Dorothy. Esther sought the counsel of Legal Services attorney Michael Fitch. Reflecting on Arnold's death, she wrote:

> [The] year after Arnold and I were married we received his 4 grandchildren to raise for 11 years. He was a logger. He wanted a home and [to] settle down and stop woods job. He didn't want me to be a nurse no more in the hospital.... [He wanted me to] take care of his grandchildren. He would give me [a] home and land if I help[ed] him to divide it. This I did—All his paper work—[I] was mother to his 4 grandchildren and then he became disabled and strokes caused by heart.... He passed on. I stood by myself at his funeral to arrange all—the services and business. No one spoke to me—but the minister.... [Dorothy] was 4 months, 6 lbs when we first took her.... [And] no one helped on expenses.[15]

Temporarily putting aside her disappointment over what she saw as Arnold's betrayal, Esther turned her attention to researching how neighboring tribes had achieved recognition. She had been told that the Stillaguamish had no legal status because they had not organized as a tribe under the Indian Reorganization Act of 1934. Yet tribal recognition under the act did not seem to be a precise procedure. The government had never precisely nor consistently defined the term "recognition." For instance, in a June 1974 letter, Commissioner of Indian Affairs Morris Thompson advised Sen. Henry Jackson that when in 1913 the government had purchased a cemetery plot for the Sauk-Suiattles and Upper Skagits to use jointly as a land base, it had, in essence, federally recognized the tribes—and thereby became responsible for giving them services. But the Upper Skagits did not receive formal BIA approval of their constitution until December 4, 1974. This approval was considered acknowledgement of their recognition. And the Sauk-Suiattle constitution was not approved until September 17, 1975, more than two months after they had received formal federal recognition. The two tribes became eligible for annual government services after their constitutions and bylaws were approved, providing democratic organization and periodic election of officers.

To counter opposition from the NTCA, Esther strongly supported—and received support from—the National Congress of American Indians. She frequently attended NCAI meetings and forged ties with its director, Chuck Trimble. Even though it was composed largely of recognized tribes, the NCAI had some twenty-one unrecognized tribes, besides the Stillaguamish, among its members.

Esther was not solely focused on gaining recognition; she still had to tackle the Stillaguamish claims award. She hoped to delay payment until it came in one lump sum so the tribe could buy property, especially Indian burial lands such as the Talbot parcel offered for $75,000. But the secretary of the interior was encouraging members to take a per capita payment, telling them they had to take the money as individuals "because only recognized tribes ... [could] take the money for tribal purposes."[16] Esther saw it as an attempt to break the tribe's cohesion.

On June 7, 1974, less than a month after Arnold's death, Esther was back in the capital, where she hoped to interview the secretary of the interior. Unsuccessful, she tried the commissioner of Indian affairs. She was allowed only to talk to Louise Perkins of the Tribal Government Service staff. But Perkins could pull no strings for her.[17] Back at Interior she badgered whomever she could find for a decision on her petition for formal recognition. Solicitor Scott Keep explained that the petition was being held up in the Budget Division. Dissatisfied with Keep's answer, she continued hammering away at Interior personnel about the need to expedite the probate of the four Gus Smith lots.

Back home, David Getches wrote the Interior Department on July 8 inquiring about recognition for the Stillaguamish. Seventeen days later, Keep sent a four-sentence reply, informing Getches that the secretary's schedule was so heavy he'd not had opportunity to personally review the petition. He was to be briefed on August 5, and, Keep wrote, "We expect a decision in the very near future."[18]

The BIA's Portland Area Office recommended withholding the claims award moneys and putting them in a trust account until the tribe received recognition. Interior's Budget Office eventually recommended approval of recognition, but the Office of Management and Budget remained opposed to Interior's recognition of any more western Washington tribes.[19] Undersecretary of the Interior James C. Whitaker delayed action on the petition until Secretary Morton returned from visits to Alaska and Washington State. Still Morton refused to see Esther. Associate Solicitor Reid P. Chambers called Getches on August 6 to tell him that Esther was still in the capital, camped on the secretary's doorstep. The staff at Interior wanted nothing so much as for her to leave town.

New contingencies developed upon Morton's return from the West. He now took a new tack: He might not be authorized to grant recognition, he said. The matter seemed to be entirely up to Congress.[20] Morton was also now uncertain, following Richard Nixon's August resignation, whether his tenure in office would continue under the new president, Gerald Ford. Esther sought help from her congressman, Lloyd Meeds, chairman of the Indian Affairs Subcommittee. Though he himself was unavailable, Meeds's staff told him Esther needed his assistance in getting Morton to authorize recognition. Meeds assured Esther he would contact Morton and urge him to extend recognition to the Stillaguamish once legal questions as to the secretary's authority were resolved.[21]

Local BIA personnel also helped Esther in her fight. The agency's Reservations Programs Officer Don Smouse even took an interest in her personal life, listening to accounts of her California years as well as those pertaining to Stillaguamish welfare. "She was no dummy," he said. "There were several things happening in regard to the usual and accustomed arena of tribes in an attempt to identify unextinguished tribal resource rights" following the Boldt decision, Smouse said. He added that "there was a tacit recognition and executive recognition that the Stillaguamishes had some unextinguished trust right in regard to some of the resources." Although the identity of these rights was obscure, the agency began taking closer notice of Esther, looking more seriously at what she was accomplishing. The agency even granted the Stillaguamish some funds as if they were a recognized tribe. Smouse justified the grant in that the agency believed the Stillaguamish were on their way to recognition. "Several times we funded tribes to make trips to Washington, D.C., to make presentation of their issues," Smouse said. All this stopped, though, when Sen. Warren Magnuson became incensed over the impropriety of the agency's paying for trips for Indians to lobby Congress. Smouse recanted, admitting that with hindsight, "We had no right to—we really went too far. . . . We borrowed and stole money out of our own agency pockets" to manage that first grant.[22]

Now that the tribe had gained visibility and a semblance of identity in the public eye, Esther found that there was an increase in the volume of tribal business. She continued paying the monthly rent for the tribal office and covered office expenses with her Social Security checks and the tribe's monthly check from OEO's Community Action Program, dispersed by STOWW and paid to her as the "community aide." The tribe could no longer operate with volunteer helpers. Fortunately, a new federally funded service called the Comprehensive Employment and Training Act (CETA) answered Esther's needs.[23] In December of 1974 she signed a contract with Rod Sayegusa to work periodically as a business manager for the tribe. Although not a full-time employee, he was paid a salary through CETA while also serving other tribes like the Quinaults and the Lummis. Frank Allen was also hired for the

Esther chats with Stillaguamish tribal consultant Rod Sayegusa. It was he who set up an office operation when some organization became necessary for the tribe's struggle to become federally recognized. From those beginnings he became a longtime friend of Esther and her family.

CETA-salaried position of office manager. Because Frank was unable to read or write, Sayegusa filled out the required reports for STOWW and other agencies and Frank signed them.

Over the next five years Rod Sayegusa helped Esther by arranging the purchase of tickets for her trips, including those to Washington, D.C. Her many trips there were to attend meetings at the headquarters of the NCAI as well as to visit offices of the BIA, Lloyd Meeds, and Senator Jackson, Sayegusa remembered. He found Esther totally uninvolved in outside interests and activities. "She was in her own little world," he said. But she excelled at getting handouts. She had to be good at that, Sayegusa noted, since her own people did not contribute to her work. "In fact," he said, "her own membership did not understand why it was so important to become recognized." Then too, there were those wanting to get their hands on the settlement award.[24]

In his position as office manager, Frank drew a monthly check from CETA for his handyman work, for chauffering Esther, and for setting up an arts and crafts shop to sell inexpensive bead work—watchbands, belt buckles, pins, and pendants he purchased from Canadian and western Washington tribes. His markup was twice his cost. Even at that, the money he spent for gasoline and car maintenance in getting the items did not leave enough profit to support office expenses, and he discontinued the effort.

CHAPTER SIXTEEN

# THE PUSH FOR RECOGNITION

Although David Getches joined Esther's crusade for recognition, he did not provide legal assistance to the Stillaguamish for other tribal matters. That help came from attorneys like Alan Stay and Cynthia Davenport at Evergreen Legal Services of Seattle, which STOWW funded. Up to this point Esther had hired attorneys in private practice and for gratis had consulted Homer Settler, an Indian with legal knowledge but not a law degree. Now, while STOWW took over providing legal help for the tribe, Esther would hire private attorneys for her personal problems.[1]

In time Esther came to appreciate Alan Stay for his knowledge, even though she was skeptical of his youth. But as she and other tribal leaders assessed their attorneys, the lawyers also assessed the tribal leaders. Stay recalled that "Esther was always an old person in the sense that she had a rough life. It showed on her because when I knew her in '74 . . . she was spry, she clearly had energy, but she did not look young. She had some life experiences that were laid down on her."[2]

Some people criticized Esther's treatment of attorneys. Though not an attorney himself, Rudolph "Rudy" C. Ryser, a Cowlitz, knew Esther well and was active in STOWW and other Indian-related organizations and programs. Her approach, he said, was to use attorneys by telling them what to do and how to do it, and then, rather than awaiting their responses, proceed to inform them of the solution. "She was persistent," he recalled, adding that "any attorney working for her, she considered *her* attorney. She wanted him to do what she was interested in doing."³

Stay continued to advise Esther on various problems, even when his official tenure as Stillaguamish counselor had ended. He traveled with her on various trips, including what he called her "regular confrontations" with Gov. Daniel Evans. And Evans, Stay said, always treated Esther with respect, "always giving her an ear."⁴

Attorney Michael Taylor, funded by Legal Services, described her at this time as always on the go, attending meetings and soliciting funds and other assistance:

> Our meetings included discussions of recognition as a tribe by the federal government, fishing rights in specific areas, obtaining a specific parcel of land for a reservation, obtaining BIA and Public Health Service services, obtaining return of the Tribal cemetery, Tribal water rights, obtaining welfare payments for specific members, and employment of a specific claims attorney. At the annual meetings, decisions were made by the membership regarding enrollment, membership of the Tribe in the Small Tribes of Western Washington, an attempt to obtain recognition, the election of officers, the participation by the Tribe in fishing rights litigation, and the position of the Tribe with regard to the Claims Commision and a specific claims attorney.⁵

Esther's momentum to promote tribal fishing was slowed after STOWW took its time granting a Stillaguamish request for funds to purchase a fishing boat. Rod Sayegusa wrote the grant proposal to purchase the craft, and the tribe eventually received $13,000. With this money, Frank had the Raven Boat Company of Issaquah, Washington, build a boat to his specifications. It was to be used for gill netting. The boat builders must have shaken their heads at the unorthodox dimensions Frank ordered—a width of twenty-two feet, a beam of eleven feet, and questionable draft, all of which resulted in a higher, wider, and bulkier craft than one customarily used for fishing. But Frank reasoned that its higher hull sides would prevent the inexperienced Stillaguamish from falling overboard. He named it *Wide Load* and ordered a forty-five-gallon gasoline drum placed on one side of the boat. With the gasoline drum counterbalancing his three-hundred-pound frame, he expected the craft would float on an even keel. With little interest in using it for commercial purposes, he intended instead to teach the inexperienced Stillaguamish how to net-fish. This plan died when, after three trips, only one person wanted anything to do with subsistence or commercial fishing. Frank hauled the boat behind the Lummi house where it would stand dry-docked for some five years.

When CETA funds failed to cover all expenses for trips, office supplies, telephone, and other services, Esther approached Rod Sayegusa about seeking nongovernmental sources of money. "Esther had her hand out. She was good at that," Sayegusa said. And he confirmed that she never received financial help from those nearest her—her own people. "They did not want their neighbors and friends to know they were Indians at that time," he explained. "They did not want to be associated with Indians or called Indians. These folks who qualified for a share of government claims money wanted that without any show of demonstration of the fact, because it was bad at that time [to be Indian]."[6]

With little hope of raising moneys elsewhere, Esther increased her trips to the BIA's Everett agency office. She and Frank would arrive in late afternoon to talk with its superintendent and other officers. By now it was not unusual for Esther to send Frank in to have an agency staff member come outside to talk with her in the car to spare her the discomfort of climbing stairs. When unable to find satisfaction in the Everett office, she and Frank visited the BIA's Area Office in Portland. While in Portland, Esther would also visit Roy Sampsel, special field representative for the secretary of the interior, often having him come down to street level from his office in the Bonneville Power Administration building. "Esther held you responsible," Sampsel recalled. "If she had talked to you three months earlier and you said to her, 'Well, I will check into this,' . . . the next time you saw her she remembered, 'What did you do about that? Remember when we talked about that?'"[7]

Her persistence in dealing with Sampsel was matched by her persistence in communicating with personnel up and down the BIA ladder. And frequently she got action. Governor Evans finally wrote Secretary Morton, listing the several nonrecognized beneficiaries of the Point Elliott treaty and asking that these "accidents of history" be rectified with recognition. He further informed Morton of Stillaguamish incorporation under state law as a nonprofit organization and noted that Esther had been a member of his Governor's Indian Advisory Council from its inception. Since the tribe had continuous dealings with both federal and state agencies, the state was soliciting the secretary's action on the tribe's drive for recognition.[8]

Though now in her seventies, Esther was still clearly in charge of tribal affairs. Time had scarcely diminished her loud and insistent demeanor. She wasted little time on small talk or personal concerns. Linda Bryant, a reporter for the *Everett Herald*, was one of many who chronicled Esther's career over the years. She first met Esther when Esther was seventy:

> To see Esther in the eyes, and to know her in the heart [were] two different things. She was an older woman then. She was very diminutive in size. She was small physically . . . about 5-2 or 5-3. She was medium-built and she was obviously old. . . . She had hair that was braided, silverish braids. She always had it back and I've seen it hanging. It was quite long [as it had been in her childhood]. I remember that face. I don't ever remember seeing makeup on her. Her face had lines. And when you saw her alongside her son Frank who seemed to be well over 400 pounds . . . she had this dignity, this kind of grace, and when she spoke it was [as] though

she were a person of value and importance, and what she had to say to you was very important. . . . I remember they came to the newspaper office and I went out and here were these two people, you look at Frank and think, "Here we go," and then Esther. She was deliberate in her speech. . . . It was a very deliberate pattern of speech. . . . [She was not] someone who was . . . trying to curry my favor or trying to impress me. She simply had something that she wanted to discuss. She felt she should discuss it with the newspaper because at this time the *Herald* had significant stories about her and the tribe for the next decade and a half, showing the importance of the tribe and its business.[9]

All the while, the Stillaguamish petition continued gathering dust on the desk of the Interior Department's solicitor. After spending several weeks in the capital in the summer of 1974, Esther was frustrated. The department evidently feared Stillaguamish recognition would "open the floodgates" to other unrecognized tribes. David Getches countered the argument that services for existing recognized tribes would be thinned by recognition of additional tribes by observing that funds for less than one hundred Stillaguamish members would be "miniscule" compared with those spent on larger tribes. "If the tribe is entitled to be recognized it would be an abuse of discretion to deny it for budget reasons alone," Getches said.[10]

Getches believed that it was not just a question of the budget; he believed that the courts could not deal with the "political question" of Stillaguamish recognition. What had to be decided was whether the secretary's authority was legal. He countered the department's claim that only Congress had the power to recognize tribes. He argued that exercise of such power required direction from one of "the political departments of the government [in this case the Department of the Interior]." The Senate, explained Getches, had determined Stillaguamish qualification for treaty rights as it had for other tribes under the March 8, 1859, Senate confirmation of the Point Elliott treaty. Further, under the Boldt decision the Stillaguamish had been found to be a tribe.[11]

Getches telegraphed Morton on October 2, 1974, with these arguments favoring recognition and questioning Morton's contentions on the issue. The secretary responded, telling Getches he did not have the authority to grant recognition to the Stillaguamish—even though he had already extended recognition to five tribes.[12]

Home from D.C. that fall of 1974, Esther traveled with David in Arnold's old Plymouth to the thirty-first annual National Congress of American Indians meeting in San Diego. NCAI director Chuck Trimble welcomed her, and at the convention, the general assembly unanimously passed Resolution No. NCAI-74-11, supporting federal recognition for the Stillaguamish.[13]

While in California, Esther turned once again to her search for her stepfather. She hired Gary E. Adkinson of the Field Services Bureau of the Ventura, California, Police Department. His investigation revealed that Oscar George Reid had been born in Canada on October 24, 1871. His wife, Mary Jane Bell Reid, had also been born in Canada. A death certificate for Reid was on file at the California Department of Health with the Registrar of Vital Statistics. Adkinson suggested Esther send two dollars for a copy of the death certificate. From that, she learned that Reid had died on September 3, 1945—some twenty-two years after Esther had last seen him—of a stroke. Reid and his wife, who had died on April 6, 1962, were buried in the Cherokee Memorial Park Cemetery in Lodi, California.[14] Esther wondered when Mary Jane had entered the picture. Reid had died four years after Angelina's death. Did Reid marry Mary Jane after Angelina's death? Could Reid and Mary Jane have married before coming to the United States? Did Reid leave Mary Jane to marry Angelina? Or was it possible that Mary Jane followed Reid to the States and persuaded him to leave Angelina?

Arnold's will soon distracted Esther from the puzzle over her stepfather. A hearing was held on January 24, 1975, in Bellingham before Judge Robert C. Snashall of the Portland Office of Hearings and Appeals of the Department of the Interior. Peter Arkinson, a Bellingham attorney, represented Esther. Dorothy Baker was in court, accompanied by her mother, Margaret. Outstanding bills were presented for payment of Arnold's medical and burial expenses. Esther asked compensation for her care of Arnold. The judge denied the request. Arkinson objected to introduction of the will on the grounds that Arnold's lack of mental capacity had rendered him incompetent. Esther insisted the 1974 will was made when Arnold was mentally incapacitated, when he was heavily medicated and under undue influence to change the will. Esther insisted the will he made in 1958, leaving all property to her, was the one that should be probated. Judge Snashall ruled that he would consider only the 1974 will. But because Esther challenged Arnold's competence, he ordered that the hearing be continued. Snashall appointed Margaret guardian *ad litem* of Dorothy, who was still a minor.[15]

With the delay in the probate of the will, Esther returned to Washington, D.C., to attend an NCAI meeting. While there, she again visited the people at the Department of the Interior. But the change of personnel with the new Ford administration meant that she found only strangers on the staff. But she also found a new policy in place: A tribe no longer had to own property to become recognized. Nevertheless, she still wanted the Smith estate probated and the property transferred to the tribe. Tribal recognition or not, she wanted the land put in trust so the tribe would not have to pay taxes on the property.

In the spring of 1975, Getches renewed his pleas to the secretary of the interior and to Senator Jackson, contending that lack of standards for recognition was not a viable excuse for governmental delay in acting on the Stillaguamish petition. The Boldt court had ruled that the tribal government was capable of administering the exercise of its treaty rights and that the Stillaguamish were beneficiaries of a claims commission award that Interior was in the process of paying off. Getches claimed once more that his

Stillaguamish clients were "descendants of treaty signatories... hav[ing] maintained a non-dissolved tribal organization" and that only Congress had power to abrogate a tribe's treaty rights, which it had not done. He reminded Senator Jackson that "For years Interior has made determinations of which Indians are recognized by the federal government," and there was no reason to hesitate now. He asked the senator to intervene by calling on the secretary and the solicitor to act on the petition.[16]

In the meantime, Esther finally succeeded in convincing the tribe to vote to accept a single lump-sum payment, but Interior could make no such payment since the tribe was still unrecognized—and since the secretary of interior was still insisting on per-capita payments. He stuck to his position that only recognized tribes could take money for tribal purposes. Esther wrote a five-page letter in longhand to "Congressmen and Senators." It took the form of a resolution, using terms like "whereas this and whereas that" and asking the legislators to intervene with the secretary to grant the tribe recognition. She informed those to whom she wrote that she spoke "for my council and the members of my Tribe as chairperson and [formerly] Secretary and doings of the Tribe for Fifty years now."[17]

Since the favorable Boldt decision, Esther had found herself mired in so much office work she was unable to perform all the chores for the tribe. STOWW therefore agreed to fund two more positions, a fisheries patrol officer and an office clerk. Esther hired her former son-in-law, Ed Fitchen, as fisheries patrol officer and his girlfriend, Ardeth Wells, as clerk. The two did the office work. In addition, STOWW funds continued to provide a Legal Services attorney when necessary. Fitchen ran up and down the Stillaguamish in his Volkswagen when not chauffering Esther or helping in the office. Some of Fitchen's work involved photocopying records, filing, and some typing. He also answered Esther's mail, and when driving her to meetings, he made notes for her. The position of fisheries patrol was really just a title devised so Esther could get CETA funds to pay him while keeping him close. "Esther and I had a very special, very unique relationship," Fitchen said. "I loved her and she loved me." Even after his divorce from Marion, they had nothing but "respect for each other"[18]

With a few weeks of free time, Esther decided to go to California for a Memorial Day visit to the Hayward cemetery where her biological father was buried and then to Reid's grave in Lodi. There, at the Cherokee Memorial Park Cemetery, she left flowers on an unpretentious ground-level, rough-poured cement slab that bore the words, "Oscar Reid 1871–1945." They appeared to have been scratched in with a stick after the slab was poured. Finding Reid's resting place seemed to serve as a catharsis for Esther, though she would continue to wonder why he had left her and her mother.

CHAPTER SEVENTEEN

# THE CHIEF AND THE WAGON TRAIN

From June 4 to June 7, 1975, Esther attended a meeting of the Affiliated Tribes of Northwest Indians in Port Angeles, Washington. Hosted by the Lower Elwahs and the Makahs, the meeting drew 450 Indians from twenty-two tribes.[1] One of the conference's objectives was to review and discuss Public Law 280, enacted in August of 1953 in a congressional attempt to resolve certain issues involving jurisdiction of states and their police power over Indian reservations.[2] Enforced during the sixties, when the government sought to terminate its relationship with tribes, the law lessened federal control and gave the states broader powers over Indians. In the wake of complaints from both the tribes and the states, Congress modified the law in 1968. The tide had thus turned from federal protection of the Indian, and the states were given the heavier hand.[3]

At the Port Angeles meeting, there was heated discussion over the scope of the states' power and how it affected Indian self-determination. Then discussion turned to issues of importance to reservation tribes.

After testing the waters in early sessions, Esther began to make her presence known. In one session, she pointed toward Steve Lozar, superintendent of the Western Washington Agency. "Now we have a Superintendent here and he never does anything for us," she said, launching into a verbal assault and accusing the government of not helping her Stillaguamish. Following the session, Lozar cornered her. "Esther," he said, "I bend over backwards to help you people." "Oh, I know it," she replied casually. "That was her way," Lozar said. "Some of her tactics were [designed] to get the limelight and get in print. Esther was a pushy woman, [but] not . . . mean or anything. If she had a goal, she would do everything she could to make sure that there [were] . . . answers to her questions. She had a way . . . of getting a lot of attention."[4]

Unlike the good feelings she had for Lozar, she held the commissioner of Indian affairs in low esteem and voted in favor of a resolution passed in the final session of the ATNI meeting, asking the commissioner to explain his lack of attendance at the Port Angeles conference. In the same resolution the participants objected to his giving more attention to Indians in other areas of the country than to those of the Pacific Northwest. Another resolution asked for an explanation as to why the funds granted under the Johnson-O'Malley Act for special educational needs of Indian children had been reduced without consultation with the tribes involved.[5]

Esther regarded one action as the centerpiece resolution of the meeting—a call for the secretary of the interior to unconditionally recognize the Stillaguamish tribe and a call for the ATNI, the NCAI, and the NTCA to throw their support behind the Stillaguamish petition for recognition.[6]

While Esther was in Port Angeles, events unfolded that would do more to advance recognition for her tribe than had anything previous. On Sunday, June 8, 1975, three horse-drawn wagons and a train of men in buckskin assembled in Blaine, Washington, just below the Canadian border, to begin the journey eastward in celebration of America's upcoming bicentennial. The train wheeled out that day, southbound on Interstate 5 on its one-year, three-thousand-mile trek. Wagons from other states would join the caravan along the way. The train planned to stop for the winter in Laramie, Wyoming, and resume its journey in the spring.

On the drive home from Port Angeles, Esther read several newspaper reports of what would become known as the Bicentennial Wagon Train. "Tulalips Too Busy with Master Plan to Attack Wagon Train," headlines in the *Everett Herald* read. Tulalip business manager Wayne Williams was quoted as saying his tribe had too much to do with industrial and residential development to "attack" the train.[7] When Esther and Frank arrived home late Sunday, they heard TV reports that the Lummi Indians would join the celebration of the trek the next day. Esther was still sleeping that next morning when Frank hatched a plan. Without waking his mother, he called Superintendent Lozar at the Everett agency to inform him that the Stillaguamish were going to "hold up" the train. Frank next called KRKO Radio in Everett, and radio-station employee Shirley Bartholomew called Seattle TV stations KING and KIRO about the planned "attack." When Esther awoke, Frank told her what he'd done. He told her the train would be waylaid to call attention to the government's failure to answer the Stillaguamish petition for recognition.[8]

The media began calling for information about the Stillaguamish threat to hold the train hostage. At this point the BIA and other Indian regulatory agencies became involved, fearing an "attack" might prove more than symbolic. The Indian activism of the earlier 1970s was still fresh in the memories of government officials. At that time, militants had taken over BIA offices, members of the American Indian Movement (AIM) had laid the seventy-one-day siege at Wounded Knee, South Dakota, and there were Indian-government confrontations in Nebraska and elsewhere. Indian militants dispossessed non-Indian businesses on reservations. There were Indian takeovers of Alcatraz in California and Fort Lawton in Washington, and the Kutenai tribe of northern Idaho declared "war" on the United States, resulting in the closure of U.S. Highway 2. At the time—September 20, 1974—Roy Sampsel, reservation programs officer of the Interior's Portland regional office, was attending an ATNI meeting in Spokane. He drove to Idaho, and with other government officials sought to end the "war" and open the highway. A few days later the Indians backed off, satisfied their challenge to the government would result in some benefits, and they did receive some concessions.[9]

Now the Department of the Interior sent Sampsel north again, this time to the Stillaguamish Island Crossing office, where Esther planned to stop the train. On his daily newscast, Paul Harvey announced to the nation the impending Stillaguamish attack. Soon after Frank had set things in motion, he and Esther found a note a tribal policeman had left at their house just before they arrived back home from Port Angeles. It notified them that Arnold's granddaughter Dorothy had been killed in Toppenish on the Yakama Reservation. Dorothy and another woman, both of whom had been drinking, were driving with five children when their car ran a stoplight, was struck by another car, and slammed into an irrigation ditch, killing Dorothy.[10]

Esther headed for the Yakama, leaving late on Tuesday, but planning to return to Island Crossing on Thursday, June 12. She should be back before the train arrived late that afternoon. Headlines in Tuesday's *Everett Herald* announced, "Stillaguamish Indians Eye Bicentennial Wagons." Under this headline was the report that the train's itinerary called for an overnight stay at Island Crossing, "just an arrow's flight away from the combination office and souvenir store." In their absence, Esther and Frank asked Rod Sayegusa to locate Alan Stay to help in mediation with wagon-train master Ken Wilcox. Sayegusa and Stay arranged a Wednesday evening meeting with the train people, who by then would have driven their wagons as far south as Mount Vernon. At the meeting they intended to apprise the train people of the "attack." The plan was to hold up the train until the government granted the Stillaguamish recognition. TV crews arrived in Mount Vernon to film the meeting.

While Esther and Frank were still on the Yakama, Stay and Sayegusa prepared to go up to Mount Vernon to meet with Wilcox and other train leaders, Chuck Funderburg of Winthrop, Washington, and Harold Magelessen of Camano Island. On the Yakama,

Esther sought out Homer Settler to write a speech for her to deliver when she met the wagon train. Settler, a friend and frequent legal counselor, was permitted to represent Indians in Indian courts. His mentor was Felix Cohen, an authority on Indian legal matters and author of the *Code of Federal Indian Law*.[11] Settler grabbed a yellow legal pad and a sleeping bag and rode with Esther and Frank back over the Cascade Mountains, all the way writing and rewriting Esther's speech.

On discovering that other Indians were to attend the Mount Vernon meeting, Sampsel, joined by Paul Weston, a Choctaw and BIA tribal operations officer for the Portland Area Office, met with Stay and Sayegusa. The men then had a long talk with Wilcox. After that, according to Sampsel, the wagon master "started calling folks at the Centennial offices in Washington, D.C. . . . They had images of a great problem. . . . They didn't know Esther. . . . There was some concern within the government structure . . . [that] this could be one of those issues that AIM . . . would decide was a good thing to do." Allaying such fears, Sampsel assured the train leaders there would be no incident in camp that evening.[12]

Reporter Linda Bryant would later recall that "the guys running the wagon train weren't stupid." "Here they got national TV [coverage]. Why had they gotten on national TV? . . . Because an Indian tribe—a lowly little nothing tribe with a woman as its chief . . . , not that anyone gave . . . [the title chief] to her, is about to stop the wagon train. Well maybe it was that she had national attention and . . . they were milking it for all their worth."[13]

Esther did not attend the Wednesday evening meeting, of course, and there was some question as to why Stay and Sayegusa did not explain her absence to the media. Linda Bryant's story in the *Herald* the next day read: "The Indians failed to show last night in Mount Vernon for a much ballyhooed pow-wow set up by members of the city's bicentennial promotion group . . . [but instead] tribal attorney Allen [sic] Stay and business manager Sayegusa, a Lynnwood management consultant, arrived at the wagon train encampment to confer with Paul Weston of the Bureau

The Bicentennial Wagon Train, June 12, 1975, en route to Valley Forge, Pennsylvania. Esther forced the train to stop a night near tribal headquarters until the wagon master promised to deliver a message to the Interior Department. *Reprinted courtesy of the Skagit County Historical Museum, La Conner, Washington.*

of Indian Affairs' Everett office and Roy Sampsel, special assistant to the Secretary of the Department of the Interior, who flew up from Portland for the occasion."[14]

Roy Sampsel hoped his friendship with Esther from the time they first met in 1971 would now diffuse any problems. Interviewed by Linda Bryant for *Everett Herald*, he reiterated his belief that the Stillaguamish had legitimate reason to voice their disenchantment with the federal government because of the inordinate amount of time it had taken for Interior to respond to the tribe's petition for recognition, which had been filed in early 1974. According to Sampsel, the department was unprepared to grant the recognition at that time since all necessary information was not yet in order. But he felt recognition would be a high priority on the agenda of Stanley Hathaway, who had replaced Rogers C. B. Morton as secretary of the interior.

Bryant also interviewed Ken Wilcox. "Our position is we're just passing through and not parties to the issue," he said, adding, "We hate to see the train used as a political tool. We're in this project to extend friendship to all people." George Cardinet, national director of the North American Trail Ride Conference, also sought to avoid a political showdown. Bryant reported on June 12 that "Wagon train leaders were still trying to stave off the pending confrontation late into the night." But many people feared it could turn nasty.[15]

After spending sleepless Tuesday and Wednesday nights, Esther arrived at Island Crossing on Thursday before the train did. The drama had been building, and Esther walked in and "played it like a master," Bryant said. Despite her lack of sleep she was unusually composed. She was alone in the tribal office when Sampsel came forward to greet her. "Why have you come?" she asked. "I did not send for you." Explaining that the document granting her tribe recognition would be ready in thirty days, Sampsel urged her not to stop the train but rather to ask Wilcox to carry her letter to the Department of the Interior.[16]

Some two hundred people were gathered on that warm Thursday at the Crossing when a patrolman delivered a telegram from the train's Pennsylvania headquarters inviting Esther to come to Pennsylvania where the Bicentennial people would negotiate with her.

Now the train of four wagons and numerous horseback riders was coming into view. TV cameras and news photographers were poised, ready to record the event. With queenly aloofness, Esther remained in the tribal office, sending Frank out to step in front of the train and invite Wilcox to come into the office. Following her orders, Frank stepped forward and grasped the reins of one of the lead horses. He informed Wilcox that the wagons would stay in nearby Silvana until the Stillaguamish received recognition. So saying, he escorted Wilcox and some of the other train members into the tribal office where Esther sat, poised and dignified. After a few brief words of welcome she stepped outside to read the

Esther outside the tribal office, surrounded by onlookers and press reporters, reading an address to members of the Bicentennial Wagon Train. *Reprinted courtesy of the* Stanwood/Camano (Wash.) News. *Photograph by Howard Hansen.*

speech Settler had written for her. Just as leaders of the train had come in peace and friendship, she said, her ancestors had welcomed white men to their valley a century earlier. As the Bicentennial Train symbolized the strength and determination of the American people, for Indians it meant broken treaties on a trail of tears, broken promises, lost pride and dreams, and, finally, the destruction of her people. She warned, "We stop this Bicentennial wagon train to bring to the attention of the nation that we have no other alternative short of violence that would bring our plight to light and produce action."[17]

After Esther ad libbed several more comments about Stillaguamish treaty rights, Wilcox replied, "You have our goodwill. We will carry your message back to the people."[18] She presented him a good luck medallion featuring a thunderbird. This she hung around his neck. She then handed him a letter for the secretary of the interior, which Wilcox was to carry back east. Esther hoped the publicity would reach the national press, making readers aware of the Stillaguamish's quest for recognition. Wilcox then moved on to the Stanwood-Camano Fairgrounds for the night. The train leaders invited her to ride with them in one of their wagons to Everett the next day. She declined the invitation but said she would visit them when they arrived in Tacoma, where she would be attending a meeting.[19]

Later, when writing his memoirs of that wagon train journey, Ken Wilcox remembered Esther as a "sweet wrinkled little woman, but a fighter." "She had her day," he recalled.[20] Linda Bryant recalled the wagon train episode and Esther's role in it:

> It was . . . moving . . . because here she was just an old lady in the middle of the road. She [wore] Indian clothing. It was really a moving speech. I remember the emotional impact it had on the crowd that day. There had been all this hoopla and all this tada and then there . . . was this small woman speaking in a sing-song voice. It was a voice that had great impact at that time. It suddenly stopped being a circus and

for those few moments that she spoke there was this dignity about her that everyone there had to respect. . . . Even the reporters in those few minutes noticed something about her presence, in her voice, and in her words that commanded respect for who she was and where she [was] coming from and what she was asking.[21]

Sampsel said the Department of the Interior was surprised at the attention it got. "What I tried to do," he said, "was get the parties together and then tell Esther that I would follow up on it afterwards, but I didn't want this [to get] into a Department of Interior discussion . . . let her make her point . . . , let the wagon train acknowledge her. . . . It was a little bit of . . . strategy on my part. If you could get the Bicentennial Wagon Train master to acknowledge this as a tribe, then it would be difficult for the Department of the Interior to answer why *it* hadn't."[22]

Activist Hank Adams, in a critique of the wagon train episode published in the June 22 issue of the *Tacoma News Tribune*, cited Esther as "one of the great ladies of Washington state history," lauding her for having brought attention to her tribe. On the other hand, Adams noted that the Bicentennial Wagon Train benefited from the publicity. "In fact," he wrote, "federally recognized tribes further down the trail [to Washington, D.C.] had been requested to stage an 'attack' for that purpose." But Esther had, as usual, stepped to the center of the stage. "In not being asked, the long-forgotten Stillaguamish were acting on their own initiatives—as usual," Adams observed. "There is little question but that people in America and elsewhere learned of the Bicentennial through Esther's 'attack.'" He pointed out how Esther helped others with their claims while lobbying for her own, how she had developed the form of a national task force on Indian problems at the community level. "It is ludicrous that anyone participating in the symbolism of commemorating the anniversaries or life of a nation could consider it an acceptable answer for Esther Ross to be told, 'Our nation and government shall decide within 30 days whether or not you should abandon yours.'"[23]

Shortly after the train moved on, Esther attended a meeting in Tacoma of tribal representatives at the Office of Native American Programs (ONAP), a federal funding program under the Department of Health, Education and Welfare (HEW). This meeting was assembled to hear George Blue Spruce, ONAP director, and the Puyallup George Clark, an ONAP staff member, explain their funding of Indian health programs. Esther spoke of the recent wagon train incident, citing Sampsel's promise of a decision from Interior in thirty days. "I hold the hammer for my tribe and they are to be recognized. I am not waiting for no thirty days with promises from Sampsel." Blue Spruce told Esther that if the tribe was a member of STOWW, it would be eligible to receive support and assistance from ONAP because of participation in the Boldt case. However, many unrecognized Pacific Northwest tribes were excluded. Recognized tribes were the predominant users of ONAP funds.[24]

On July 4, 1975, Esther and Frank entered their "float" in parades in Sedro-Woolley and Arlington. They rode in the Stillaguamish patrol car with the American flag placed upside down on its antenna. In a subsequent release to newspapers, Esther stated that the tribe "Received no prize because the U.S. flag was flown upside down." Frank defended this display of the flag as representing a signal of distress for the tribe.[25] The editor of the *Arlington Times* took a different view of the situation:

> We may not be the greatest American patriots in the world. But we are patriots. And it galled us—really galled us—to view the American flag being flown upside down by the Stillaguamish Indians in the Arlington 4th of July Grand Parade, the theme for which was "Arlington Honors the American Flag."
>
> Frank Allen, tribal policeman, declares this was a sign of distress felt by the Stillaguamish Indians. Actually, it indicates a life or death situation and is usually applied only to the maritime. What few members of the controversial tribe remaining look pretty healthy to us. Frank must tip the scale

at more than 300 lbs. and his mother, Tribal Leader Esther Ross, has lived to be an energetic 70 plus.

And their "distress" at not being recognized as a legitimate tribe is minute compared with the distress felt by spectators who viewed their contempt for this country by flying the flag as they did. Their cause was certainly not furthered by this deed. Some people who had given it little thought before are beginning to wonder if the Stillaguamish Indians aren't about as authentic as Alice in Wonderland.[26]

CHAPTER EIGHTEEN

# WHILE WAITING FOR RECOGNITION

A month after the wagon train rolled out of Island Crossing, there was still no word from the secretary of the interior on the Stillaguamish petition for recognition. David Getches had received no word either, which reinforced Esther's belief that the federal government did not keep its promises. Politicians encouraged Esther and continued to profess to be in favor of Stillaguamish recognition. Yet the Washington State attorney general and other state officials and legislators were reticent to openly support Stillaguamish recognition, fearing political fallout.

Much of the support Esther received came from activists for landless and urban tribes in the state.[1] It came as well from personal friends like James "Jim" Heckman, a federal fish and wildlife employee during the Boldt case and now executive director of Northwest Indian Fisheries Commission (NWIFC). Heckman had left federal employment to work for Indians because of political attitudes. Esther never had to schedule a meeting to talk with Heckman or another friend, NWIFC biologist Michael "Mike" Grayum. She often simply dropped in to their offices in Olympia to talk.[2]

During this stalemate over recognition, Esther worked closely with Chuck Trimble not only because he was a friend, but also because as executive director of NCAI he had contacts with other

Indian and governmental organizations. In midsummer 1975 she convinced him to write a letter to BIA commissioner Morris Thompson to get him to push for recognition. Trimble advised Thompson that, at the previous fall's annual NCAI meeting, members had passed a resolution supporting federal recognition for the Stillaguamish. Now Trimble asked for a meeting with Thompson, attorney David Getches, and representatives from STOWW and the Stillaguamish. Trimble also asked the BIA for a "complete statement as to the obstacles that hinder full recognition and assistance to this Tribe . . . as soon as possible."[3]

Esther's work earned less than enthusiastic response from Stillaguamish tribal members. Their lethargy was apparent in a meeting she called that August, when scarcely more than a dozen were present to meet with Rod Sayegusa and STOWW representative Ike George, who had come to discuss an approved minigrant. This grant paid for office rent, for office expenses, and for maintaining *Wide Load*. Sayegusa asked the group to consider acquiring firearms and uniforms for tribal officials patrolling the river and to consider buying a new patrol car. Members adopted Donna Soholt's motion calling for a packet of tribal fishing regulations in the fishing ordinance and the constitution. Frank's motion that the tribe take "full responsibility" to maintain *Wide Load* also passed.[4]

Trimble finally received a response to his letter to Thompson, though not from the commissioner himself. Instead, Interior solicitor Kent Frizzell wrote that the former secretary of the interior, Rogers Morton, did not feel sufficiently convinced that he had the legal authority to extend recognition to Indian tribes without congressional action. He concluded that "the 'recognition' concept appeared to be an exceedingly murky one," and attorneys at Interior were in the process of reviewing their findings. The changeover with the incoming Ford administration had prompted "unavoidable" delay.[5] Intending to force the issue, David Getches filed suit against Thomas Kleppe in October 1975. It was a ploy to get the new secretary of interior to make a decision on the Stillaguamish petition for recognition.[6]

At the 1975 annual NCAI meeting in Portland, Esther had no problem getting attendees to adopt a resolution reaffirming "their support for the recognition of the Stillaguamish Tribe," and demanding that the secretary of the interior "unconditionally recognize the Stillaguamish." Then, at a banquet on the last evening of the meeting, she was honored for fifty years of service to her people. Ramona Bennett presented her with a shawl. Esther introduced Getches and surprised him with the gift of a beaded belt buckle. Getches admitted that only a few other times in his life had he been so touched.[7] Though Getches had recently left NARF for a position in the law school at the University of Colorado, Boulder, he assured Esther he would continue to represent her in the struggle for recognition.

The case of Arnold Ross's will had been simmering for months. It came to boil again on September 24, 1975, when Judge Robert Snashall called his court into session. Dorothy's death almost four months earlier had left her mother, Margaret, as heir to the property if Arnold's will was upheld. Michael J. Fitch of Legal Services represented Esther, and Bellingham attorney Jon E. Ostlund represented Margaret. Testifying on Esther's behalf were Dr. Arthur Watts, the Bellingham physician who had attended Arnold; Rose Mary Placid, a Lummi friend of Esther's; William Genschow, who'd been the family's case worker since 1970; and Art Jorgenson, a heavy-machinery contractor. Those testifying for Margaret included Willifred Cooper, director of the Lummi Alcohol Program; her husband, Kenneth Cooper, who was Arnold's cousin and a Lummi police officer; and Roy Paul, also Arnold's cousin and a nightwatchman and pastor.

Rose Mary Placid testified that Esther's step-grandchildren constantly confused Arnold by asking him to change his will. She also testified about many conflicts in Esther's house. Arnold did not like Frank, Placid said, and Esther did not like Dorothy. When it came Art Jorgenson's turn to take the stand, his testimony did not support Esther's case. Jorgenson, who'd done some bulldozing in the yard, testified that he came by to collect monthly payments from Arnold and found him fully competent to discuss business.

Esther anticipated that Dr. Watts's testimony would show that Arnold was *not* competent to execute a will. But Watts admitted that though Arnold was desperately ill during intermittent office visits, he was not disoriented. He testified that Arnold's last stroke had affected part of his brain, but that there was no marked deterioration in his mental state during his last months. Margaret's attorney got Watts to admit Arnold still had the ability to handle money even though he might have spent it on whiskey rather than on medicines and food. Watts also said Arnold was lucid enough to recognize property he owned and to whom he wanted it to go, though he could not certify as to Arnold's competency at the time the will was executed.

William Genschow confirmed Placid's testimony that Arnold abused his medication as well as alcohol. Genschow also testified that George Felshaw, then superintendent of the Everett agency, had contacted him in 1972 and told him Arnold wanted to change his will. Genschow had advised against it and suggested Dorothy could be cared for some other way. Genschow testified that Dorothy's siblings were disruptive and brought whiskey over from the Yakama, and that on one occasion, Dorothy's brother, Donald Baker, broke down the back door of the Lummi house.

Kenneth and Willifred Cooper testified that they had been close to Arnold in his final years and that they considered Dorothy almost their own daughter. The Coopers said that for some time Arnold had wanted to change the 1958 will to leave his property to Dorothy, and moreover, that Frank and Esther were hostile toward Dorothy. Arnold, they said, was afraid Dorothy would be treated improperly after his death. Kenneth Cooper went on to state that Dorothy had cared for Arnold with compassion—in the "Indian way" he said. They testified that when Arnold was sober he was lucid and competent. Roy Paul testified that Dorothy returned intermittently to care for Arnold days at a time in his last years.[8]

Genschow's redirect examination ended the day's hearing, and Judge Snashall ordered a continuance until November.[9] It was actually December 11 before the next hearing was held. Testimony of Frank's and Esther's long-time friend George Smith did nothing to change the case. Smith said he had seen Arnold three or four times during his illness, and Arnold was able to recognize Smith when he came. When Esther finally testified, she characterized Arnold as ill and confused. She and Frank, who also testified, contradicted other witnesses. She said Arnold was taking large doses of drugs at the time he executed the will. Her words conflicted with testimony of probate clerk Sharon Redthunder, who testified that at the agency Arnold walked on his own and appeared to have been well when making out his will. When Dorothy had brought him in, Redthunder said, he talked with her and clerk Inez MacNamara in private. Dorothy was not a witness to the change of the will. Redthunder's testimony was corroborated by scrivener Earl Allen. He said that although he knew Arnold was in poor health, he was competent to change his will. No evidence was presented of undue influence by Dorothy and others to induce Arnold to change the will. Exhibits were presented showing that Arnold wanted none of his land to go to Frank. The day's hearing ended with a decision pending.[10]

Esther decided to request a rehearing and should that fail, ask for an an appeal, claiming prejudice on the part of Judge Snashall. Indeed, at times, Snashall had become irritated with Esther. "If we proceed on the basis on which we are proceeding she can come up with any kind of statement [nonresponsive to the question] she wishes," he had said, and at another point he had asked her, "You are a Chairman of the Tribal Council or are you just a busybody?" Becoming impatient with Frank's testimony, he had once interrupted him, scolding, "I don't know why you just can't answer the thing instead of going through a long discourse. Why don't you simply tell us . . . the point?" To this, Frank replied, "I learned it the white man's way, to explain everything." The judge responded, "That's not the white man's way. That's the Indian way, the way you are doing it. Now please get to the point the best you can."[11]

In January 1976, while the judge had the case under advisement, Esther returned to the capital in an attempt to break the logjam that blocked things moving through the bureaucratic mill. Before making her usual rounds, she visited Chuck Trimble's NCAI office. At that point Trimble noted that although Esther "seemed quite old," nothing had dampened the fire in her spirit. Like Esther, Trimble was aware of "tension between the federally recognized tribes . . . over fishing." Esther's awareness of the stance of these more powerful groups only heightened her sense of purpose.[12]

Photojournalist George Ortez, who photographed Esther in meetings in the capital, remembered her as making "a nuisance of herself . . . [saying] the same thing over and over. Sometimes, to be honest, I'd like to go the other way," he said. The Snohomish Jack Kidder remembers Esther on this trip to the capital as being "bound and determined" to brush off any negative responses.[13]

Focusing on the details she wanted to get across, she ignored signals in Senate hearings that her allotted speaking time had lapsed. Malcolm McLeod, who accompanied her on three different occasions to Senate hearings, coached her on how to present her testimony. As he manipulated her words, she manipulated both her hearing aid and her audience. Much of her brazenness stemmed from a disregard of rules and protocol in the conduct of the nation's business. Some of her brashness came from willfully ignoring what she believed to be useless.[14]

Esther's conversations were almost always tied to her hearing aid. Ken Hansen, a Samish, remembered her working this "repulsive instrument" with a bulky alkaline battery the size of a pack of king-sized cigarettes which, instead of being discreetly positioned inside her clothing, was pinned to the front of her dress. When something was said that she wanted to hear, she would turn on the aid, but if she disagreed, she would say, "Oh, let me turn it up. I can't hear you." When the raucous feedback from the aid drove people from the room, she would turn it off and proceed with a speech or sit there oblivious to others. Hansen says, "She

Meeting held in offices of the Department of Interior, Washington, D.C., January 21, 1976. Quinault tribal chairman Joe DeLaCruz is on the left. *Photograph by George Ortez, N.E.W.S. photo NW.*

used it as a weapon. Where some elderly ladies would use a hat pin to spear our attention, Esther used her auricular weapon."[15]

Esther sought advice on hearing aids from the U.S. Public Health Service. William A. Murdoch remembered Esther breezing past receptionists to his office in the former Marine Hospital in Seattle. There she stood before him with "her fairly long day dress, her gray hair somewhat tucked up, her clear-eyed gaze, firm challenging attitude yet with a quizzical sense of humor—with the subtle but strong, not to be turned aside pressure." Before Murdoch could explain the complex government agencies, she reminded him that his job was "to help the Indians." "That 'hearing aid,'" Murdoch said, "came between Esther and me a number of times. She appeared one day telling me it didn't work and Indian Health should fix it. I suggested that Esther and Frank take off a couple of hours and leave her hearing aid to get fixed. I discovered that its batteries were dead."[16]

On February 13, 1976, Judge Snashall entered his decision on the Arnold Ross estate, ordering acceptance of Arnold's last will and testament as executed on January 16, 1974. Although Washington

Esther in a meeting. Her cumbersome hearing apparatus is apparent. Hard of hearing, she used her son, Frank, to hear for her if she was without her hearing aid or her battery was dead. *Photography by George Ortez, N.E.W.S. photo NW.*

was a community property state, under Indian law and on Indian reservations one could disinherit a spouse. Following the decision, Esther demanded that attorney Michael Fitch appeal it, but Fitch advised her that the case merited no appeal. "The . . . decision denying your challenge to the will will be almost impossible to change at this point," he told her, and he withdrew from the case, returning her documents and correspondence. Should she proceed, he said, she would have to retain another lawyer. Undeterred, Esther hired attorney Alan Stay from STOWW to resume her case.[17]

As David Getches prepared for the Stillaguamish suit against Interior, the Tulalips decided to intervene on the side of the government. Tulalip tribal chair George S. Williams prepared an affidavit supporting their intervention on the government's side. Stillaguamish recognition would mean the Tulalips would have to share the fish resources of Puget Sound and would be excluded from their "usual and accustomed" fishing stations along the Stillaguamish River. The Tulalips feared another recognized tribe would dilute the economic and physical resources they received from the BIA.[18] When attorney Donald B. Miller, representing the Stillaguamish, filed a memorandum to block the Tulalips' intervention, it was denied.[19]

CHAPTER NINETEEN

# THE CASE OF THE FLYING FISH

More than eight months had now passed since Roy Sampsel had promised action in thirty days on the Stillaguamish petition for recognition. The delay prompted Esther to "introduce" herself to President Ford's newly appointed secretary of the interior, Thomas S. Kleppe.

At a meeting of the Non-Recognized and Terminated Task Force, held the first week in March 1976 in Olympia, Esther and others under her leadership proposed a plan as bizarre as that of "attacking" the Bicentennial Wagon Train. She would air-freight a frozen steelhead trout to the new interior secretary in order to familiarize him with her drive for recognition. After John Smith, son of Gus Smith, brought in an eighteen-pound steelhead from the Stillaguamish River, it was packed for delivery and labeled: "Fresh Washington Salmon. The Best That Swims. Danger: Eating My Be Habit Forming." Esther would have been aware of the deceptive labeling—"salmon" instead of "trout"—but she figured the fish's recipients would not.[1]

After sending the frozen fish off in dry ice on March 4, Esther called the *Washington Star* to alert the paper to its arrival. She also called Secretary Kleppe—twice. There was no reply. The fish lay unclaimed in the freight area at Washington's National Airport. Esther finally reached BIA Commissioner Thompson, who told

Kleppe of the arrival. Inside the shipping box a letter explained that this particular fish was first blessed and sent on its way by unrecognized tribes. The gift-givers asked Kleppe's help so their children could "stand proud knowing full well of their heritage." The blessing read, "May the Great Spirit walk with you and yours now and in the future along the path of life beautiful." It was signed by Esther, Clifford G. Allen and Kathleen L. Bishop of the Snohomish tribe, Robert Comenout of the Snoqualmie, and Beulah Wilson of the Cowlitz. The Saturday edition of the *Washington Star* contained a writeup of the fish incident headlined, "Uh, Mr. Kleppe, There's This Fish Here to See You."[2]

Like a salmon bruised by its upstream passage to its parent stream, the once-blessed fish arrived in the capital in poor condition. Workers at the loading dock wanted someone from Interior to take it off their hands immediately. Department officials sent someone scurrying to retrieve the fish, which "was aging quickly."[3]

Secretary Kleppe's response to Esther was rumored to have been "Thank you for the fish but I prefer beef." In a March 8 letter to her he indeed stated that beef was his preference, that he had given the "beautiful fish" to his neighbors, but that he appreciated the thoughtfulness and civility of those who had sent it. Esther was pleased with her flying-fish strategy. It seemed to have gotten the publicity she was seeking. An article in the March issue of the STOWW publication, *Indian Voice*, determined that fish or no fish, "The Stillaguamish had legitimate reasons for being disenchanted with the federal government because of the inordinate amount of time it has taken to respond to the tribe's most recent request."[4]

Before leaving for Boulder, Colorado, to visit Getches and give her depostion in the forthcoming suit against Kleppe, Esther was in Taholah on the Quinault Reservation attending the March conference of LaDonna Harris's Americans for Indian Opportunity (AIO). The conference focused on issues of timber and other natural resource issues. Harris recalled Esther's consistency in seeking support for her cause: "She reminded you of the struggles of her

Esther with Sam Cagey (left), Lummi, and Roger Jim (right), Yakama, at an Americans for Indian Opportunity meeting, Lake Quinault Lodge, near Taholah, Washington, March 16, 1976. *Photograph by George Ortez, N.E.W.S. photo NW.*

people and she just—she would just be there and right in your face. She made sure you'd make some commitment to help her. To help the tribe. She would travel, I don't know how. She was so impressive that she put that much energy, that she'd make you commit to help her. . . . She had it all mapped out what we should do."[5]

Getches made arrangements for Esther to fly Continental Airlines on March 22 to Denver, where someone from NARF would meet her and take her to give a deposition that day in the Stillaguamish suit against Kleppe. Hank Meshorer of the attorney general's office in Denver met her at Getches's office. Meshorer "was endeared to Esther during the deposition," Getches said, "and told me privately that he would try to convince his superiors in Washington that something should be done." Getches also arranged a meeting to introduce Esther to Don Clark and Wayne Chattin of the American Revolution Bicentennial Administration at the Denver Federal Center. These men were interested in Esther's exploits and wanted to publicize them. Getches gathered information on the wagon train and flying-fish episodes and sent it to Chattin, commenting, "Your willingness to take the lead in trying to bring to the public eye the historical significance of this small tribe and their long battle to remove the indignity and the administrative problem of not being considered an Indian tribe by the United States will be a great boost to the Stillaguamish."[6]

Before Esther returned home, Getches took her to Boulder's swankiest restaurant for dinner. At well-dressed tables at which sat equally well-dressed people, Esther ordered a one-course meal of bread and milk.[7]

On her return from Boulder, Esther was eager to know if the mood had changed in the capital. On March 24, the day she arrived home, she wrote to Secretary Kleppe. A month passed before the secretary answered her. It was, in her words, "the same old story." "Unfortunately my Solicitor and I have not yet resolved the question of whether this Department has legal authority to extend Federal recognition to your people as an Indian tribe," Kleppe wrote, but he was expecting that legal opinion any time.[8]

CHAPTER TWENTY

## THE WAIT GOES ON

Even as she besieged federal agents and agencies, Esther did not slacken her efforts to control the tribe. In a May 1976 letter she informed Leo J. LaClair and Gary Johnson of STOWW that in April the Stillaguamish council had defied her position as chairman and denied her the "authority to hire and fire." She threatened to take up the matter with a higher office of CETA. In the meantime, she went on record as having fired "Edward Goodridge from any office he may hold now. He shall be removed from his office of Planner. I also fired Llewelyn [sic] Goodridge off of his Patrolman job." She advised STOWW that Ed Fitchen was now helping Frank patrol the river. Even though he was office manager, Frank had bolstered his authority in fishing patrols. Because of a shortage of funds, Esther had to let her eighteen-year-old grandson David go.[1]

As could be expected, Esther drew strong criticism of such nepotism from the Goodridge-Smith group, and they found support from the Office of Native American Programs, one of the watchdogs of tribes that received federal funds. When ONAP warned her about the nepotism on her staff, Esther wrote another letter to STOWW:

> The Stillaguamish Tribe of Indians hereby formally request that the Mini Grant committee of STOWW waive and grant

Tribe participation without the interference of the ONAP rule regarding nepotism. The main purpose of this request is that the Tribe presently has as its executive administrative staff, Esther Ross and her son Frank Allen doing the majority of the Tribe's business. Due to the Tribe's size and lack of qualified personnel to carry out the business, the Tribe has had to employ a mother and son team. Through the Mini Grant of STOWW, the Tribe is able to actively travel to the various meetings that are necessary for Indian Country. Approval of travel vouchers and expense reports must be done by either Ms Ross or her son. This is in violation of the nepotism rule. Past Mini Grants have shown that Esther and her son have not misused their authority or privilege regarding any funds received from STOWW.

Because of the unusual and unique circumstances of the Tribe and the Mini Grant program, the Tribe [asks] that this request be granted.[2]

A year after the wagon train event, Esther handed a letter to a Bicentennial Pony Express rider headed for Valley Forge. It was addressed to Secretary Thomas Kleppe, who acknowledged that he or his representative would accept the letter during July 4, 1976, ceremonies. The July 1976 edition of STOWW's *Indian Voice* carried the text of the letter:

To the pony express:

We, the Stillaguamish Tribe of Indians of Snohomish County, State of Washington, do hereby stop the Pony Express to deliver our request to the Secretary of the Interior Hon. Thomas Kleppe in Washington, D.C.

We stopped the wagon train as it went through our tribal territory a year ago. We were given 30 day [commitment for an answer] by the secretary of the Interior Department. The new secretary, the Hon. Thomas Kleppe, through his under secretary promised to sign our recognition paper for us in a few days. Those have long passed!

> We do not want to delay the U.S. Mail, but we do want immediate delivery of our . . . letter to the Secretary of the Interior [requesting recognition of] . . . the Stillaguamish Tribe at once without delay.
>
> Thank you, Honorable Esther Ross, chairperson of the Stillaguamish Tribe of Indians.[3]

Along with others from western Washington, Esther was invited to the capital to participate in the Festival of American Folklife sponsored by the Performing Arts Division of the Smithsonian Institution. Guests were to discuss a wide range of topics, including national and international cultural folklore, anthropology, ethnomusicology, social history, and area studies. The program for Native Americans included three groups: the Alaska Federation of Natives, composed of Aleuts, Athabascans, Tlingits, Haidas, and Tsimshians; the Confederated Tribes of the Siletz; and the Confederated Tribes of the Warm Springs Reservation of Oregon. Representatives from western Washington weren't listed on the program, possibly because of late filings. The festival, first held in 1967, usually ran about ten days. However, during this centennial year, it was to run all summer.

In mid-July Esther filled out an acceptance form, giving the Smithsonian permission to reproduce any part of her performance. She listed newspapers to which news releases could be sent and specified her dietary requirements: oatmeal, Cream of Wheat, potatoes, milk, bread, eggs, and cottage cheese.[4]

Robert Comenout and Kathleen Bishop joined Esther in the capital on July 26 for orientation and a rehearsal for the July 28 and August 1 presentations. Each talked about their respective tribes. One of the major topics at the festival was "Can the Indians cut themselves off from the rest of Americans?" Other questions concerned whether or not Indians could exist communally without being federally recognized. On Sunday, August 1, Esther appeared in two sessions. In the first, she presented the background of the music of the late Gus Smith. In the second, she, Bishop, and Comenout discussed their tribal histories.

The wheels in the capital were turning slowly in regard to the Stillaguamish suit. In September the NCAI filed an amicus brief with the district court in Washington, D.C., on behalf of the tribe. It said that as "the nation's largest and most influential [Indian] organization," it agreed with the plaintiff's position on the issue, the Indians having been constantly victimized by the "unresponsiveness and arbitrariness [of] . . . the bureaucracy that wields great influence over legal rights, their lives and fortune." The brief also stated that the Stillaguamish were indeed a bonafide Indian tribe and were recognized by other Pacific Northwest tribes. Furthermore, their status was confirmed by the state and its governor, Daniel Evans. The tribe functioned under a constitution and bylaws adopted on January 31, 1953, and revised on June 5, 1974, and was willing to design and implement a regulatory plan for fishing.[5]

Although Interior had once informed Esther that her Stillaguamish could not be recognized because they were landless, the department had already recognized a number of landless tribes. Since the land ownership requirement has been abandoned, it was now conceded "that the ownership of land is immaterial." While the secretary continued to question his authority to extend recognition to *any* Indian tribe, he received recommendations that he do so from the commissioner of Indian affairs, the Portland area BIA office, and the associate solicitor for Indian affairs.[6]

The Stillaguamish case—Civil Action No. 75-1718—was scheduled for a hearing before Judge June L. Green in U.S. District Court for the District of Columbia. At that point, David Getches turned the suit over to Jeanne Whiteing, a young attorney for the Native American Rights Fund, whom he had coached over several weeks. "I was getting her prepared because I wanted her to do some or all of the presentation to the court," Getches said. "We had done the briefs. She worked hard with me on that . . . I wanted her to have her first court appearance in Washington, D.C., and have it go well."⁷

At the hearing, Esther found several Tulalips in court as intervening defendants. Their presence irritated her. "I'm not going to become a Tulalip or anything else," she said. "That's not what I am."⁸ But the Tulalip were in court in defense of their own interests. According to Roy Sampsel of the BIA, there could have been fifty or more tribes beside the Stillaguamish wanting recognition at this time. If they achieved their goal, their claims were bound to dilute the funds and services due the tribes already recognized. And those recognized tribes jealously guarded their own interests in dealing with unrecognized tribes.

The hearing lasted one day, and neither Esther nor the Tulalips testified. The Stillaguamish moved for summary judgment after the government had so cross-moved.

Getches described Whiteing's performance as "effective." She was "a very soft-spoken, deliberative person," he said. "[She] thinks deeply about things before she speaks and she speaks quietly." Judge Green asked hard questions of the government attorneys, some of whom Getches had known before but who now were not particularly friendly and who seemed to treat the case "as if . . . the whole idea . . . [was] a bother." "The demeanor [of the government attorneys] *after* the case . . . was, I think, a little more humble than before when they thought we were just wasting their afternoons," Getches said, and he believed their attitudes affected the judge's order. As for Whiteing's presentation, Getches was more than satisfied for she definitely "clicked" with the judge.⁹ It may have been no accident that he had turned the case over to Whiteing to try, for then the plaintiff, her attorney, and the judge were of the same gender.

In her ruling, Green mentioned four times that the NCAI favored recognition. The tone of the judge's remarks, Getches notes, seemed to indicate that if most of the nation's tribes accepted the Stillaguamish as an Indian tribe, then the United States government should too.¹⁰ But instead of resolving the issue of recognition itself, the court hearing intended merely to force Interior to respond to the Stillaguamish petition. In her "Memorandum Order" issued on September 24, 1976, Judge Green noted that the Stillaguamish maintained that theirs "was and is a 'recognized tribe' entitled to the rights, privileges and services enjoyed by other recognized tribes and their members." She further noted that the "Defendant's unexplained failure to act on plaintiff's petition for almost two and one-half years is arbitrary and capricious and an abuse of their discretion." With this, she ordered the matter remanded to the Department of the Interior for a period not to exceed thirty days to allow the secretary to act on the petition and report back to the court. The court retained jurisdiction over the matter, holding in abeyance the cross-motions for summary judgment.[11]

Interior finally responded on October 27 in a nine-page letter from Acting Secretary Kent Frizzell to Getches. The department agreed that the tribe had treaty rights and was eligible for funded services:

> As set out herein, the Department has determined that: (1) the Stillaguamish Tribe of Indians is an Indian tribe entitled to exercise treaty fishing rights, and that the Department has a trust responsibility with respect to the protection of those rights; (2) the Stillaguamish Tribe is entitled to continue to function as an organized government outside the Indian Reorganization Act of 1934, and to have its constitution and tribal roll provisionally approved by the Department (subject to a study of the Bureau of Indian Affairs to confirm that members listed on the tribal roll satisfy the membership requirements in the constitution) and (3) the Department has authority subject to availability of appropriations to provide certain services to members of the tribe as set forth in greater detail herein. My authority to take land in trust under Section 5 of the 1934 act, 25 U.S.C. 465, is expressly discretionary. The Solicitor has some doubts that Section 465 applies to the Stillaguamish and that there is no other authority for the

Department to take the lands willed to the tribe in trust. I am not convinced that I would be justified in taking land in trust for this tribe at this time.

Frizzell further explained that since the Ninth Circuit Court of Appeals upheld the Boldt decision, he was directing the commissioner of Indian affairs and his staff to meet with Esther to determine if Interior, depending on applicable acts of Congress, had authority to extend other services to the tribe. Two recent statutes, he pointed out, appeared to have provided certain other services to the Stillaguamish as an indirect result of the Boldt decision. These were the Indian Financing Act and the Indian Self-Determination and Education Assistance Act. Both acts provided for contracting and managing major federal programs for eligible tribes and for providing economic development grants and loans. The two acts defined an "Indian Tribe" as "any tribe . . . which is recognized by the Federal government as eligible for services from the BIA." The Self-Determination and Education Assistance Act was designed to cover "any Indian tribe . . . which is recognized as eligible for the special programs and services provided by the United States to Indians because of their status as Indians." Frizzell noted that, "unlike . . . [some] statutes applying generally to Indians, these laws base their application on some form of federal 'recognition.'"

The secretary concluded that his department had trust responsibility to provide services to protect Stillaguamish fishing rights. It also appeared to him that under these special statutes "the tribe 'is recognized as eligible' for federal Indian services," though they did not suggest "*how many* services or *what* services." In practice, the bulk of services due the tribe was authorized by the broadly worded Snyder and Johnson-O'Malley Acts. The Department of the Interior had established criteria for benefits under the Snyder Act that delimited eligibility for Indian people to those "on or near reservations or trust lands." Authority under the Johnson-O'Malley Act—providing for state and local education agencies to assist Indians beyond reach of BIA-operated schools—was broad in that the secretary could enter contracts for such funds. However, over the years, the contracts had been restricted to providing education to eligible Indians "outside the BIA-operated school system."

Although Frizzell was uncertain as to whether the Snyder Act would provide services for the Stillaguamish, he promised to request appropriations under that act. He would also seek appropriations to provide Johnson-O'Malley services to members of the Stillaguamish tribe "to the extent [that] they have more than one-quarter degree Indian blood," explaining that since 1974 "Indian" had been defined as "an individual of 1/4 or more degree of Indian blood and a member of a tribe, band, or other organized group."

The department accepted the 1953 Stillaguamish constitution as it was. Frizzell ordered the BIA to verify people listed as Stillaguamish descendants; most important, he accepted the minimum one-sixteenth degree of Indian blood as prescribed in the constitution. But he denied the tribe's request to take land in trust. As far as the Gus Smith property was concerned, Frizzell explained, the solicitor for Indian services interpreted that under the law tribes not administratively recognized on the date of the Indian Reorganization Act of June 18, 1934, were ineligible to hold land in trust, and he knew of no other provision that could be used for transferring fee patent land into trust.[12]

From NARF headquarters in Boulder, Getches dictated a letter to Chuck Trimble, director of NCAI, expressing his delight with the decision in Esther's case, adding, "I wanted to let you know how important NCAI's participation in that litigation has been. . . . You certainly can count your efforts on behalf of the Stillaguamish among the very important ones of the NCAI in the past couple of years and list it proudly in the success column. Thank you very much on behalf of NARF and the tribe for your valuable continuing support."[13]

Tulalip service manager Francis J. Sheldon issued a statement on behalf of that eleven-hundred-member tribe. From now on, the Tulalips would have to make their peace with a bona fide tribe and not with a group of "wanna-bes," Sheldon said. But it was still the Tulalip position, he added, "that if a group of people have left their culture, disappeared into the general society, and only now are resurfacing because there is money around, then the question of 'recognition' becomes destructive of Indian culture, identity and continued existence as an Indian Tribe." In much the same way, he said, the Tulalips had objected to recognition for such groups as the Snohomish, Samish, and Snoqualmie, whose culture has blended into the general society. "Everyone wants to be Indian now," Sheldon remarked. "But when the blood line is watered down so much, and there is apparently no effort being made to check out whether the claims of individual Indians are actually valid as to being a member of any tribe, what do you expect us to do who have maintained our identity, in the best way we know how?"

Having spoken his piece, Sheldon was ready to accept the Stillaguamish as a fully recognized tribe. He hoped they would "get what they want from the federal government and the courts. ... They are fine people, and I have particular respect and affection for Esther Ross, their leader, a great lady and a remarkable Indian woman."[14]

Although Getches and Sheldon—and everyone else—seemed to accept Frizzell's letter as tantamount to federal recognition of the Stillaguamish, Esther remained somewhat uneasy about the situation. Frizzell had touched upon all the rights owed to the tribe without using the exact phrasing that would indicate that the tribe indeed had recognition. Because Frizzell's letter did not contain any statement to the effect that the Stillaguamish were hereby recognized, Esther remained unsure of her tribe's *exact* status. This insecurity reinforced a mistrust that would color her attitude toward the government the rest of her life.

Uneasy as she may have been in this regard, she also had personal problems to deal with: She had so far failed to secure Arnold's property. Her rival, Arnold's daughter and heir, Margaret, was battling alcohol abuse; Margaret's son Donald had a baby by his half-sister; and Margaret's house on the Yakama had burned down.

Margaret's troubles did not soften Esther's attitude toward her: "[My] home was built for me and Mr. Ross free Grant from BIA and I done paperwork to help him divide said heirs property, and sign well and septic tanks—I was yet his wife at death—but although the Dr. and neighbors testify he was incompetent to make a will at any time [in the] last 3 years of his life, the BIA Judge gave everything to other side."[15]

Working with Alan Stay on Esther's appeal of the decision, attorney Cynthia Davenport filed an appeal despite the fact that Judge Snashall had earlier denied a rehearing. The appeal was filed with the Interior Board of Indian Appeals, Office of Hearings and Appeals in Arlington, Virginia.[16]

Whatever the outcome of her own personal claims, Esther had gained much for her tribe—and she knew it. "It took a long time to get our Identity through the Secretary of Interior that we Existed," she wrote in an undated memorandum to tribal members. And later she reflected, "I did my bit—I got fishing rights and . . . recognition for my tribe, being all these years at labor." She seemed finally to be ready for an easier life. "I'd like to relax with a [companion.] . . . Travel when I wish and visit . . . friends I used to know."[17]

Linda Dombrowski of STOWW acknowledged Esther's accomplishments. She was all by herself until she caused Washington to cave in, Dombrowski said. "Finally they recognized that tribe and since that time . . . because of her accomplishment they changed the federal acknowledgement process." Roy Sampsel believes the wagon train incident was the impetus behind her final success and should not be overlooked. "It raised some consciousness and forced people to deal with the issue—and not only that, but herself, to deal with it," Sampsel said. Bill Black of the Everett agency felt she accomplished what she did because she "dealt directly with decision makers in Washington." In the words of Malcolm McLeod, who had long advised her in legal matters, she "was the only woman who could bring the United States to its knees."[18]

CHAPTER TWENTY-ONE

# A Celebration at Muckleshoot Hall

The achievement of recognition for the Stillaguamish tribe called for a celebration. A dinner was planned for December 4, 1976. The event would have to be held at a large facility because Indians and others from all over the Puget Sound area and people from across the nation were to be invited. The close-by Tulalips had a gathering hall that would have been a good place to host the event, but since that tribe had been on the opposite side of the issue, it seemed better not to ask to use their hall. Instead, Esther chose the community hall on the Muckleshoot Reservation. It was plenty large enough, and it was close to the Seattle-Tacoma International Airport. In honor of Esther, the Muckleshoots agreed to loan their hall for the occasion.

Some of those invited to the celebration were unable to attend, such as Bud Lozar, who was now superintendent of the Crow Agency in Montana. He sent his regrets, though in doing so, he overestimated the enthusiasm of her own people for what Esther had done:

> I am sure your fellow tribesmen are very proud of you for your untiring efforts over the years to finally achieve this goal. I'm also sure that members of tribes, who know you and those who don't personally know you, are equally proud

of you. I know for sure I and my family are. . . . Throughout your long struggle many . . . sad things happened that would discourage a normal person to junk the entire effort. However, Esther, you are not one of the normal persons, you are an extraordinary person and this is why you pushed on.[1]

Rudy Ryser, executive director of STOWW, accepted Kathleen Bishop's request to serve as master of ceremonies. Bishop was the program planner; she arranged for the food and the donations. No Stillaguamish served in the planning. Native foods eaten in traditional wintertime festivities and more modern foods were served. While celebrants dined on macaroni salads, salmon, venison, and beef, Esther ate only her customary bread and potatoes, washed down with milk. Two hundred seven-inch wood-carved salmon inscribed with the words "Stillaguamish 1855–1976" decorated the tables. It had taken Frank, with the help of son David and an aunt, three days to craft them.

Among those receiving these tokens was attorney Jeanne Whiteing, who flew in from Boulder with David Getches. The occasion gave Getches an opportunity to reminisce about his relationship with Esther: "There were a lot of times when she was hard to get along with. It wasn't just at first when we were getting to know her, but I must say that later, probably after the [Boldt] trial and its decision when I worked with her on recognition she was much more congenial and the relationship was almost familial at that point." "There was a certain trial by ideal factor in gaining her confidence," Getches recalled. "She [was not] impressed by the fact that I had gone to school and was an attorney who was working. . . . She expected the best and wasn't going to stop short of it."[2]

Chuck Trimble, the director of the NCAI, was there too, and he reminded Esther that she had mistrusted him until he had proven himself. Also present was another favorite of Esther's, Forrest Gerard, now a counsel on the Indian Affairs Committee on Interior and Insular Affairs of the U.S. Senate. Anthropologist Barbara Lane came from British Columbia. Even Llewellyn Goodrich

At the Muckleshoot tribal hall dinner honoring Esther and recognition for the Stillaguamish, December 4, 1976. In the foreground, Sam Cagey with the drum, Catherine Tally, Esther, Margaret Greene, and, on the far right, his back to the camera, the Lummi spiritual leader, Joe Washington.

was there and, so it was reported, were representatives of nearly every Pacific Northwest Indian tribe. However, no representative of the Governor's Indian Advisory Council was in attendance. Esther also felt the absence of her cousin, the now-deceased John Silva, who had served as tribal chairman from 1945 to 1970.[3]

Esther's daughter Ruth came from Seattle; her daughter Marion, who had rarely spoken to her mother in twenty years, came up from the Vancouver, Washington, area. And, of course, Frank was there. To Marion, the event was somewhat of a shock. "You wouldn't believe it," she recalled. "There were what seemed like thousands of Indians. And then there were the Stillaguamish . . . all blondes and redheads, claiming to be Indians. And I thought, 'Oh my God.'" She admitted to being impressed with the jewelry, the Pendleton blanket, and the other beautiful gifts her mother received.[4]

In the enthusiasm and goodwill suffusing the Muckleshoot hall, there was a plethora of talk about how Esther should be pensioned by the tribe, given an annual stipend. But after the evening was over, there was no more talk of tribal largesse for Esther.

Now that the Stillaguamish were a federally acknowledged tribe, Esther wanted to have a chief in the traditional manner, one who would take the name of her great-grandfather Chaddus. She believed the dinner was the time and place to make such an announcement. The long-deceased Jackson Harvey had already used the name in smokehouse activities. His son Paul, now a Sauk-Suiattle, was no longer identified with Stillaguamish. Esther had long wanted Frank to become chief, but she decided on John Smith, a councilman, who was active in tribal affairs, and the son of Gus Smith. However, even though she had told John to be present at the dinner, he failed to attend the event.

After everyone else had spoken, it came time for Esther to respond. Rather than making her usual pointed remarks, this night she reverted to reflecting on the tenets of her Adventist faith. But as her words reached her surprised audience, Catherine Tally, Margaret Greene's sister, interrupted her and escorted her out of the hall, informing her she was to prepare for her formal presentation. Minutes later, under escort of Tally and Greene, she reentered the hall. She was wearing her customary chiefly vestments—Indian clothing with a headdress band with star in front and a shawl over her shoulders. Since the bestowing of a title was a spiritual affair, Lummi spiritual leader Joe Washington conducted the presentation. After a few remarks, he asked an unrehearsed question of the audience: "Who wants Esther as the chief?" The response was loud and positive. At that point, Washington initiated Esther as chief of the Stillaguamish. Reporting the event, the *Indian Voice* noted that he conducted "an initiation ceremony for a new chief, Esther Ross, the designated chief [John Smith] having been absent." Unflappable, Esther accepted the honor—without giving up the long-held wish to someday see her son take his great-great-grandfather's mantle. From this point on, she signed letters and tribal documents, "Chief Esther Ross," finally able to use the title that matched the role she'd effectively assumed almost fifty years earlier.[5]

When David Getches returned home to Boulder he wrote Esther that the December 4 affair was "truly magnificent," that he was glad Esther received comments "long gone unsaid" by national Indian leaders as well as local people of importance. He wrote that he was proud to have been associated with Esther and her tribe. He sent his thanks for the blanket and the carved fish, which was an "especially important remembrance" of his work with the Stillaguamish tribe and which would be a "constant reminder of the spirit of determination and purpose which you manifest."[6]

Esther was now expected to offer input into BIA agency decisions in addition to leading her own tribe. She was invited to a meeting at the Everett agency to discuss applications for the superintendent's position and a possible division of the Western Washington Agency. She was invited to attend a meeting of the Affiliated Tribes of Northwest Indians in Portland to consider reorganization of the educational branch of the BIA, to discuss the Indian Health Care Improvement Act, and to offer input regarding the Federal Regional Council and candidates for key positions in the upcoming Carter administration.[7]

Rod Sayegusa helped Esther prepare a self-determination grant application to fund a program for the tribe titled "Technical Assistance and Start Up." Esther was also preparing for another trip to the capital in the new year. These kinds of activities and plans buoyed her when she received word that the Interior Department's Board of Appeal had upheld Judge Snashall's ruling. Margaret Baker was rightful heir to Arnold Ross's property.[8]

CHAPTER TWENTY-TWO

# RECOGNITION BRINGS MORE TROUBLES

Now Esther's primary concerns were to implement the recognition process and to organize her tribe as a functioning entity. In Washington, D.C., in January of 1977, she visited the BIA and the new Congress to make sure that no strings were attached to federal recognition. She discovered that strings did appear to be attached. Interior personnel were upset with the numerous news accounts that the Stillaguamish had been extended "federal recognition." Technically Kent Frizzell's letter of October 27, 1976, to David Getches did *not* extend recognition. The letter was merely intended to acknowledge that the Stillaguamish had treaty rights and that Interior was responsible for seeing that such rights were provided. Forced by the suit to make a determination on the tribe's petition for recognition, the Interior Department came to the conclusion that since the ruling in the Boldt case had called the Stillaguamish a tribe and determined that they had a right to fish, they then had other treaty rights and were entitled to other governmental services. According to a letter the BIA office sent to David Getches in mid-January 1977, while Esther was in the capitol, Frizzell's response "on behalf of the Tribe had been misunderstood." The term "recognition" as applied to Indian tribes had never been adequately determined legally. What "recognition" meant at this time in history was open to speculation. In more recent years, it has often been used to mean that a group of Indians was eligible for the full range of BIA services in the broadest sense of the word. In the October 27 letter to Getches the acting secretary determined to follow the more precise practice of determining eligibility for BIA services on a case-by-case, statute-by-statute basis. The letter implied that "the Stillaguamish tribe was [already] 'recognized as eligible' for federal Indian services."[1]

This most recent interpretation disturbed Esther, but Getches assured her that the Stillaguamish would be functioning as a recognized tribe.

For Esther that winter was unpleasant; she had periodic health problems to deal with. It began with abdominal distress experienced during her visit to Washington, D.C. The trouble began the day President Carter was inaugurated. Esther had positioned herself along Pennsylvania Avenue at a place where she could move out into the street and unfold her tribal banner as the Carters passed by. She hoped TV cameras would capture the picture for the world to see. However, severe abdominal cramps (she attributed them to french fries eaten the night before) brought a colonic response forcing her to make a hasty retreat to her hotel room before the new president and his wife strolled by.

Once she was back home, accolades and honors began to come her way.[2] The Shoalwater Bay Indians wanted to honor her with a reception at a meeting of tribal leaders from throughout the state. The meeting, held in mid-February at the Doubletree Inn in Sea-Tac, was to address fishing rights, and Washington's governor Dixie Lee Ray was scheduled to give the opening address. A Democrat, Ray had dismissed Fisheries Director Don Moos, a high-profile Republican, and she planned to bring on board Esther's friend, Jim Heckman, the former government fish biologist who was now executive director of the NWIFC. But, three days before the Sea-Tac meeting, Esther came down with severe cramping again. This time she believed it to be the flu. Even so, she was determined to attend the meeting to receive the Shoalwater Bay award and meet Governor Ray. Eugene Crawford, administrator of the National Indian Lutheran Board, was also coming to the meeting. Esther had earlier approached the board for funds to buy a small boat to patrol the river, and Crawford was coming to the meeting to hand her a check for forty-five hundred dollars to purchase an eighteen-foot boat, *Smoker Craft*. With it, Frank, whom Esther had appointed fisheries enforcement officer for the tribe, could patrol the Stillaguamish River. Sleek and small, able to move swiftly over the water, the *Smoker Craft* bore little resemblance to the dysfunctional and abandoned *Wide Load*.

The morning of the Sea-Tac meeting, despite recurring abdominal cramps, Esther ate the breakfast of eggs and toast her grandson David prepared for her. Soon thereafter an unpleasant feeling engulfed her left leg and arm, and her voice took on a strange quality. She had suffered a stroke. Frank tried to dissuade her from going to the meeting. But, despite the weakness in her left arm and leg and her slurred speech, she was determined to go. Frank and David got her into her wheelchair and into the car. At the hotel, Frank found Eugene Crawford and Ken Hansen. Making a human arm chair, they lifted her out of the car and into her wheelchair and took her in to the meeting. By now her speech was barely discernible. Because of her condition, the Shoalwater Bay award was given to her without fanfare.

From the meeting she was taken to the Seattle Indian Health Board Clinic and then to the Public Health Services Hospital on the Old Marine Hospital grounds in Seattle.[3] The staff at Public Health Services pleaded with Esther to remain at the hospital, but after about two hours, she insisted on returning to Bellingham. En route there, her condition worsened, and Frank drove her to Bellingham's St. Luke's Hospital, where her doctor, Arthur B. Watts, was called. Esther refused to budge from the car until talking with him. By now she was able to speak well enough to make her wants known. Dr. Watts ordered her admitted to the hospital, and she relented, too exhausted to fight the catheter and intravenous fluids. "I don't take medicine," Esther informed the nurses. "I haven't taken any pills for 30 years—I won't now."[4]

The next day her speech was much improved and she had regained some movement in her left leg and arm. X-rays showed there was marked deterioration of her left hip, but she refused physical therapy. On Friday more blood tests revealed normal counts and chemistries but her chest X-ray showed possible congestive heart failure. On Saturday she had Frank take her home. She left the hospital against medical advice, of course, but refused to sign a statement to that effect. Frank went to the Lummi Indian Health Clinic for a hospital bed and a noncollapsible wheelchair to move her about. She resolutely opposed medication and the care of visiting nurses from the reservation clinic.[5] Over the next month, Esther spent most days in bed reading the Bible and straining to sing hymns. Gradually her speech improved, as did the strength in the left side of her body. She was now getting around reasonably well with her walker and wheelchair.

Even though Esther held the title of chief, she needed a spiritual ceremony to validate it. The Muckleshoot dinner had not been the appropriate place or time. Joe Washington, the spiritual leader of the Lummis, picked a comfortable spring evening under a bright, clear sky to conduct the ritual at the shore of the Stillaguamish River. Indian and non-Indian friends alike were invited to witness the event. Esther was moved from the car to the shore in her wheelchair. During the ceremony, a loud clap sounded in the heavens. She looked skyward for rain, but none came. Some decided it was a heavenly acknowledgment of the affair.[6]

Gone were the days when Esther used her personal funds to support the tribe. Now rules and regulations were imposed on her management of tribal affairs. A Futures Task Force composed of consultants Ken Hansen and W. Sherwin Broadhead; attorneys David Getches, Charles Kerry, and Cynthia Davenport; Rudy Ryser; Esther; and others met on May 27 to plan the restoration of the tribe, to establish administrative and organizational capabilities, and to determine Stillaguamish needs. On June 6, 1977, the tribe adopted the written report of the plan. Phase I of three phases for tribal development was to begin in July 1977. The first phase, funded by STOWW, called for a budget of $173,000, and the BIA imposed strict guidelines for submitting applications for funding. The tribe would receive its first appropriation of $99,000 in June 1977 for the fiscal year operations and services. The appropriation required Esther to meet with Reservations Programs Officer Don Smouse and Tribal Operations Officer Bill Black of the Everett agency.[7]

All the while, Esther was strengthening her relations with Supt. Peter Three Stars, who had replaced Steve Lozar. His "open door" policy fit perfectly with her forceful way of dealing with agency officials. At their first meeting, she presented herself as chief of the Stillaguamish tribe, but she showed enough restraint to assure an audience with him. Immediately, Three Stars became aware of how strongly she felt about what she was doing. That was enough for him. Esther and Frank were frequent visitors to his office, always crusading, but always in harmony with each other. Three Stars was determined to respond in kind.[8]

At the Stillaguamish tribal office, operations were now more formal. Ed Fitchen and his friend Ardeth Wells had been laid off for a year now. Esther hired an acquaintance, Valda Orr, a Tulalip who was remotely related to Frank through his father, as her secretary. Orr had on occasion visited Esther, tidying her house and watching Frank's five-year-old daughter, Sandra, when Esther found such duties difficult to perform. Esther also hired Miriam Levin as bookkeeper. Esther assigned herself to a salaried position in charge of organizing the rolls, choosing Margaret Greene as her assistant. This task involved locating legal documents, filling out applications to certify membership, and getting signatures on affidavits to substantiate ancestries. In July Esther was notified that the Stillaguamish application for a contract for a Fisheries Management Program had been reviewed and approved. The contract would be awarded on or before August 11, 1977. Esther handed out another salaried position to Frank as fisheries enforcement officer.

Esther still had to complete the tribal membership roll, as required by Acting Secretary Frizzell in his letter of October 27,

1976. Interior's "provisional" approval of the Stillaguamish roll, subject to BIA studies to confirm memberships, meant that Esther had to provide proof of her peoples' blood degrees and tribal affiliations. Confirming vital statistics of members in the enrollment process was not without its difficulties. Increased confrontation with the tribal council in the decision-making process complicated her task. According to Frank, "We got hung up on the enrollment feature after recognition, spending more time fighting memberships and who was an Indian."[9]

Esther found Margaret Greene's help invaluable. Greene helped her on weekends, holidays, and summer vacations from Evergreen State College. Some tribal members looked askance at the position Greene, a non-Stillaguamish, held, especially since she was paid staff, not a volunteer. Since the tribe now had funding and annual appropriations, Esther was paying Greene twenty-five dollars an hour for herself, her car, and travel expenses to search out vital tribal statistics in county, state, and federal records. But Esther struck a deal with Greene whereby she would accept partial pay until the end of her employment, when she would be paid the balance. Greene was also to lend Esther the tally of hours worked so that Esther could use it to collect her own pay. Greene accepted these conditions because the work offered her insight into the difficulties of organizing her own tribe, the Samish, and because of her friendship with Esther.[10]

Esther spent hours being driven around in Greene's Volkswagen. "I wasted a whole car on Esther," Greene once said. This left Frank to himself with a used 1970 Jeep Wagoneer from Hinton Motors in Mount Vernon. On each side were painted the words "Fisheries Patrol." Frank equipped the vehicle with an overhead light bar and siren. He took to using it away from the river until the agency disciplined him after the state highway patrol complained of his unwelcome assistance on the roads. Not long after, Frank sold the equipment to the Lummi and let the vehicle itself go for defaulting on payments. Then, in the name of the tribe, Esther leased a new 1977 Ford E-150 Club Wagon from Diehl Ford, the first and only new car the family had ever driven. Tribal funds paid the monthly lease.

To complete the recognition process, Esther needed to obtain family background information to confirm relationships and blood quantums. Some candidates lacked birth certificates and proof of their correct names. Ardelle Preston, who was familiar with the National Archives on Seattle's Sand Point Way, helped her sort out enrollment statistics. Esther, Greene, and Preston sometimes worked in that facility. On occasion Esther went to Kate Johnson's home in search of the tribal business records Johnson had kept when she was tribal secretary. Because of the old rivalry and because Johnson believed Esther had treated her brother Llewellyn Goodridge unfairly in firing him from his position as office planner, the visits were usually unpleasant. The confrontations for Esther were mostly dry runs; Johnson had no intention of giving Esther the papers. Even so, Esther's "computer mind" enabled her to make the most of what little access she had to the papers. "If she saw them once," Margaret Greene said, "she remembered . . . them."[11]

Esther needed to have affidavits taken when vital statistics and other membership documents weren't available or were incomplete. Although some candidates for membership cooperated with her in her searches, some did not. Still unwilling to be identified as Indian, they brushed Esther aside. Greene observed that many of her contacts had had no previous status as Indians and were unfamiliar with reservation life. Others feared the ridicule of friends and neighbors. Others saw Esther as a trouble-maker. Yet some of Esther's and Greene's contacts, even those who bore little resemblance to Indians, came forward to establish their degree of Indian blood adequately enough to qualify for tribal membership.[12]

If Esther found an Adventist church when traveling with Greene on Saturdays, she paused to be alone to meditate in peace. She didn't embrace the twentieth-century revival of traditional Indian religions. However, when she faced problems, she would say to Greene, "Let's do it the old [Indian] way."[13]

After finishing all the legwork for enrollment, Esther, Greene, and occasionally, Ardelle Preston had still more work to complete. Often working into early morning hours at Esther's house, they sifted through affidavits and filled out questionnaires and application forms for those who were reluctant to identify themselves as Stillaguamish. And all the while, Esther was still somewhat limited by the physical residual from her stroke. She used a walker or wheelchair at times. On August 19, she had a rare home visit from the clinic health nurse for the Lummi Reservation after she had fallen from her wheelchair. By the time the nurse arrived ten days later to assess the situation, she found Esther up with her walker and looking better. Esther complained that the reservation clinic did nothing for her, that William Murdoch of Public Health Services did more for her, and the nurse duly recorded on her chart that the patient was "very disinterested in services here at this time. Does not listen to what CHN [Clinic Health Nurse] says. Difficult to carry on conversations with."[14]

The Lummi house became the focal point again in the contest pitting Esther against Margaret Baker over Arnold's 1974 will. Margaret tried to evict Esther or to get rent from her and Frank. The house was not trust property, so Judge Snashall had not included it with the land in any of the hearings. He made no decision on the house, leaving it separate from the 21.3 acres of land Arnold had owned. Esther took the matter to Lummi court, seeking full ownership of the house. Attorney Cynthia Davenport urged Esther to negotiate some agreement with Margaret to live there for her lifetime, with Margaret being paid a token sum for use of the land while the house remained there. With a hearing scheduled in the Lummi court on September 22, Davenport advised Esther to work out an agreement with Margaret and her attorney, Jon E. Ostlund, before that date, to avoid going to court. A week before the court date, Davenport wrote to Esther again, telling her she had an offer from Margaret's attorney—either Esther could buy out the land or Margaret buy out the house. Because Esther would be in Dallas, Texas, for the annual NCAI meeting on the day she was to have been in court, the date was moved up to October 6. That date would also be postponed. No settlement was reached and the situation languished since neither woman had the money to buy out the other.[15]

The painfully forced changing of the guard under tribal reorganization that summer of 1977 strained relations between Esther and the council. The council not only blocked her every move, it also ignored her input. Council members were concerned about initiating an accounting system to bring themselves in line as a BIA-recognized tribe. Mark Diefendorf and certified public accountants of the firm of Knight, Vale and Gregory of Tacoma helped set up an accounting system. Esther became increasingly defensive of her actions. Even though Frank was on the council, he was of little help to her since its deliberations were usually conducted in his absence: He had become so frustrated over the council's blatant attempts to wrest power from him and his mother that he simply began attending meetings only sporadically. Esther began meeting challenges of the council by deranging the filing system, removing pages from reports and letters and placing them in a separate filing system she devised to aid in her own searches. Lack of space at the office also forced her to pack papers not pertaining to immediate tribal operations into her Lummi house.[16]

The council had outlined steps to be taken for running the office and administering tribal affairs. Hiring and salaries needed discussion and contracts had to be written and let. Some of the council had met in an unannounced session on August 30 at the Sea-Tac Holiday Inn. Esther learned of the meeting the next day and had Frank sign a letter to the Superintendent Three Stars, complaining that the council had violated the constitution since a special meeting required that a majority of the council call it and give a seven-day notice. The council had been concerned about Esther's handling of tribal funds. Council members Donna Soholt, Marie MacCurdy, John Smith, and Llewellyn Goodridge decided to hold another meeting on September 8 at the Holiday Inn in Everett. They invited agency personnel to help institute the new office setup.

Now that Esther was aware of what was going on, she rescheduled the meeting for September 14 and mailed out the notices. Discussions centered on the spending of grant moneys and on a Natural Resources contract for the tribal fisheries program. Superintendent Peter Three Stars attended, along with Bill Black, Winifred "Win" Blodgett of the Natural Resources branch, Don Smouse of Reservation Programs office, and Marianne Bennickson of the contracting office. The council appointed Marie MacCurdy to the position of tribal enrollment clerk and Llewellyn Goodridge as tribal fisheries manager, each at a salary of $650 a month. The resolution for these appointments passed with only Frank's negative vote. The next special meeting was called for September 29 in the Natural Resources office at the agency. At this meeting the council voted to require that Esther have two co-signers, Goodridge and John Smith, on all checks issued by the tribe, though she retained her status as chair and chief and primary signatory. She signed this resolution after its acceptance by the unanimous vote of the council.

Immediately after that meeting, Esther left for California in search of more answers to Oscar Reid's disappearance. She had learned the whereabouts of Etta Chamberlain Bechthold, the daughter of Mary Jane Reid and her first husband. The woman was living in Auburn, so Frank, Esther, and Sandra started for that central California city. Arriving in Auburn, Esther approached the house. An hour later she emerged, slammed the car door shut and sat sullen and silent in the back seat. It was evident that she had been crying. Only gradually did she begin to talk about that meeting with Bechthold. Esther had learned that on February 19, 1934, some dozen years after walking out on Angelina and Esther, Reid, then a rancher, had married Mary Jane Chamberlain (nee Bell). On the marriage license Reid listed the marriage as his second and listed himself as a widower. Esther also learned that Reid had lived his later years on state welfare. Esther asked Bechthold if she had any personal items of Reid's but the woman had none.[17]

Over the years, Frank assessed bits and pieces of that conversation, connecting them with family history he had heard from Angelina. For Esther's sake, he did nothing to dispel her theory that Reid must have suffered from amnesia after he left the Eureka hospital that day in 1922.[18]

Despite her personal and tribal problems, Esther went to Dallas for the annual NCAI meeting. After the meeting she wrote, "I am a little stronger than I was in Texas. I have forced myself to do some of my work [at home in spite of a painful] left hand, walk with walker. My left leg is a little short—my spine curved from walking too early from the hospital."[19]

Llewellyn Goodridge and Marie MacCurdy continued to question Esther's use of funds for travel and other expenses. Now that they had official tribal appointments, they were spending more time than Esther in the office. And whenever she and Frank did appear, they were ignored. Decisions and policy were made without informing her or asking for her input. At the annual meeting on November 7, 1977, the council questioned Esther's accounting of tribal funds and requested an audit.[20]

Reflecting on the turbulence of 1977, Esther sent a poem as a Christmas greeting to Gov. Dixie Lee Ray. The governor responded, "I was very interested in learning about your work, Chief Ross, and was impressed with your fine poem. I appreciate your sharing it with me." Esther then submitted the poem to the *Everett Herald*:[21]

> Stormy winds may rage and roar, nations rise and fall.
> Men through space may upward soar, answering to each other's call.
> Aged chiefs, our native blood, are gone.
> Gone our virgin timber which stood 250 feet high.
> Gone our villages and burial grounds, on land we claimed our home.
> For the young braves, our chiefs, the history gave.

An aging Esther in Indian regalia. She believed that if one was Indian, one should dress like an Indian, especially when attending important meetings. *Reprinted courtesy of the* Everett (Wash.) Herald. *Photograph by Jim Leo.*

To carry on, mocked by tribes, government and non-Indians
Who claimed our dead to show the world their finds.
They we live around and hear the words,
"Who is an Indian?"
If you would know an Indian look at his spirit and not his skin.
Look at his heart and not his hair.
Look at his relationship to his father and his brothers, not his bloodlines.
Look at him as he is, not like you would like him to be.
To us who live on, it's just another day.
Still our love for our own native blood will ever be.
Soon life's race will run, life's work well done.
Soon will come our rest.

CHAPTER TWENTY-THREE

# CALLING THE ROLL: A TROUBLESOME TASK

At the first Stillaguamish council meeting of 1978, on January 16, the atmosphere was heavy with tension. The new year brought to the surface problems long brewing between Esther and the council. The members had trouble accepting Esther's style of leadership. They'd had no answer from the agency to their request for an audit of tribal accounts. They disapproved of the continued employment of Margaret Greene, a nontribal member. And they wanted an end to nepotism. Now that the tribe was recognized and receiving annual federal appropriations and no longer dependent on Esther's financial management, members wanted to assert their rights in tribal operations.

This tug-of-war with the council left Esther in an unusual—and uncomfortable—position. Having been the dominant force in the re-creation of the tribe and its survival, it was not easy for her to accept ideas and input from others. She also found it difficult to follow federal protocol and conform to federal regulations, which was now a necessity. Tribal relations were at the point where the leadership was passing to the membership.

On the evening of January 16 the council came prepared to assert control. The first item on the agenda was Margaret Greene's invoice of thirty-nine hundred dollars for her intermittent eighteen-month service chauffeuring Esther from the Canadian border south to Vancouver, Washington, interviewing potential members and confirming those already enrolled before the Interior Department approved the membership requirement. The council voted to pay Greene only nine hundred dollars for her work. Councilwoman Marie MacCurdy wanted Greene fired, but that hardly seemed necessary. Green's job was nearly over.

Esther's request for pay for herself brought the council's harshest response. She had already appropriated large sums of moneys, they said, to which she was not entitled. The council then passed a resolution that all vouchers for payment required council approval. Another resolution authorized Lew Goodridge to sign all payroll vouchers and vouchers for CETA funds. The council also added a fisheries secretary position for Valda Orr and raised her salary to a thousand dollars a month.[1]

Tempers flared, angry words were thrown about, and fingers were pointed as Goodridge and Kathleen Johnson accused Esther of padding her expenses. Donna Soholt and Marie MacCurdy, acting secretary, joined in with more accusations. Long-suppressed feelings about appropriations and the use of CETA moneys were vented. Finally the council relented and passed a resolution that "all papers, documents, contracts, grants etc. of the Stillaguamish Tribe must be signed by the following two (2) Council members: Esther Ross, Chairman, and Llewelyn [sic] Goodridge, Vice Chairman." The council passed one final resolution approving the submitted enrollment list as the official and current membership of the Stillaguamish tribe. In all, a record eight resolutions were presented and passed that evening, the largest number in any single meeting thus far. Though the air had been cleared, Esther knew she would no longer have absolute say in tribal matters, especially in the hiring and firing of her staff. But she also had the impression that the next-to-last resolution passed gave her consignatory powers on pay vouchers. This was *not* the intention of the council.[2]

Esther was only partially prepared for what would transpire at the next meeting, held two weeks later. Expecting it to be stormy, Frank took along a tape recorder. In the meeting, one resolution, the sole item of business, was put before the council. It called for rescinding Esther Ross's signatory powers on all tribal documents and appointing Lew Goodridge, vice chair, and John Smith, secretary, as sole signatories. Virtual bedlam erupted. Esther and Frank challenged the council, and both sides hurled charges at each other. Profane words were used. In the end, Resolution 39-78 was passed by the council. It read: "Resolved ... that Stillaguamish Tribal Council ... does rescind *all* of the Chairperson's, Esther Ross, signatory powers on all Tribal documents and papers from this day on; [and] ... that the Vice-Chairman Lew Goodridge and the Tribal Secretary, John Smith, will sign all documents, checks and papers, except payroll and time sheets which will be signed by the Office Manager [Valda Orr]. The Office Manager's time sheets and payroll will be signed by the Vice-Chairman, Lew Goodridge, from this day on."[3]

Esther and Frank refused to sign the resolution. Those who did included Llewellyn Goodridge, Marie MacCurdy, Donna L. Soholt, and Gail K. Abel (Kathleen Johnson's daughter). On the line where the chair's signature should have appeared were the words "Refused to sign."

After the meeting, Esther went down Cagey Road to Margaret Greene's house to talk things over. Greene patiently and compassionately tried to ease the impact of the evening. She assured Esther she would continue to assist her from time to time. And she did—though she never did collect the pay her friend had promised her when she hired on.[4]

Through sheer coincidence, Peter Three Stars answered Lew Goodridge's request for an audit on the same day as the tribal council's vote went against Esther. According to the superintendent, Esther Ross was "the only bonded tribal official to whom tribal checks are issued, and who ... has portions of the tribal accounting material." Three Stars could not honor the council's request for an audit "without a Resolution from the Council, including the signature of Mrs. Ross."[5] Goodridge knew it would be impossible to get Esther to sign such a resolution.

One week later Lew Goodridge was in Everett to meet with Bill Black, the agency's tribal operations officer, to try to persuade him that an audit was needed before he took over as signatory for paying vouchers. Black went to the superintendent, who now advised that an audit committee be appointed to request an audit of the books. Three Stars also advised Goodridge that he believed Resolution 39-78 relieving Esther of her authority was in conflict with Article IV, Section 3(a) of the Stillaguamish constitution, which authorized the chairperson to preside at all meetings of the council, to call special meetings, and "to have a general supervision of all affairs of the organization." He informed Goodridge the resolution would only undermine the work of the council: "To maintain a strong tribal government all tribal leaders must work toward a common cause. Mrs. Esther Ross had been the leader and champion of the Stillaguamish tribal cause for nearly half a century. Without the persistence of this grand lady the tribe would not have attained the recognition it now enjoys. Mrs. Ross is recognized nation wide by high government and tribal officials as the traditional and elected leader of the Stillaguamish Tribe. We urge you to seek her counsel and not thwart her continued efforts to work toward tribal advancement."[6]

Nevertheless, council members now used their majority to fire her appointees—and offer the positions to members of their own families and friends. Some of these positions, such as Valda Orr's as office manager and fisheries secretary required experience and training, and Orr was retained. Esther believed Orr had turned against her, that she had been cooperative with the council all during the preceding months, being privy to office conversations, tribal plans, and agendas. Esther was now convinced that majority decisions were made before they were ever formalized in meetings.

The stroke Esther had suffered nearly a year earlier contributed to her feeling of dwindling power. It had kept her out of touch for several months, and by the time she recovered, the council had become more managerial in the conduct of tribal business. From that point on, she received the "cold shoulder" treatment at her own office. When she and Frank would drive up to the tribal office doors, the staff would warn, "Here come Esther and Frank!" Such treatment caused her to spend more time at home than in the office.[7]

Over the next few months Kathleen Johnson would be hired as property manager as well as a delegate to STOWW; John Smith was hired as a fisheries patrolman; Donna Soholt's brother Dennis, as a part-time fisheries aide; Terry Martin, biologist; and Goodridge, fisheries manager and delegate to the Northwest Indian Fisheries Commission. Though Esther lost her official position as the tribe's delegate to various groups, she continued to attend meetings anyway.

And the tribe continued to strip Esther and Frank of privileges and functions. It banned the use of tape recorders in council meetings. Marie MacCurdy spearheaded a move to stop any further payments on the Ford Wagon Frank leased for tribal business.

On February 13, 1978, the council passed a resolution that Donna Soholt, tribal treasurer, would be designated the sole person authorized to dispense tribal funds. At that time salaried office personnel included MacCurdy, Goodridge, Miriam Levin, and Orr.

Although stripped of official power, Esther set out to revise tribal rolls in a last-ditch effort to oust the Goodridge-Smith group. She reasoned that her opponents were not true Stillaguamish, but really only a mixture of Upper Skagit, Sauk-Suiattle, and Snohomish ancestry. In such reasoning, she was conveniently overlooking the fact that almost all tribal members lacked pure Stillaguamish blood. On her new mission she sought help from Lena Smith, an elder herself and, most importantly, Jimmy Dorsey's granddaughter. Though Smith's support carried little, if any, clout, she wrote a letter on February 20 to Superintendent Three Stars on tribal stationery. "I review[ed] the enrolment with Esther," Lena advised him, "[and] found the enrolment not right."

The council had already approved the membership rolls Esther and Greene had gathered. Now Cecelia Myrick, charged with overseeing enrollments in the Puget Sound area, had to go over them, adding or deleting names and researching what else might be needed before certification by Bill Black for submission to the BIA in Washington, D.C. Myrick was also responsible for confirming documentation sent with membership lists. On occasion she drove to Esther's house to use source materials stored there. Myrick made these trips herself instead of sending her assistants, since none of them wanted to visit Esther. She found Esther's home more like an office than the tribal office at Island Crossing. When she'd arrive, Esther would greet her, invite her in, offer her coffee, and if it was around lunchtime, prepare a light meal for her. Esther would visit with Myrick for awhile. She revealed more information to her in a short time than she usually revealed to others. Myrick found her friendly and talkative and a very determined person. "I just sat there and listened to her," Myrick said, and "when she was finally ready, she got me the things I needed. I didn't push her or throw black and white paper in front of her and say 'I don't have time and I need this and that.' . . . I enjoyed listening to her and so I figured as long as I got what I wanted I'm not going to worry about that."[8]

Instead of padding the enrollment lists, Esther now informed the agency that she wanted forty-two names deleted from the list of ninety-eight she had first submitted. Those she had in mind for removal were supportive of the council, of course, but, denying any questionable motive, Esther claimed the forty-two should be removed on the basis of having too little Stillaguamish blood.[9]

In mid-February on tribal letterhead, she wrote Superintendent Three Stars asking that he "hold in abeyance" the tribal rolls. She reiterated her role as tribal leader: "I have been hurt. I am not dumb, or I could not have accomplished the work for the Stillaguamish with the help from those who graciously gave of their services. Why can't my people cooperate with me like they did before the recognition and before the money came to us?" In many situations, the quests for money and for power were indistinguishable. It was "a family affair," Ed Fitchen said, with members of the council all intermarried. He described it as "a greed thing, with all wanting the money it brought . . . all cutting each other's throats."[10]

On February 21, the agency completed its certification of the membership roll. In an undated notice intended as a press release, Esther wrote:

> Notice to the Public to People of State of Washington.
>
> I, Esther Ross the Chief and Chairperson of the Stillaguamish Tribe, . . . would like to tell you what's on my mind regarding fishing. I went to Judge Boldt's Court to get rights legalized for Indians of my Tribe, and [the] Judge agreed. I also went to Court for recognition in D.C. and got it.
>
> Since then [some members] of my tribe [have] not been able to prove their Identity. Therefore they are working *illegally* . . . as Treaty Indians with background of whites down the line and all married whites and their children married whites and their white husbands take over.
>
> A Treaty right can not be socially . . . Transportable.

Esther wrote Judge George Boldt, asking him to withdraw fishing rights for the tribe. She also wrote her congressman to withdraw recognition and wrote Peter Three Stars questioning the accuracy of the certification and objecting to submission of the roll to the Portland Area Office and to the assistant secretary of the interior.[11] In her letter to the superintendent, Esther quoted from the Interior Department's letter to David Getches in October of 1976: "The Secretary [of the Interior] directed the Bureau of Indian Affairs to 'verify that each person listed is a Stillaguamish descendant possessing the degree of Indian blood prescribed in the constitution.'" It was her understanding of the Stillaguamish constitution "that members must possess a minimum of 1/16 degree of Stillaguamish blood in order to be full members of the tribe." She questioned the certification of some members who had provided neither affidavits nor birth certificates. "How can you certify a roll when the information needed is incomplete or non-existent?" she asked. "Although I previously voted to approve the roll, it was not made clear what the approval was for, nor did I understand the result of my approval," she added. She sent a copy of her letter to Interior Secretary Cecil Andrus, to his assistant, Forrest Gerard, and to Vincent Little, director of the Portland Area Office.[12]

Esther followed up the letter with a visit to Three Stars in Everett. While waiting to talk with him, she met Winifred Blodgett, the agency's Natural Resources officer. Esther asked her for the check Blodgett was holding, a check Esther had written to herself and one the tribe wanted returned. She wanted to hand it to the superintendent, Esther said. She informed Blodgett that she was canceling the lease on the Island Crossing property. Blodgett informed her, as had Three Stars, that its disposition was up to the tribal council.[13]

Stillaguamish fisheries operations at the time was in the process of renting another site for its expansion. With help from the NWIFC, the tribe had repealed fishing ordinances and amendments enacted over the previous few years and had adopted instead a law-and-order code for fisheries enforcement. Sandra Gabb—again a non-Stillaguamish since none of the tribe qualified for the position—replaced Valda Orr as fisheries secretary. In a council meeting, Lew Goodridge had appointed Marie MacCurdy's husband, Joe, a non-Indian, fisheries manager and technician and delegate to the Northwest Indian Fisheries Commission.

Because of Esther's successes, NCAI officials had consulted with her for the previous two years, working to iron out protocol in the processing of petitions for tribal recognition. NCAI had opposed Senate Bill 2375, which had to do with recognizing landless tribes, believing it inadequate. The bill was now being debated in Congress. A meeting to bring groups together to strategize was arranged for March 1978 in Nashville, Tennessee. Esther was invited. She found the funds she needed to get to Nashville. She welcomed this brief respite before she would have to return to resume her struggle with her opponents in council. Now twenty years of age, grandson David went with Esther. She was also buoyed by the way NCAI officials welcomed her input.

On March 29 the organization voted to oppose the bill as it was written. As it was, the Interior Department had already made changes in the petitioning process to acknowledge the existence of Indian tribes and empower them to write a constitution and form a tribal government.[14]

Back home, Esther sought the advice of her old friend, Seattle attorney Malcolm McLeod, as to how to handle her problems with the tribal council. McLeod turned her complaints over to attorney Shirley Saulnier, who asked the council to restore Esther's authority. When her request was met with silence at the March 13 meeting, Saulnier wrote Lew Goodridge, insisting that Esther's power be restored. She questioned the validity of the March 1 meeting, which had been held without notifying Esther and Frank. Saulnier advised the council to rescind Resolution 39-78 at the upcoming March 23 meeting. She told Goodridge that she had spoken with Win Blodgett at the agency regarding a position for Esther as tribal historian. At a meeting on April 21, the council finally did rescind Resolution 39-78. Esther could now sign documents. At the same time, the council appointed her to the unpaid position of tribal historian.[15]

Cecilia Myrick shortened the final agency-approved list by sixteen people, none of whom were the forty-two Esther had wanted deleted. Esther immediately denounced the list as incomplete, and she asked Bill Black and Peter Three Stars to delay certifying the list until she had taken the fight to Washington, D.C.

Esther flew to the capital to persuade BIA officials to reject the list until it contained only the names of those who she believed eligible for membership. She called Frank to tell him the good news: The BIA had advised her they would not honor the first list and that she could prepare a second one. Back home, Frank drove to the agency on April 13 and informed Black and Three Stars of Esther's call, only to find they had already certified and signed a second list, identical to the first, and were preparing it to send to Washington, D.C. Undaunted, Esther continued her crusade to remove the forty-two names from the rolls. In a letter campaign, she contacted people she trusted, believing they could help her reduce the membership. She continued talking with Don Smouse and Jim Heckman, who sympathized with her cause. She also made frequent visits to Black's office, even though she realized it was probably counterproductive.[16]

CHAPTER TWENTY-FOUR

# A WAR OF WORDS AND WILLS

In spring 1978 the council met to sanction Esther for failure to turn over the tribal records it had requisitioned on February 13. The memorandum read, "These reports have not been received by the Tribal Council. After the request for these reports there have been other irregularities and activities of the Chairperson, Esther Ross and Council member, Frank Allen that are not in the best interest of the Stillaguamish Tribe. . . . Therefore the . . . Council and . . . members do hereby ask for the immediate resignation of Esther Ross and Frank Allen." It was signed by the council: Llewellyn Goodridge, vice chairman; John Smith, secretary; Donna L. Soholt, treasurer; Marie A. MacCurdy, council member; and fifteen members. Esther did not respond.[1]

The council continued to press Esther to turn over to them all the tribal papers she had in her possession at home. It seemed more than ironic to her that they had, on the one hand, appointed her the official tribal historian—by their own admission, she had "collected and kept vital records" of the tribe for over fifty years—and yet they wished to remove from her the very records she needed to carry out the project.[2]

On June 30, 1978, Esther wrote up an "Enrollment Report" for the tribe. "Report of last few months on Enrollment. . . . I find [the affidavits] incorrect, unfinished. Have not received any affidavit forms that were supposed to be sent back to me that the BIA wanted me to send out." Then she went on to explain:

> No one knows their background. The folders contain white Man's history that Cecelia [Myrick] and [Bill] Black put together and none of the old affidavits. . . . Mr. Peter Three Stars and Mr. Black have been in the wrong for signing a second time your Enrollment sheets without my orders. . . . My orders now are to send them to [Washington] D.C. . . . [To qualify as a] Stillaguamish Indian, [a person] must be over 1/16 or more [blood quantum]. I have found about 45 who do not have that blood quantum. Without money I can't pick up records for the file that I see fit to place on record books. I worked on each folder each affidavit long hours at night and day. . . . Those hours have never been counted up. I will have to report later when I make up the roll. I spent my pension the last few months besides borrow[ing] money to keep going.

With the new fiscal year beginning on July 1, Rudy Ryser sent materials to start Phase II of the three-phase restoration plan inaugurated a year earlier. The grant money for this phase was to be used to cover fisheries management and enforcement, enrollment, tribal government development, education, and tribal administration. Following Superintendent Three Star's lead, the council called a special meeting on July 17 to request the agency to provide funding for the tribal historian's position, the contract to become effective on August 1, 1978. The position would pay nine hundred dollars a month, less taxes, and would end on January 30, 1979.[3] The agency agreed to fund the project.

In late August, Esther visited Three Stars, carrying with her a "Stillaguamish tribal resolution number 1," dated August 24. It was a resolution prepared solely by Esther and signed only by her. The resolution stated that the superintendent had affirmed in a letter dated August 8 (Three Star's letter was actually dated August 1) that Esther Ross had constitutional power as chairperson to supervise all affairs of the tribe. The resolution also stated that the

BIA approved the tribal roll under her signature only because pressure had been imposed upon her by "various members" of the Stillaguamish tribe or its "agents." It went on to state that the tribe's fishing contract was hereby held in abeyance until all blood quantum inaccuracies on the tribal roll were corrected. Esther had already presented all this at the ATNI meeting that week, making a point of a telegram sent by ATNI president Roger Jim, a Yakama, verifying that, as chair of the Stillaguamish, Esther had "the rights and privileges to represent the Tribe at the Affiliated Tribes Northwest meeting."[4]

Three Stars attempted to defuse further confrontations by responding to Esther's resolution two weeks later. In a three-page letter, he advised her that Article II, Section 1(f) of the membership section of the tribal constitution permitted the one-sixteenth blood quantum for membership. He also wrote that the records revealed that she had recorded each name in tribal minutes and that she had verified that each person on her submitted list was a Stillaguamish descendant with allowable blood quantums and was considered a tribal member. He emphasized in the letter that the eighty-two people authorized for membership would remain permanently on the rolls. He would be happy to assist in updating the rolls, he added, whenever the need arose. Ending his letter on a conciliatory note, he wrote, "Mrs. Ross, you have been very active in the affairs of the Stillaguamish Indian Tribe since its beginning. Your perseverance and active involvement in seeking federal recognition for the tribe has made a permanent landmark not only to the Stillaguamish membership roll. I will always be ready and available to provide assistance to you and your membership whenever the need arises."[5]

Even though Esther and Frank rarely attended council meetings that summer, the members ended up adopting tribal plans that Esther had espoused. They planned to set up measures to handle the judgment money from the Indian Claims Commission. They voted to acquire the Gus Smith property and property in Oso to put in trust. But they also adopted a resolution to remove

Esther as the registered tribal agent and appoint Lew Goodridge to that position. Another resolution designated Goodridge as the signatory on various contracts and other funding-related documents. The council proposed a "land consolidation area" to protect the tribe's natural resources and to develop lands for the economic benefit of it and its members. They asked for funding under the Snyder Act. Continuing with the fish propagation and management program, the council entered into a lease for a hatchery site on Harvey Creek. And they did all this without Esther's input or involvement.[6]

Esther was not entirely excluded from duties. She had begun her job as tribal historian, and the council agreed she would be the Stillaguamish representative to the annual NCAI meeting in Rapid City, South Dakota. Frank drove Esther to Tacoma, where she was to meet other delegates for the ride to Rapid City. Six-year-old Sandra rode along to Tacoma with them. Arriving there, Sandra asked her grandmother if she could go along on the trip to South Dakota. When Esther told her no because she had no suitcase, Sandra pulled out a small bag packed with clothing and toilet articles. There was no way Esther could refuse her, and so the child accompanied her grandmother and the other delegates to the meeting.

On November 20, 1978, Esther wrote a letter to Forrest Gerard at Interior, citing her opposition to tribal membership of the Goodridge family and asking to have them deleted from the membership rolls that had been submitted in April. She also informed Gerard that Goodridge was performing tribal functions that she believed were her prerogative as chairperson. She complained that BIA audits were sent to the tribal office before they were sent to her. And despite her own sins in this regard, she accused the council of nepotism. Finally, she asked that a BIA representative be assigned to assist the tribal council in resolving "problems standing in the way of progress."

Theodore Krenzke, director of the Office of Indian Services in Washington, D.C., answered Esther, informing her that the council had to determine a need for assistance and request help through the agency superintendent. He wrote that the BIA appreciated her "long-time service to the tribe." He expressed his hope that she would "work with other members of the tribal council to advance the cause of the Stillaguamish people."

Having as yet received no pay for her job as tribal historian, Esther fired off a letter to Forrest Gerard; Vincent Little, the BIA's Portland Area Office director; and to contracting officer Cecil Brenner in Portland. She described the lack of pay as "inexcusable," and, having heard a rumor that she would not receive her pay until after Christmas, she wrote that she had a "rather urgent need," since she had no money to buy gasoline to travel "even as far as the local grocery."[7]

Demanding reports from tribal employees covering their activities of the previous three months, Esther called for a meeting on December 14. There were no reports forthcoming from the council. The only action taken was to criticize Frank, who had issued a news release to KRKO radio in Everett and to the *Seattle Post-Intelligencer* that the State Departments of Fisheries and Game had authorized the Stillaguamish to sell steelhead to non-Indians. Frank's action spurred the council to pass a resolution regulating sales of steelhead to non-Indians. Goodridge berated Frank because the council not only opposed fish sales to non-Indians but even lacked the facilities to do so. The Fisheries and Game Departments were also displeased. In his own defense, Frank claimed he had been misquoted in the paper.

Turning its attention from Frank, the council focused on Esther's November letter to Gerard. Esther reiterated her claim that Lew Goodridge and others could not be members of the tribe because they were "white people." James Sovak, Jr., now tribal operations officer for the Everett agency, was in attendance at the meeting to remind Esther that any effort to remove persons from the roll was unauthorized, since only the tribe could update the list with additions or deletions based on recommendations and eligibility requirements. Frank threatened to go with his mother to the news

The small, onetime realty office served as the Stillaguamish tribal office during Esther's tenure with the tribe. The building was just off present U.S. I-5, three miles west of Arlington. In the early 1980s the tribe would acquire land north of Arlington where they built a much larger tribal headquarters. *Reprinted courtesy of the* Everett (Wash.) Herald. *Photograph by Ray Watters.*

media with the story that the BIA was allowing whites to be members of the tribe. He was warned that he would subject himself to lawsuits by those "who he thinks are not qualified members of this tribe."[8]

Esther's six-month position as tribal historian ended on January 30, 1979. By the end of February she had been paid $4,500 for five months' work. Because Gary Pertram, her secretary at a monthly salary of $650, had quit after only two and half months on the job, Esther asked for her remaining month's worth of pay and for the balance of Pertram's since she had been left to do secretarial work. Superintendent Three Stars denied the request, notifying her that "The rest of the contract dollars were used by the tribe for fringe benefits, travel, reproduction expenses and supplies and materials." If she had more questions, he suggested she contact the tribal operations officer, James Sovak.[9]

In March 1979, the BIA finally sent Robert Farring of its Washington, D.C., office to investigate Esther's dissatisfaction with the council and office staff. In trying to impress Farring with the importance of her role as tribal chief, Esther persuaded him to call Lena Smith. When he did, Lena was no help for Esther. "According to tribal tradition, the position of a chief can only be held by males," Smith told him. Facing what she considered tribal harassment, Esther asked Farring for a court order to allow her to tape meetings. The 1978 resolution banning the use of recorders in council meetings had put a stop to this occasional activity of Esther's and Frank's.

After talking with council members and agency personnel about Esther's concerns, Farring reported to M. E. Seneca, acting deputy commissioner of the BIA. Seneca wrote a four-page letter to Esther, listing the various complaints she had related to Farring and responding to each one. "You oppose the inclusion of the Goodridge family on the Bureau approved tribal roll and favor replacing it with one you feel can be supported by historical research," he began. "In that certain persons bearing the Goodridge name have been verified by historical documents to meet the tribe's membership requirements, there is no basis for excluding them from enrollment. Accordingly, we continue to recognize as tribal members those persons determined to be members by the tribe whose names appear on the roll submitted to the Bureau and approved by the Superintendent on April 13, 1978."

Seneca then addressed the role of the chief. "Our dealings with the tribe are based on terms of the tribe governing document rather than tribal tradition," he explained. "Other than the limited authorities granted to the tribal chairman, the governing power of the tribe is to be exercised by the board of directors [the council]." As for the use of the tape recorders: "In that the board of directors has refused to permit the use of tape recorders in its official meetings, you have asked the Bureau to make available to you the services of a court reporter to preserve the record of deliberations." This, Seneca explained, would be an inappropriate involvement for the BIA. As for reimbursing Esther for the outside meetings she attended, Seneca explained that the BIA was unauthorized to make such payment and suggested that she look to private foundations for such funding. He also notified her that the BIA had no input to change how she was paid for her work as tribal historian, since the agency superintendent had chosen the contract. Esther did receive one concession from Seneca. He authorized Supt. Bud Lozar, who was now in Montana, but who had worked closely with her on the cemetery issue when he was with the Everett agency, to come to Washington and do what he could to help her acquire Indian burial sites.[10]

The council would have been pleased with Seneca's report but for his recommendation that they establish "definite procedures with the view toward effective operation of the tribe's administrative and governing functions." Seneca specifically advised an updating of the constitution, which permitted nepotism and other practices. "The hiring of relatives is generally not conducive to effective administration of tribal programs," he warned them.[11]

On July 2, 1979, the U.S. Supreme Court's six-to-three decision upheld the Boldt ruling, which commercial and sportfishers had appealed. By this time, six other tribes had joined the original fourteen, so twenty tribes stood to harvest 50 percent of western Washington salmon. The Northwest Indian Fisheries Commission had been a party in *United States v. Washington*, and Esther was a faithful attendee at their meetings, even though Lew Goodridge was the official Stillaguamish delegate. Esther found NWIFC forums not only a good place to discuss fishing matters, but also a place to advance her dream of acquiring tribal land ownership and reclaiming the cemeteries. Though uninterested in Esther's battle for trust status, the NWIFC commissioners tolerated her interruptions of its proceedings.

CHAPTER TWENTY-FIVE

# STRATAGEMS FOR LEADERSHIP

At Island Crossing council members were getting frustrated trying to operate tribal business in Esther's absence. They had discovered the awkwardness of trying to operate without a functioning chair. However, when Esther did come to the tribal office she was ignored. The council never attempted to create an environment to draw Esther into a cooperative relationship. Marie MacCurdy wrote Superintendent Three Stars in February 1979 that they needed to know how to get around the constitution's quorum requirement, because Esther and Frank were absent from most council meetings. The council had attempted to alter the constitution a few times since 1973, but up to this time changes had always been initiated by Esther.

The bumpy journey for revision of the constitution had begun six years before, when the tribe was seeking recognition. Esther always maintained that the tribe operated with bylaws from 1926 until it adopted a constitution in 1953. If they were ever written, no bylaws exist now. In early 1973 the tribe wrote a set of bylaws to add to the 1953 constitution and presented them to the membership on March 9. Because of a poor turnout at that meeting, they were not accepted until an October 6 meeting. Months later, David P. Weston, the BIA's Portland area tribal operations officer, wrote Leo LaClair, then director of STOWW, that the draft of the new Stillaguamish constitution needed to incorporate changes from the existing constitution in order to conform with IRA requirements.[1] Esther had her own view of the problems the tribe faced in updating the constitution. "[Bylaws] are white mans rules," she wrote David Getches and Barbara Lane. "Only a few leaders go by it. An Indian . . . goes by his own feelings and time."[2]

At a meeting on August 23, 1979, a record thirteen resolutions were passed. The tribal council hired Marie MacCurdy as property manager and Joe MacCurdy as fisheries technician. Shirley Oman was designated primary delegate to the Puget Sound Health Board, and her sister, Marie MacCurdy, was named her alternate. Miriam Levin Hillaire was appointed to represent Stillaguamish at meetings of the Affiliated Tribes of Northwest Indians. The tribe also approved a resolution to adopt a revised law-and-order code for fisheries enforcement effective August 23. Other resolutions pertained to writing descriptions of positions for current employees; reestablishing their personnel, policy, and procedures manual; and continuing the civil suit in the Lummi tribal court to have the boats *Wide Load* and *Smoker Craft* returned to the tribe, even though there were no plans to use them.[3]

The battle of the boats had begun in 1976 when Frank asked the tribe to sell him *Wide Load*, which lay in the back of Esther's Lummi house. He had a chance to sell it to someone else and hoped to profit from the transaction. When he approached the tribe, attorney Alan C. Stay advised him by letter of the state's complicated regulations. Because the tribe was incorporated under the Washington State nonprofit corporation act, the sale of the boat would fall under the Revised Code of Washington Annotated (RCWA). Frank dropped the matter. Now in 1979, when the tribe tried again to retrieve the two boats and met Frank's refusal, the council filed suit in Lummi court. Esther wrote Superintendent Three Stars, asking that Bill Black appear in court to represent Frank. On August 21, 1979, in a hearing before Chief Judge Charles Finkbonner,

"Frank Allen, Esther Ross, and David Allen, Respondents," were ordered to refrain "from destroying, removing or selling the boats" until final disposition of the case.[4]

In the fall of 1979 the council prepared a grant for funds to train and inform appointed officials under the new constitution being formulated in committee. The grant also was for funds to investigate a platform from which government services could be received. Having virtually assumed the chair's duties, vice chairman Lew Goodridge requested and negotiated grants for funding. His signature was accepted on council-approved resolutions instead of Esther's, and only his signature was accepted on contracts, which were no longer sent to Esther's Bellingham address. Threatened and wearied by Esther's determination to cling to the title and position of chair, the council, in essence, sought to empower other tribal officials to perform duties which formerly were hers. To further their efforts, they requested a BIA grant for strengthening tribal government. This would allow the tribe to refine its business control system, enable it to submit grant and contract applications to outside sources, and to update policies and procedures on adoption of a new constitution.

The draft of the constitution called for regular meetings to be held quarterly. Special meetings, requiring a week's notice, could be called by the chair and the majority of the council. The new constitution called for a five-member quorum; over the years a mere majority vote had been accepted by the agency, even if the majority was constituted by two of three council persons at the meeting. The council hoped the new constitution would solve problems like this. However, efforts floundered, and for another six years the 1953 constitution would serve as the standard.[5]

Esther suffered a loss when Charlie Smith, one of her favorite non-Indian friends, died on July 30, 1979. A Snohomish County commissioner for many years, Charlie was familiar with county history, and he was a reliable source as Esther gathered her information. Esther visited him and tape-recorded the visits. He gave her details on Indian burials, and at his death, she was in the process of consulting him for a historic marker honoring the Stillaguamish. She had wanted the marker erected along Interstate 5, but no final decision had been made.

Gertrude Alexander, Charlie Smith's sister, planned to scatter his ashes on the Stillaguamish River on October 20, 1979. Esther would not have missed the service, which was conducted by Indian Shakers, even though it was difficult for her to make her way to the riverbank. Alternating between her walker and her wheelchair, she reached the site where the ceremony was to be held. She had invited Bud Lozar, newly arrived in Everett to help her acquire Indian burial sites, to join her at the river. Politicians and Indians from around the country came, including Mad Bear, the legal spokesman for the eastern Iroquois. Children of all sizes, colors, and ethnic backgrounds were also reportedly there. During the service Smith's ashes were spread on the river. "Today, landowners have agreed, because of Charlie's work and that of Esther Ross and other tribal leaders, to sign over land for two cemeteries at Hazel and Trafton," the *Indian Voice* reported.[6]

Unfortunately, Indian burial lands were *not* turned over to the tribe. Lozar spent two weeks in western Washington to seek an agreement with property owners of two Indian burial sites to "effect a gift deed to the Stillaguamish tribe for both burial plots in a tax-free status." His efforts were nonproductive. He found one owner who would gift some land, but the title was clouded. He doubted the BIA would accept it. On returning to Montana he summarized his visit; "I called Esther Ross to update her on what happened. I thought Esther should know first hand what transpired. Frank [told] me . . . that there are 29 other grave sites and I should not have left the Area. He also said I am being sued. For what reason, I don't know. I attempted to advise Frank and Esther that my job was to return two cemeteries. I also advised them that they have a Superintendent and Realty Staff in Everett for their other problems."[7]

A disappointed Esther found Lozar to have been no help and considered his visit a waste of time, but the tribe continued working toward developing a land base plan to submit to the BIA for approval, even though Superintendent Three Stars thought they would have little success. "As far as we can tell," he advised them, "the Stillaguamish tribe does not have the authority to obtain Trust Status."[8]

The council opened 1980 with plans for a general election to be held within ninety days. Lew Goodridge appointed Miriam Levin Hillaire to seek technical assistance in setting up and carrying out the election. However, by the end of the month she had been fired for having been convicted in 1974 of embezzling from a previous employer, a charge the council had been unaware of when they appointed her. Three Stars supplied Goodridge with copies of election ordinances of other tribes. He also offered Bill Black's services to provide technical assistance to an election committee. Esther was aware of this, having received a copy of Three Stars's letter to Goodridge.[9]

In 1978 the tribe had decided that instead of holding an election, it would continue the five-year sequence, as provided under the 1953 constitution. However, the previous 1975 election was out of sequence because earlier elections had been irregularly held as vacancies occurred. The previous fall the tribe had asked Cynthia Davenport to do an analysis of the constitution and the election practices. In her report, a memo to the council, she wrote, "Unfortunately, the current Stillaguamish Constitution contains several ambiguities which make it difficult to give a definitive answer to this question." The constitution's intent was clouded with variances. Davenport interpreted the constitution to read that elections for the council members and for the chair were to have been held in separate years, and elections were to be held every five years. Figuring from the time the constitution was approved in 1953, the last election for chair should have been held in 1974, and the last election for council members should have been in 1978.

The 1978 election had been for both council members and chair. Either the constitution would have to be amended or a resolution passed each time there was a variation. In May, the council drafted an election ordinance and Three Stars officially endorsed the selection of a group of members for an election committee. In his words, this was to "encourage you to expedite your [overdue since March] election process to prevent future confusion concerning council membership."[10] The council proposed a tentative election day of August 22. On July 15, Lew Goodridge, council members Marie MacCurdy and Donna Soholt, and secretary John Smith signed a letter to Three Stars stating that the council had tried to get Esther and Frank to its meeting to set a firm election date and adopt a tribal election ordinance. They did not show.

The election ordinance called for the council chair to appoint five people to serve on an election board to administer and conduct the election and called for council-certified candidates to fill out applications. The ordinance stipulated that tribal officers were to be responsible for delivering or accounting for all tribal documents and equipment in their possession to the newly elected tribal chair immediately upon the swearing in of the new officials.[11] This provision was clearly aimed at Esther.

All this time Esther remained outside the circle, largely unaware of what was happening. On August 12, after learning that an election was scheduled for August 22, Frank phoned the Everett agency to inform Lew Goodridge that since there was no previous meeting to discuss it—there actually had been—Esther wanted the election postponed. She got her wish. The election was postponed until October 18.[12]

Three Stars chided Esther. "Several meetings were scheduled to discuss the adoption of a proposed Stillaguamish Election Ordinance over the past several months," he wrote her, adding that he would encourage her and Frank "to take a more active part in tribal activities, especially Tribal Elections." He also informed Esther that candidates who wanted to appear on the ballot had to file for office by September 15.[13] Neither Esther nor Frank filed.

Esther protested the tribe's handling of the election. She cited a lack of quorums at meetings, which were, in her words, "done

[in] secret without notifying us." She contended that three of the people on the election committee had left the tribe and one of its members, a white, was not even a tribal member. She further complained that there should have been a meeting "as in early days" to vote on members turning in affidavits of their tribal affiliations before elections. She called for a tribal meeting at the Everett agency because the tribe's office was now a place where she and Frank were shunned and ridiculed. This letter of complaint addressed to Superintendent Three Stars was signed "Chief Esther Ross and Frank Allen Councilman" and was notarized.[14]

Three Stars passed the letter on to Lew Goodridge, who refuted Esther's claims. Esther and Frank, he said, were in violation of Section 4A of the constitution in failing to respond to notices of council members, and further, "there was at no time any effort on the part of Esther Ross and Frank Allen to sit down with the Board of Directors to establish Election procedures." He denied that there had been any secret meeting. He did not respond to the accusation that a nonmember white person sat on the election committee.

Seeking some way to bring order out of the tangled Stillaguamish tribal affairs, Three Stars, at Esther's request, arranged a meeting of the council and tribal members at Everett. On September 10 they met with Bill Black at the Everett Yacht Club to discuss the election ordinance. At that meeting, the ordinance was adopted after protracted discussion of the deadline for filing for a council position. Wanting to defuse a cut-and-dried election—only six people had filed for six council positions—Three Stars pressed for an extension until October 14. Esther stalled, but eventually the change was made. In spite of the extension, however, no more people filed.[15]

In the midst of the commotion, the council passed Resolution 25-80, authorizing a contract to complete the history project without naming an individual to do so. As he'd done before, Three Stars recommended that they consider a contract directly between Esther and the Bureau of Indian Affairs. "Mrs. Ross is the only person in the Stillaguamish Tribe competent enough to compile the history of the tribe," he reiterated. "Her home has been the storage place of tribal documents and records for several decades. It would be expedient to allow Mrs. Ross to complete the last phase of the project."[16] If Esther was offered the contract she did not accept it.

Instead, she continued her counterattacks. On September 22 she sent a letter to the agency, protesting actions of the Stillaguamish tribal office and stating that the provisions of the election ordinance were being put into effect without a vote of all tribal members. She called for a meeting of the full membership on October 9. Three Stars responded to that letter, telling Esther that since elections were a tribal function, he was forwarding her letter to the tribal office.[17]

When Esther and Frank appeared at the office on October 9 for the meeting, only Marie MacCurdy and Shirley Oman were there working, and they left quickly. Frank phoned the agency, wanting to know why federal workers could walk off the job and avoid them. Frank said that Esther had prepared a full agenda for the meeting: She wanted to pass resolutions that would authorize her to attend the upcoming NCAI meeting in Spokane, call for a vote on new memberships before the voting, approve of work Frank had done in the National Forest, and request a public hearing on the court of claims award. Having lodged their complaints, Esther and Frank went home.[18]

Gearing up for the October 18 election, Patricia Rudd at the agency printed sixty-five ballots that the Enrollment Office had prepared and numbered with a voter sign-in sheet. The agency advised Rudd to see that nominations were called for from the floor prior to the opening of the polls.[19]

On October 18, Rudd arrived at the tribal office at 8:45 a.m. to find Lew Goodridge, Marie MacCurdy, and John Smith already there. The polls opened at 10 a.m., and twenty-five of the fifty-six eligible to vote cast ballots. Neither Esther nor Frank showed up to vote. Marie MacCurdy was elected the new chair, Goodridge was reelected vice chair, Kathleen Johnson, secretary, and Shirley

Oman, treasurer. Mildred Claxton and Edward Goodridge were elected council members. The tribe sent notice that following the swearing in of the new officials, outgoing officeholders were responsible for delivering or accounting for all tribal documents and equipment in their possession.

The tribe was still trying to get land in trust. A reconsideration of their rejection in 1978 was requested. The renewed effort brought a new interpretation of the law. The dialogue recordings during the 1934 hearings on the IRA (Wheeler-Howard Act) were combed for passages to add an acceptable twist to the law. The interpretation was modified. The Stillaguamish qualified as a tribe under Section 5 of the IRA. The Interior Department wrote the commissioner of Indian affairs in October of 1980, "Thus it appears that the fact that the United States was until recently unaware of the fact that the Stillaguamish were a 'recognized tribe now under Federal jurisdiction' and that this Department on a number of occasions has taken the position that the Stillaguamish did not constitute a tribe in no way precludes IRA applicability." The new conclusion was that the Stillaguamish composed "a tribe for purposes of the IRA."[20] On December 15, 1980, solicitor Scott Keep informed Jeanne Whiteing, Marie MacCurdy, and attorney Cynthia Davenport that the tribe was eligible to take land in trust and that it would be up to the secretary of the interior to act on the request. Esther's hopes of acquiring Indian burials to put in trust status were rekindled.

Legal problems regarding the tribe's boats were still unresolved. In the spring of 1980 Frank told Patricia A. James, clerk of the Lummi Tribal Court that he intended to sell the boats. James advised Chief Judge Charles D. Finkbonner, who instructed her to "strongly remind" Frank of the order Finkbonner had made in open court on August 21, 1979, in which he had, in effect kicked Frank, Esther, and David out of his court.[21] Eugene Crawford of the National Indian Lutheran Board, the agency that had provided the money to buy the *Smoker Craft*, was so disappointed in the lack of its care and use that he wrote Esther of his concern: "The

NILB helped purchase that boat for the tribe to use to patrol and enforce fishing codes," he reminded her. "If you and your sons [sic] have impounded the boat[,] it is not being used for the function intended." The boat was to benefit the whole tribe, he continued, adding that it would be detrimental to the National Indian Lutheran Board, as well as Lutheran supporters of Indian work, if the charges became public knowledge. "I hope, Esther, that you and Frank sit down and work this out," he concluded.[22]

The court ordered Frank and Esther to release the boats to the county sheriff who would turn the boats over to the tribe.

CHAPTER TWENTY-SIX

# Exit and Exile

Under virtual exile from Stillaguamish tribal administrative circles, Esther was both hurt and angry that the tribe had not consulted her on her unfinished projects, which included action on the tribal fish hatchery and other fishing matters. Lew Goodridge remained her primary opponent. She accused him of "selling out" the tribe's fishing rights by asking the Tulalips to assist in the Stillaguamish fisheries program.

According to the Boldt decision, each tribe was restricted to fish in their own usual and accustomed places and not outside the area unless invited by a host tribe. The Stillaguamish tribe's usual and accustomed fishing places were the Stillaguamish River and the upper part of Port Susan, the bay in the sound into which the river empties. Because the Stillaguamish had been assigned to their reservation by treaty, the Tulalips had always fished upper Port Susan. Now the Stillaguamish wanted their own fishing place back, but the Tulalips did not want to give up Port Susan. It was contention over Port Susan that had led to Tulalip intervention in the Stillaguamish suit against the Interior Department in 1976.

The Boldt decision had affirmed the Stillaguamish right to fish in their aboriginal fisheries to the exclusion of other tribes. However, they were in limbo from the time of that decision until recognition because they were without means and assistance from the government to establish a fishing program. Once the Stillaguamish began to receive assistance in 1977, the Tulalips were shut out. It was then that Goodridge, as Stillaguamish fisheries manger, negotiated an agreement with the Tulalips that the latter could fish Port Susan in exchange for their assistance with the Stillaguamish fishery planning and enhancement program. Though she was no longer a tribal officer, Esther gathered information on the arrangement and vented her anger on the negotiated contract. She believed that, with their fishing expertise, large boats, and fancy equipment the Tulalips could easily exceed the harvest arrangement between the two tribes.[1]

Esther's numerous physical ailments made her fight all the more difficult. Her debility, now more pronounced than earlier, diminished her arsenal of weapons. Still, she pushed her crusade to have the tribe "unrecognized," a crusade she'd begun in 1978. Her weapons included letters, the telephone, and, occasionally, automobile trips, all to urge Judge George Boldt and Congress to rescind Stillaguamish recognition and fishing rights.[2]

She stood guard over her most prized weapons—the records and other tribal papers in her house. Meanwhile, the council was proceeding on its own. On October 31, 1980, it passed Resolution 44-80 to purchase the 2.3 acres it was leasing for a fish hatchery. Members also passed Resolution 46-80 to submit an application to the Housing Improvement Program (HIP) to put homes on the twenty acres that the tribe wanted to purchase and develop. And then passed Resolution 53-80, calling for "legal action against any and all persons or person harassing tribal council members and tribal office staff members." The resolution clearly pointed a finger at Esther.

Since Esther had always used her home address for much of the tribal correspondence, she still received considerable mail that she did not bother to forward to the office. Marie MacCurdy sent out notices to various organizations and to the agency and other groups with whom the tribe did business. The notices listed names of Stillaguamish officers and other tribal members, along with the tribal address and telephone numbers. "Please mail all correspondence concerning Tribal business to the above address," MacCurdy wrote, "not to Esther Ross in Bellingham as she is not a representative of the Tribal Government at this time. Thank you."

One incident reveals just how serious the council was in its dealing with Esther. As Frank describes it, one of his children was alone in the Lummi house when there was a knock on the door. Opening it, he was confronted with two stern-looking plainclothesmen who flashed identification badges and demanded to see Esther Ross and Frank Allen. They charged Esther and Frank with embezzling five thousand dollars from the Stillaguamish tribe.

In response to the charges, Frank drove Esther to the Everett agency to talk with Don Smouse. Smouse told her to bring in receipts for travel to various meetings, gasoline for their car, and any other expenses to substantiate her innocence. When she produced the receipts that proved the tribal funds had been spent on tribal business, the agency cleared her of any wrongdoing.[3]

Esther's friends agreed that moneys she was accused of taking in no way matched the value of her service to the tribe. Don Smouse himself said, "If five thousand dollars disappeared along the line, it doesn't even stir the surface of what she gave to the Tribe." When Bill Black, after a year away for special training, returned to the agency as superintendent in 1982, he would say of this incident, "so many allegations were gong back and forth at that time . . . we couldn't take any of them seriously."[4]

Esther found in Mike Grayum, an employee of the Northwest Indian Fisheries Commission, a good and understanding listener. Visiting with him in his Olympia office, she shared her evolving view of things. Instead of seeing Stillaguamish development as a cultural process, as she once had, Esther now saw such development in the context of wrongs against the tribe, a legacy stemming from the Point Elliott treaty of 1855. Tribal fishing, for instance, she now regarded as a simple matter of rights under the treaty. She believed the same applied to Indian burial grounds, once regarded as sacred terrain but now viewed as battlegrounds symbolizing wrongs perpetrated by the treaty. Whenever Esther and Frank showed up, Grayum said, "I allowed them to speak their piece. I think a lot of people don't do that, and so when [they found] somebody ... that would listen to them they would talk."⁵

Esther rued not having established membership standards and requirements different from those of 1926. She would have made them strict enough that even her own descendants would find themselves outcasts, and she encouraged these descendants to enroll in other tribes, abandoning the Stillaguamish entirely. When Ramona Bennett reminded her that blood quantums could be increased in just one generation, Esther retorted, "They don't even look like Indians. They certainly won't be marrying Indians and having children that are more Indian." Bennett countered, "Well, don't be too sure, Esther. I'm in social work because I believe in miracles. And you have made a few miracles yourself so don't give up any hope."⁶

Esther's stormy family relations continued. At this point she and her daughter Marion had ceased communicating. Ruth occasionally visited the Lummi house, but the visits grew increasingly farther apart. An October 1980 visit was Ruth's last. Frank spoke with counselors at a Bellingham rehabilitation facility, where he wanted to take Ruth for her alcohol abuse. She refused. On April 27, 1981, five days after her fifty-sixth birthday, Ruth died of alcoholism. That night Esther awoke and thought of Ruth's last visit and recalled her goodbye as she left. Then Esther wept.⁷ Marion wanted Ruth's body cremated. Esther insisted it be embalmed and buried near Arnold in the Lummi cemetery. Since Ruth was childless, her estate embroiled Esther and Marion in further conflict, with Marion contending that Ruth's will had named her as executrix. The problem became moot when no will was found. Esther subsequently hired Malcolm McLeod to represent her. Under court order, both parties agreed to Marion's appointment as administrator since Esther had hearing problems and Frank could neither read nor write.

Marion spent two weeks in Seattle closing up Ruth's house. On arriving, she found many household furnishings had been removed—or so she told Esther and Frank. They believed Marion had taken them. Esther sued Marion in May 1981 for Ruth's household property. Because of a fall, she missed some of the court hearings on Ruth's estate, which were covered by McLeod until he was hospitalized for a few days and his son took over for him.[8]

Following the attorneys' arguments, the judge threw the case out of court. In a final estate settlement Esther was awarded proceeds from the sale of Ruth's house, undervalued at some eighty thousand dollars with about twenty thousand dollars still owed on it. The house was sold to an attorney friend of McLeod's. Esther received a first payment of twenty thousand dollars, which vanished in paying previously unpaid repairs of aluminum siding, installing a new roof, and covering Ruth's medical and funeral bills, plus attorney fees, realty commission, and closing fees.

The purchaser agreed to assume the twenty thousand dollars outstanding on the mortgage. Thus Esther was left with a buyer's contract for approximately forty thousand dollars that would pay her on the balance and accrued interest at the monthly rate of five hundred dollars until it was paid out. Esther sold the contract for half the amount in cash, which gave her an instant twenty thousand dollars.

To spare Frank the difficulties she had just endured—and wanting her papers safeguarded from the tribe—Esther drew up a will, stating that even after her death she did not want the tribe to have her records. On July 28, 1981, she went to the offices of attorney Jacob Smith to draw up a will designating Frank her sole heir, stipulating, "It is my desire to leave nothing to my daughter, Marion L. [Byrum]." She took along Margaret Greene to sign as a witness. Over the years the tribe's efforts to acquire Esther's files failed.[9]

Esther was soon in court again. Her stepdaughter Margaret wanted to rent the Lummi house out. But Esther was not budging. Once again she hired attorney Jacob Smith. The matter was heard in July of 1981 before the Lummi Tribal Court. Chief Judge Charles D. Finkbonner ordered that, though each had a half interest in the house located on Margaret's land, Esther could reside in

Esther bends the ear of former governor Dan Evans, May 4, 1982, in Bellingham, Washington. *Reprinted courtesy of the* Bellingham (Wash.) Herald. *Photograph by Martin Waidelich.*

the house for the rest of her natural life. Since Frank was needed to provide for her, he and his family could stay with her rent-free.[10]

With all her troubles, Esther commiserated with others who had experienced similar reverses. Among them was Janet McCloud, who had founded the Survival of American Indians Association (SAIA) in the 1960s, only to be ousted from it after she had built up the organization. McCloud felt a kinship with Esther. "[She] worked so hard for her people . . . [and they] kicked her out," McCloud said. "It happens all the time. It happened to me, too. That's the way it goes. It's life. Don't ask me to talk about perverse human nature." But a fight with Indians was worse, McCloud claimed, "It's their wounds in my back that hurt."[11]

On May 2, 1982, Esther attended a town hall meeting in Bellingham's Holiday Inn with Northwest Power Planning Council members and former Governor Evans. The meeting was held to test the public mood on the energy question facing the council, which had to project power needs from 1982 until 2000. The meeting was to address whether or not to cut back hydroelectric power in order to provide more Columbia River water for salmon. *Bellingham Herald* photographer Martin Waidelich snapped a picture of a pensive Evans with Esther, her finger waggling in his face. The cutline of the picture on the *Herald*'s May 5, 1982, front page read, "Former Gov. Dan Evans speaks with Chief Esther Ross of the Stillaguamish Tribe." On a copy of the *Herald*, Esther wrote, "Gov. Evans knew me at once. Promises never fulfilled."

Because of Esther's increasing disabilities, she visited the Lummi clinic on April 13, 1982, where she ordered the doctor to sign her up for disability parking privileges. She believed the clinic staff should have been aware of her condition, but at the same time, she would not subject herself to examination. She did concede to being weighed but refused to sit for a blood pressure reading. Snatching a medical form, she marched out of the clinic, announcing, "I will go elsewhere. I was a nurse, so I know what is wrong with me."[12]

A year in advance of the event, in June of 1982, Esther attended a planning meeting for the July 4, 1983, celebration at Marietta at the entrance to the Lummi Reservation.[13] It would be the hundredth anniversary of the town's founding. By now Marietta had lost its post office and businesses and had developed into a clutter of rundown quarters with abandoned cars surrounded by piles of garbage. Esther and Frank called for the meeting at the Marietta Elementary School to discuss ways to celebrate what had been the town's glory. Frank's great-grandfather Solomon Allen, originally from Illinois, had homesteaded at Marietta in 1873, then called Lummi. A decade later, he founded the town.[14] Plans completed, Esther and Frank needed funding. Eugene Crawford on the National Indian Lutheran Board gave Esther five hundred dollars to finance the event—despite Crawford's earlier disappointment over the pair's handling of the boats. Albertson's Stores and the Seventh-Day Adventist Church donated food and chairs and tables for the meal, which extended from noon until

Esther in 1987, a year before her death, surrounded by Frank and three of his children. Left to right: Clyde, David, Frank, and Sandra.

early evening. Sixty-nine people attended. The *Bellingham Herald* on July 10 described the affair as a quiet celebration of historic significance.[15]

During Marie MacCurdy's tenure as tribal chair, Stillaguamish holdings increased markedly. Investing the claims funds the tribe received in toto, as Esther had wished, instead of on a per capita basis, members purchased the Island Crossing property and the 2.3 acres on Harvey Creek for the fish hatchery program and five acres near Bryant for a second hatchery. They also acquired sixteen acres northwest of Silvana at the confluence of Pilchuck Creek and the Stillaguamish River. During this period, the tribe moved its headquarters from Island Crossing to the twenty acres it had purchased northwest of Arlington, where a new tribal office was built and a housing development begun.[16]

Housing and Urban Development (HUD) offered to erect twenty houses next to tribal headquarters. The monthly rent would be sixty-five dollars for ten years, after which occupants would own the houses. Taking advantage of the offer, Frank and his son David both applied for houses in the fall of 1983. When they were ready, David, Frank, and Sandra moved into the two homes. But they found themselves too near the tribal offices for comfort. When Frank brought Esther to spend the weekend, he discovered what he believed to be axle grease smeared on the wall of his house, and the rear-door window was broken. After two stressful hours, Esther asked Frank to drive her home. Shortly thereafter, Frank and David gave up their tribal houses.

CHAPTER TWENTY-SEVEN

# DEBILITY AND DENOUEMENT

Esther now spent considerable time reading her Bible. She also read and fingered spiral-bound copies of the 1974 petition for recognition. From her bed that she had pushed up to the large window in the living area she watched cars driving past on Cagey Road, about eighty yards from the house. She welcomed a few visitors from places as close as Bellingham and as far away as Vancouver and Mission, British Columbia. She mourned the loss of her little Mexican chihuahua, Peanut, which was killed when a hawk attacked it. Several dogs had been a part of her life at various times. Peanut was her last. In addition to burying her beloved Peanut, she buried near her home the bones from the Indian burial ground outside Milltown, though she never told Frank exactly where she had buried them.

The search for Oscar Reid, which had run like a raveled thread through the fabric of her life, still haunted her, though she had by now given it up. Her mother's wedding ring, which had long graced her own left hand, an ever-present reminder of Angelina, slid away one day as it slipped from her soapy finger down the kitchen sink drain. It was never retrieved. Another treasured reminder of the past was the worn-out fur coat purchased with the death benefit money of her beloved Walter. Tattered and torn, **it still covered her bed each night.**

Esther continued to lose weight. She was now unable to bend over and she was increasingly immobile. Valda Orr Elixman, with whom she had reconciled her differences, came frequently to tidy the house and care for her, as did Madge Slaughter of Bellingham.[1]

Esther had always been concerned for Frank. Now she took heart that his plans would finally work out. In 1982, he began thinking about launching a new bus line. Though Esther was unable to help him financially, having spent all of her inheritance from Ruth's estate, Frank borrowed two thousand dollars from the bank to purchase a twenty-passenger school bus from Bellingham Junior Academy. He also planned to purchase a twelve-passenger 1976 Plymouth van to add to his fleet. Jim Thomas, a former aide to Vice President Spiro Agnew and now a Lummi resident and active Democrat, jumped in to assist Frank. On May 30, 1984, the Washington State Utilities and Transportation Commission issued license M.V.C. No. 1448 and approved the Allen Bus Line. Superintendent Bill Black gave his blessing to the project, which he described as "the only all Indian owned bus and charter services in the Northwest."[2]

Under Frank's plan Esther would keep the records and David would help operate the buses. The line ran between Gooseberry Point and Bellingham via Haxton Way, Lummi Shore Road, Kwiana Road, and Marine Drive, serving the off-route point at Marietta. Frank and David ran the line for a few months and then quit. The venture had been opposed all along by the Lynden Stage & Charter Lines, Inc., and when his business folded, Frank blamed the Lynden lines.

On one rare occasion Esther broke her isolation to attend a retirement party for Jim Heckman at the Tulalip Senior Center. She wanted to express her gratitude for Heckman's help during implementation of the Boldt decision and his subsequent interest in Stillaguamish affairs. Esther joined others in praising him and acknowledging his service on the Northwest Indian Fisheries Commission and his other work on behalf of Indians.[3]

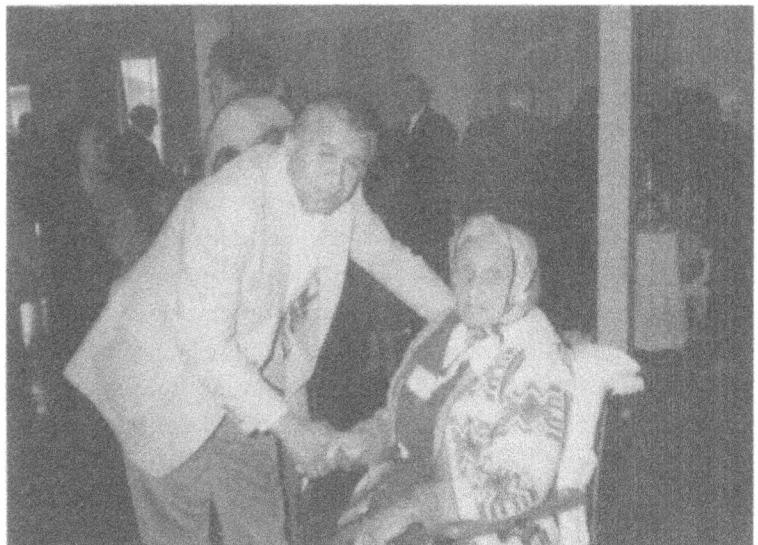

Nisqually tribal member Billy Frank, Jr., chairman of the Northwest Indian Fisheries Commission, greets Esther. Even after she had been forced out of tribal office, Esther on occasion attended the commission meetings until it became too difficult for her to leave home.

Suffering the dreary days of December 1984, Esther wrote a letter in response to Mike Grayum's notice of an NWIFC meeting to be held the middle of the month on the Tulalip: "I [am] 80 yr old ... I am with wheelchair now and when [the] wind blows and [there is] rain ... I can't go out of the house. I don't [know] just what to say [about attending the meeting]. My son Frank Allen would have to drive ... me. I don't have any money neither does he for the rest of this month." Admitting that she got some help from STOWW in paying her bills, she complained that "Nobody comes to see me here at the house. ... I never hear from your office ... anymore."[4]

Her isolation was somewhat relieved by visits from Doug and Maria Venn on behalf of the Adventist Church. She had long been sustained by the firm roots planted by her Adventist upbringing. Now the Venns came to sing, pray, and read the Bible with her.[5]

Esther depended on Frank and Sandra for household chores and for preparing her meals of mashed potatoes, white bread, milk, and eggs. But on May 12, 1986, when Margaret Greene discovered Esther alone and unable to reach her wheelchair, she felt better arrangements had to be made for her care. Frank hesitated calling the Lummi clinic, mostly because his mother had always refused its help, but Greene called the clinic anyway and asked for home health care. Despite Esther's long-standing opposition to nurses, doctors, and home health care workers, she capitulated, and the clinic began sending members of their staff to her home. When offered the services of a cleaning woman from the state's Department of Social and Health Services (DSHS), Esther had Frank "fire" her. When another person replaced the discharged worker, Frank also let her go after she had made just a few biweekly visits.[6]

Visiting nurses were immediately concerned that the boxes of records and piles of newspapers in the home were potential fire hazards. Just after New Year's 1987, a Lummi police officer visited the home and judged it to be a definite fire hazard. Boxes stacked to the ceiling behind doors made the doors unopenable. R. Bruce Haley, Lummi law and order administrator, reported the conditions to the Indian Health Service and Gooseberry Fire Department and notified Frank by letter of the findings. Frank cleared the doorways.[7]

With days passing slowly for Esther, she had now lost virtually all contact with the outside world. There was no telephone service for want of payment of past due accounts. She showed little interest in television. No one from the tribe gave her the time of day, having blocked her out of tribal affairs. In fact, no one from the tribe made a courtesy call inquiring about her welfare.

When friends advocated more nursing care for Esther, Frank refused to turn over the papers necessary for admission to a rest home. Dr. Dale Haveman of the Lummi Indian Health Clinic wanted her in such a facility, but Esther was adamant on the point, telling a visiting home health care worker, "Dr. Haveman can't put me in no rest home. If you don't like the way I want things done around here I can fire you." Esther now found herself pitted against not only the DSHS and the Lummi clinic but also against Adult Protective Services (APS). All of the agencies were doing their best to get her into a nursing care facility.[8]

By December 1987 Esther was so weak that she did not want to get out of bed, even when it was being changed. Four days after Christmas, she asked the visiting nurse to remain for awhile. She gained strength temporarily in early January, but by month's end, she did not want to be bathed and again asked the nurse to sit with her awhile. With the family gone, she now seemed to want company. Once Frank locked the door against the nurse's scheduled visit. "You're not supposed to come in. Frank said to keep everyone out, . . . but I need my nails cut [and] the hair on my face [removed]," Esther yelled through the door. "If you hurry we can beat him." When Frank began locking the door more frequently, the nurse left a note for him, warning him that locking the door kept the cleaning woman and the home health nurses out.[9]

On April 27, 1988, Esther was taken to Bellingham's St. Luke's Hospital for an X-ray to determine if her left hip, which had bothered her all winter, was fractured. It wasn't. The leg pain was part of the degenerative process. Occasionally her leg would slip from the bed and hang over the side until someone arrived to lift it back up on the bed. Esther now found it extremely painful to be moved from bed, and moving her required more help from the family.

When nurse Gwen Hoshy visited on May 6, Esther's left leg was markedly swollen. On Thursday, May 10, Dr. Haveman and a clinic nurse visited Esther on authorization of APS to assess her condition. Haveman felt she now needed twenty-four-hour nursing care. APS asked for a court order to remove her from her home. Now that DSHS was involved in her case, Esther had no choice. Though Frank vociferously opposed his mother's entering a nursing home, she was taken by ambulance to Bellingham's Sehome Park Care Center on May 17. On the admission form, her occupation was listed as "retired schoolteacher." Her chart showed a diagnosis of a small CVA (cerebral vascular accident), a stroke, suffered at home prior to her admission to the center. Her chart also carried the remark, "Quite Belligerent Patient." Despite her pain, she refused medication. The nurses heard her "crying out." Esther explained it away as "singing." Aware of Esther's Indian roots, the nurse noted in her chart, "Apparently singing an Indian chant."[10]

Whenever she was home from her Adventist school, Esther's granddaughter Sandra would visit. When she had turned sixteen, she'd been accepted into the Adventist Thunderbird Academy in Scottsdale, Arizona, where she participated in a summer program in which students attended school half days and worked in the community the other half. Frank had driven her to Scottsdale in the used Oldsmobile he had acquired by trading the three Disneyland tickets Sandra won in the Washington State Easter Seal Society's basketball "shoot-out" in 1987.[11]

Returning home from Arizona around the first of July, Frank found his mother in terrible shape. She claimed she had been force-fed solid foods laced with peanut butter and jam. Frank told the center's administration that he wanted his mother removed. Telling the nursing staff he was taking his mother to church, he propped her up in his car and drove her straight home to be cared for by a Canadian woman he had hired. Arriving at the Lummi house he needed help to get her inside. An hour and a half later, she was so ill that he called Dr. Haveman, then returned her to the center. Haveman found her suffering from pneumonia. He also declared her incompetent. She would have to give over the management of her affairs, he said.[12]

On July 19 Frank was at the center to take his mother out for awhile. He said he would return her before evening; however, he intended to take her home and keep her there. He drove to the Lummi clinic to tell Dr. Haveman of his plan. Reminded that she was under supervision of APS, Frank gave in, and returned Esther to the nursing home.

When Dr. Haveman asked the court to assign power of attorney for Esther, it was not Frank the court designated, but Margaret Greene's brother Sam Cagey. The state's attorney general, Kenneth

Esther in her wheelchair, pushed by Frank. Mother and son were virtually inseparable.

O. Eikenberry, set a hearing for July 22 in the Superior Court of Whatcom County. Patricia Woodall was appointed Esther's guardian *ad litem*. Angered by Dr. Haveman's action, Frank went to the Lummi clinic where he fired the doctor from his mother's care. When notified of Frank's action, DSHS employee Francia Luesson asked the nurse to call Woodall, who retained Haveman as Esther's physician.[13]

Esther's weight had now dropped to ninety-five pounds. Her condition alternated daily between alertness and lethargy. At one point, Dr. Haveman was certain she had suffered another stroke, but he decided against a brain scan. In a lengthy discussion with the staff concerning Esther's food intake, Frank explained that she didn't eat meat because of her religious beliefs and a weak stomach. He also hired another doctor to assume his mother's care, one Kenney Spady, but on learning of the situation, Spady backed off, unwilling to become involved in the case. By July 26, Patricia Woodall had withdrawn from the case, and Hank Balderroma was designated temporary guardian. The court hearing was set for August 9.[14]

During these medical and legal conflicts, Doug Venn and Margaret Greene discussed their worries about Esther. Greene noted that she had become "lighter and lighter" from weight loss. "I'd comb her hair. I'd pull her up in bed, and I'd tell her she was going to get better," Greene said, but she didn't. On July 30 she was reported as being in "poor general condition." She could sit in a chair but she was refusing food. Her condition spiraled downward. At 3:05 p.m. on Monday, August 1, 1988, one month short of her eighty-fourth birthday, Esther Ross died. Unbeknownst to Frank, her remains were sent to the Moles Funeral Home in Ferndale. Lummi police left a note at his house advising him of her death.

Frank's first response was anger. He decided to sue Dr. Haveman. However, in a few weeks his anger subsided and he dropped plans for a suit. Ninety dollars from the Adventist Church enabled Sandra to fly home from Arizona to attend the funeral. Esther's embalming didn't please Frank. He had wanted an autopsy performed to ascertain if she had gallstones or a liver problem. Dr. Haveman had recommended a postmortem exam, but Frank was never asked to sign the authorization papers.[15] Sam Cagey and his sisters Margaret Greene and Catherine Tally, who worked at the Lummi Center, were able to calm Frank to the point that he changed his mind and decided to allow viewing of Esther's body.

They arranged for the funeral to be held in the Lummi gymnasium. Frank wanted his mother buried in full Indian regalia, but Greene dissuaded him from that, since Esther had let Sandra wear it in March 1986 when she appeared on television as top fundraiser for the Washington State Easter Seal Society.[16] It was believed that clothing should not be buried with the owner if another living person had worn it. Frank allowed the older of two morning star headbands to be placed on his mother's head.

Frank wanted Doug Venn to preside at the funeral, but Venn thought it best to have an ordained minister officiate. Venn agreed to deliver the eulogy.[17] Frank asked Rev. Wesley Olfert of the Ferndale Adventist Church to officiate, though Olfert scarcely knew Esther. Tommy Gobin and his band played religious music.

Services in the Lummi Neighborhood Facility began at 10 A.M. on Monday, August 8. In the Family Record page of the memorial book on display at the funeral, the space listing Esther's father was blank. Only her mother's name was listed. Casket bearers were Mike Grayum, Bill Cagey, George Adams, Lew Goodridge, Clarence Hatch, and Vernon Lane. Grayum was unable to attend the service. Honorary casket bearers were Janet McCloud, Yakama leader Roger Jim, Ramona Bennett, anthropologist Barbara Lane, attorney David Getches, and U.S. Senator Dan Evans. Evans sent a letter of regret on August 3 that Senate business would keep him from attending. Marion and her husband, Dick Byrum, also attended.

Many people eulogized the deceased Stillaguamish leader. David Getches wrote in a letter to Frank, "Chief Ross will long be remembered as one who fought for the survival of the Stillaguamish as a people when no one else seemed to care. I wish that her spirit would live on in the emerging Indian leaders of today. If it does, the future of Indian tribes and culture will be far more secure." Time dimmed neither Getches's memory nor his esteem for Esther. In the fall of 1993, he again wrote to Frank, prefacing the letter with an expression of his delight that Esther's life was being chronicled and concluding it with a fine epitaph:

I would like to think that all of our legal antics tipped the scales in favor of the battles we fought with the tribe. But when I think of Esther's determination and strategy, I am not sure that the legal wrangling really made the difference in the successes finally earned by Esther and the tribe. From the poor people's march on Washington, to stopping the Bicentennial wagon train, to the parades and news stories, to the prayers and friendships she fostered, it now seems clear to me that whatever happened right was because of Esther and not the lawyers and politicians and bureaucrats.[18]

In the *Everett Herald* of August 4, 1988, Agency Supt. Bill Black described Esther as "larger than life . . . [though] physically small, yet whenever she would come into a room, she took command of it. Whether it was the agency superintendent or the Commissioner of Indian affairs she wouldn't leave until she got what she came after. Her presence in Indian country couldn't be denied. She was so active, persistent, outspoken and she got results." In the same issue of the *Herald*, Pat Rudd, agency tribal enrollment specialist, was quoted as saying that Esther's single-handed efforts had gained Stillaguamish recognition in the landmark fishing rights decision by U.S. District Court Judge George Boldt. Characterizing her as "a very determined person who wasn't going to let bureaucracy get in her way," Rudd allowed as how she was "cantankerous" but concluded that it was her determination that "brought the tribe into the federal family." Susan Shown Harjo, executive director of the National Congress of American Indians, sent a telegram:

FOR THE FAMILY AND FRIENDS OF THE HONORABLE ESTHER ROSS ON BEHALF OF THE OFFICERS AND STAFF OF THE NATIONAL CONGRESS OF AMERICAN INDIANS I WISH TO EXPRESS OUR DEEP SORROW AT THIS TIME OF THE PASSING OF OUR FRIEND AND RELATIVE MRS ESTHER ROSS. WE ALSO WISH TO EXPRESS OUR GREAT JOY IN HAVING BEEN PRIVILEGED TO SHARE IN HER LIFE AND WORK FOR A

WHOLE AND HEALTHY PEOPLE TO CARRY ON THE TRADITIONS OF NATIVE AMERICA. WE HAVE HER FINE EXAMPLE OF PERSEVERANCE AND HOPE TO ENCOURAGE AND INSPIRE. AS THIS DAUGHTER OF THE GREAT SPIRIT NOW RETURNS HOME, WE SHALL KEEP HER IN OUR HEARTS AND PRAYERS WITH SADNESS.[19]

At the Lummi cemetery, American Legion member Paul Wrigley of Marietta laid a folded flag on Esther's casket. Then, taking it from the casket, he handed it to the family in remembrance of one he called "a warrior."

CHAPTER TWENTY-EIGHT

# EPILOGUE AND RETROSPECT

In October of 1988 Sandra Allen returned home from the Thunderbird Academy. She and Frank sorted through the things that Esther had carefully laid aside for Sandra. Among Esther's few baubles was her cherished beaded bolo from Bernie Gobin. Frank returned the bolo to the Tulalip elder.[1]

Seeking to maintain some continuity in the Stillaguamish chieftancy, Frank told *Everett Herald* reporter Linda Bryant of Esther's wish that he become chief and take the name of his great-great-grandfather Chaddus.[2] Frank organized the ceremony by which he would become chief of the Stillaguamish people a year after his mother's death. It was held at the Marietta Grange on August 5, 1989. Joe Washington, the spiritual leader of the Lummi, presided. Having earlier given his eagle-feather headdress to his son Clyde, but wanting a proper headdress to signify his exalted position, Frank had purchased a new one made of dyed turkey feathers for two hundred dollars from the Tulalip arts and crafts shop for the occasion. (Once the ceremony was over, Frank would pawn the headdress off in a Vancouver, British Columbia, shop.) Anthropologist Barbara Lane sent her regrets that she couldn't attend. But Malcolm McLeod did attend. After making a few remarks, he was given five dollars and a blanket, which he considered a symbolic gift from the tribe. Later he would admit that, after serving forty years as legal counsel for the Stillaguamish, those five dollars and the blanket—and a few salmon received over the years from Esther—were the only recompense he ever got from the tribe.³

The ceremony naturally drew the attention of Stillaguamish tribal officials. The council unanimously adopted a resolution that denied Frank the designation of Stillaguamish chief.⁴

By now the tribe's enrollment had increased to 163 and in another year would shoot up to 182.⁵ Frank who carried his mother's acquired disdain for tribal "white people," unilaterally decided to institute a new and separate tribe. They would be called the "Lower Stillaguamish Indian Nation." "I'm going to do what my mother wanted me to do," Frank said. Those whom he planned to enroll in his tribe would have to have at least a one-quarter Stillaguamish blood quantum. And he proposed a possible land base by laying claim to an area along the lower Stillaguamish for which the government had made no award.⁶

Frank prepared a tribal constitution to file with the Washington secretary of state to give his tribe nonprofit status. Seeking legal assistance in his venture, he contacted David Getches. Getches was not encouraging: "I must say that I think that it will be very, very difficult to create another tribe." He explained to Frank that at the time of the initial recognition of the tribe in 1976 there were fewer obstructions than those he faced now.⁷

Frank was not easily discouraged. He used a July 28, 1990, *Bellingham Herald* story to announce an organizational meeting on July 30 in his Lummi home. He was the only one who attended. Once he realized the new tribe was going nowhere, he decided to run for governor of the state in the 1992 election. As creative as his mother, he purchased a second turkey-feather headdress from the Tulalip arts and crafts shop. Mimicking Esther in the Poor People's Campaign, he donned the headdress and announced his candidacy. He would run on the platform of representing poor people, he said. He drove to San Francisco to attend the annual NCAI meeting in 1991. There he buttonholed Indian leaders, asking their support in his bid for governor.

Most of the reactions to Frank's gubernatorial aspirations were negative. According to STOWW's Linda Dombrowski, who was at the NCAI meeting to discuss recognition issues, she encountered Gail Greger, then tribal chair of the Stillaguamish, at the conference and they talked of Frank's campaign. Gail told Dombrowski that "it was like nobody knew what to say." "Look," Greger said, "I just deal with it in a business-like fashion. This is my cousin. I prefer it didn't happen." Back home, Greger asked tribal council members to neither support nor encourage Frank. The media reported Greger as saying, "Most people think his campaign is a hoax or something for him to get attention. This whole thing is a lark. . . . The feeling is he couldn't do us any good."[8] Opinions ranged from those of the Lummi elders who "scoffed at the prospect, saying it is an ill-conceived lark of a man with nothing better to do," to Bernie Whitebear, who said, "I think Frank's chances are slim. He doesn't have the war chest to win a race. He doesn't even have the name familiarity." But supportive remarks came from Catherine Troeh, a Chinook, who said, "He is a sincere man. He has the interest and the perseverance to put his name in the political arena. I have to admire him." Margaret Greene said her people recognized Frank as a chief, and they warmly supported his gubernatorial campaign.[9]

Frank was featured in the December 23, 1991, issue of the *Bellingham Herald* with a big headline, "'Poor People's Candidate' Will Run for Governor." He was quoted as saying, "I don't believe the [present] governor has ever picked hops for a living, searched for pop cans or stood in a food line. I am a poor man, and so I know what poor people need." In the end, Frank's ability to attract support proved so ineffective that he was forced to give up the race. He sold the headdress to a Samish friend with the understanding that he could buy it back at any time. His hopes and plans to walk in his mother's footsteps weren't working out. He lacked her energy and determination.

♦ ♦ ♦

Esther Ross sought to live and think "Indian" in her adoptive culture with a ferocious feel for Indianness. Strong as this was, her conversion to Indian ways was not totally complete. For instance, she never relinquished the deep-seated principles of her Adventist background, especially in her later years. She did not follow others who were returning to Indian religious practices and ceremonials of their heritage. She shunned aboriginal tribalism. Terms such as "shaman," "spirit powers," and others associated with nativism were not in her vocabulary. And she did not learn the tribal language.

Esther was a woman as well as an Indian. In promoting tribal causes, she pushed for equality for women. In the process she became the doyenne of women activists who were assuming leadership within their own tribes. This group included Lucy Covington, the Colville; Janet McCloud, the Nisqually; Ramona Bennett, the Puyallup; Evelyn Kanim Enick, the Snoqualmie; Kathleen Bishop, the Snohomish; Margaret Greene, the Samish; and others.

Esther's cultural background in the non-Indian community served her in the tribal rejuvenation process. She could work with the BIA and its regional agencies. Above all, she was aware that she had to understand the policies and protocols of the federal government to achieve a tribal rebirth. Her creativity prompted her to stop a wagon train, display ancestral bones, and flash her tribal banner at demonstrations.

Officials nearest her in the Everett agency and the Department of the Interior were in the best position to explain her successes. Superintendent Bill Black of the Everett agency attributed them to her ability to do business with politicians and staffers in the capital. Bud Lozar of the Everett agency and Roy Sampsel of the Portland branch of the Interior Department believe her successes were a result of media attention and high visibility. Everett agency Supt. Peter Three Stars credited her successes to David Getches and the NARF group for expertly handling her drive for recognition. Interior's Scott Keep believes her creativity was her important asset.

Esther balanced her tribal activism with an often troublesome family life. Broken relationships with her biological and her adoptive fathers, failed marriages to Fletcher Carlton and Arnold Ross almost overshadowed her love match with Walter Allen. She deeply loved her son, Frank, had an uneasy truce with her daughter Ruth, and held her daughter Marion in low esteem.

One's character often can be revealed in attitudes toward the use of money. For fifty years, Esther spent her own money nurturing the fledgling tribe. She received little if any monetary support from other tribal members. She constantly had to search for funds for travel and other expenses. Once the tribe was funded with annual appropriations, she struggled for tribal control with her opponents.

Don Smouse, a supporter, believed that the tribe should have reimbursed Esther with money or, at the very least, rewarded her with power. "The tribe should build a statue to her," he has said. Pat Rudd of the Everett agency expressed a similar view: "For years when I was working for . . . [the Stillaguamish] I'd go out there and say you should take an acre out there in the 20-acre [tribal] housing area and dedicate it to her. Without her you would have nothing."[10]

While Esther spent money easily, she hoarded documents and records having anything to do with Stillaguamish and Indian matters. These papers show her resolve, but they also reveal her conservatism in opposing any change in tribal government that would threaten her leadership. Bill Black observed that once tribal recognition was achieved, her leadership style was no longer appropriate and her personality counterproductive to a fledgling group trying to establish a small organization that ultimately will grow into a bureaucracy. "She had fulfilled her purpose," he said, "but she was not going to give up her position." As the tribe moved into a democratic-type organization, her aristocratic approach no longer worked. "It's a logical evolution," Black said.[11]

Esther's confrontations with her own tribespeople were common in Native American politics. Linda Dombrowski saw that many times in leadership among tribes. David Getches saw the problem repeated throughout the country. "New tribal governments are resentful of traditional leaders," he noted.

For Esther there was no gracious withdrawal. Aware that some in the Stillaguamish council had less than one-quarter blood quantum, she sought to remove them from the rolls, but tribal percentages could not be easily manipulated. Esther's rearguard efforts to regain her leadership only resulted in her falling further behind rather than forging ahead.

With Esther's passing it became too late for the tribe to withdraw acrid epithets and forgive in person and forget in absentia what some considered her frailties and transgressions. It is not too much to hope that with the dawn of a new century the tribe will credit Esther for her accomplishments. Margaret Greene, for one, will never forget her. She was "a rose. A fragile rose," Greene says. "She didn't die with hardening of the arteries. She died with a broken heart."[12]

That brilliant morning star that appeared in the skies on the day of her birth will long reflect the spirit and determination of Esther Ross.

# NOTES

Unless otherwise indicated, all documents cited in the Notes are found in the Esther Ross Papers at the Eastern Washington State Historical Society in Spokane.

## CHAPTER 1

1. Angelina Silva and Christian Johnson were married in San Francisco on December 28, 1902. Scattered throughout Esther's papers are her handwritten notes on photographs as well as dissertations on family history jotted on pieces of paper. However, two years following her birth, an earthquake and fire destroyed much property in the San Francisco area. Among the casualties were records of Esther's birth, which had not reached the state capital in Sacramento.

2. "Betsey" Silva's Indian name was Zis-da-gub.

3. For instance, Esther used the name Reid on the "Junior Missionary Volunteer Reading Course Certificate," April 9, 1919, signed by M. N. Helligso, secretary of the Pacific Union (Adventist) Conference.

4. "Esther's Diary," hereafter Diary. This is a plethora of random, undated personal remarks.

5. A. A. Ross to Angelina, July 17, 1923; director, Division of Motor Vehicles, Sacramento, Calif., to Angelina, February 9, 1924.

6. Diary.

7. A signed affidavit by J. Brum of Hayward attests to his knowledge of Angelina Johnson, whom he claimed to have known for twenty years; he further asserts that her stepmother, Mary Silva, had rented five acres to him in 1915–16 and that when he wanted to purchase them Mrs. Silva

refused to sell, stating that the land was for her daughter Angelina. She told Brum that John Silva had left the place to Mary during her lifetime, but after her death it would go to Angelina.

8. Dora I. Peterson, To Whom It May Concern, March 31, 1926. Peterson stated that she had known Mary Silva and that Mary had told her "a number of times" that the farm was to go to "Augua" (Angelina). In late January 1914, Mary signed a paper (which Dora in her affidavit calls a deed) giving the farm to Angelina when she died. Judge Charles Prouse drew up the document, which was signed by Dora Peterson and W. H. Stanley as witnesses. Mary gave the document to Prouse to keep until Mary's death and then to deliver to Angelina. This indicates it to be a will. Fred Mohr of Oakland to State of California, County of Alameda, January 6, 1926, wrote that he had known Angelina for thirty-three years and that she was the daughter of John Silva and stepdaughter of Mary Silva and that the latter had told Mohr and his wife, Carrie, that the Silva property was to go to Angelina on Mary's death. "I also know that John Silva objected to the adoption of the girl named Louise or Lula that was brought into the home from the orphan home by Seventh Day Adventists" Mohr wrote. "I know Lula is not the daughter of Mary Silva." In Esther's papers are many other affidavits supporting the fact that Silva intended the house and property to go to Angelina once Mary was deceased, if she outlived him.

9. Angelina communicated with Supt. W. F. Dickens of the Tulalip Reservation on January 12, 1922; February 21, 1922; July 8, 1925; etc.

10. Diary.

11. Frank Allen, interview by authors. The authors and Frank Allen have engaged in conversations spanning seven years (June 22, 1993, to July 2, 2000) and numbering some eighty-six in all. Because topics of conversation constantly recurred, we have not cited any specific date for this reference and those to follow. Tapes and their transcriptions and notes are found in the Esther Ross Papers.

## CHAPTER 2

1. Over the next forty-some years, from her move north in the spring of 1926 until she was finally able to establish a home of her own with Arnold Ross on the Lummi Reservation near Bellingham in the spring of 1970, Esther adopted what might best be described as a peripatetic lifestyle. For the better part of those years, she and the family lived in various parts of the Northwest—but generally in the Stanwood, Everett, and Seattle area—moving in and out of rentals, sometimes just in advance of

the rent-due date. It is hard to reconstruct exactly where she was living at any one time during these years.

As reported in the *Arlington (Wash.) Times*, August 8, 1925, a woman at a gathering of Stillaguamish Valley pioneers that year explained the name "Stillaguamish"; its meaning is also verified by anthropologists. The name has been rendered variously as Stoluch-wa-mish, Stolutswhamish, What-lam-amish, Steilaguamish, Solucwamish, and Stolucwamish. After the middle of the twentieth century, the tribe used the spelling Stoluckquamish for a time, and the federal government at midcentury used the spelling Stoluck-wha-mish. Anthropologist Barbara Lane says the name is generic, having been given by other tribes to the people living along the Stillaguamish River. *Stillaguamish Tribe of Indians v Thomas S. Kleppe, et al.* (hereafter *Stillaguamish v Kleppe*), deposition of Barbara Lane, March 23, 1976, 9.

2. *Duwamish et al. v United States*. The suit was authorized by an act of Congress, February 12, 1925.

3. *Arlington (Wash.) Times*, June 19, 1930. A series of five treaties was negotiated by Isaac Stevens in 1854-55; Medicine Creek on December 26, 1854; Point Elliott, January 22, 1855; Point No Point, January 26, 1855; Neah Bay, January 31, 1855; and Quinault, July 1, 1855 (formalized January 25, 1856).

4. See Robert H. Ruby and John A. Brown, *Indian Slavery in the Pacific Northwest*.

5. Diary.

6. Susan Dorsey's story was recorded by Esther Ross on May 14, 1927.

7. *Stillaguamish v Kleppe*, Lane deposition, 18-22.

8. Robert H. Ruby and John A. Brown, *A Guide to the Indians of the Pacific Northwest*, 244.

9. *Stillaguamish v Kleppe*, Lane deposition, 13.

10. Ibid., 14, 10-11.

11. Ibid., 20; Nels Bruseth, *Indian Stories and Legends of the Stillaguamish, Sauks, and Allied Tribes*, 5-11.

12. Samuel Hitchcock, *The Narrative of Samuel Hitchcock, 1845-1860*, 108-15. The Roman Catholic missionary Francis Norbert Blanchet, who came among Indians of western Washington in 1839, taught them to make the sign of the cross. See F. N. Blanchet, *Notices and Voyages of the Famed Quebec Mission to the Pacific Northwest*.

13. Alice Essex, *The Stanwood Story*, vol. 1, 1; Diary.

14. Frank Allen, interview.

15. *Stanwood (Wash.) Tidings*, July 16, 1913.

16. Special Agent, U.S. Indian Service, Charles E. Roblin, Schedule of Unenrolled Indians, Stillaguamish Tribe, January 1, 1919.

## CHAPTER 3

1. Minutes of Meetings, 15–16, Stillaguamish Indian Tribal Records, hereafter Minutes. This is a bound ledger volume in which minutes of tribal meetings were written by Esther from July 1, 1926, through 1967, with only intermittent reports after about midcentury. Esther made numerous handwritten copies of portions of the minutes. The hardcover ledger is in the archives of the Lummi Indian Reservation.

2. The Northwestern Federation of American Indians (NFAI) was organized in Tacoma, Washington, on February 22, 1914, and Angelina had been a member in 1917–18.

3. Minutes, 3–5. A copy of the news release, "Indians Organize to Enforce Treaty," is in Esther's papers.

4. Minutes, 9–14.

5. Ibid., 20.

6. *Stillaguamish Tribe of Indians v United States*, No. 207, 15 Indian Claims Commission (hereafter *Stillaguamish v United States*, 15 ICC 1), deposition of James Dorsey.

7. Roy Sampsel, interview by authors, July 17, 1994.

## CHAPTER 4

1. Letter, October 26, 1933, Arthur Griffin to Esther Carlton quoted in Minutes, 50.

2. *Arlington (Wash.) Times*, June 19, 1930.

3. Ibid., July 10, 1930.

4. Minutes, 43. With the adoption of a constitution, officers were elected for prescribed terms rather than "for life."

5. Griffin to Esther, October 26, 1933.

6. *Duwamish et al. v United States*.

7. Griffin to James Dorsey, February 8, 1935.

8. Minutes, 58.

9. The surname given on Frank's birth certificate is Carlton.

10. R. L. Popwell, regional adjudication officer, Veterans Administration, to Esther, January 14, 1931, and April 30, 1932. Esther had trouble listing the paternity of her children. On August 4, 1980, trying to straighten out records of Frank's biological father, she wrote an affidavit notarized by Karen K. Martin in which she stated, "I have two daughters by Fletcher Carlton, Ruth and Marion . . . Frank's certificate of birth reads Carlton as

Dr. [William] Scott [who delivered Frank at the house of Ella Lovejoy in Seattle] delivered my previous children." Note, however, that Ruth had been born in Oakland, California, not Seattle.

11. Popwell to Esther, June 13, August 2, and 17, 1933; and July 29, 1946.

12. Frank Allen, interview.

13. Diary; Frank Allen, interview; Marion Carlton Byrum, interview by authors, June 11, 1995.

14. Frank Allen, interview.

15. Ibid.; Byrum, interview.

## CHAPTER 5

1. Diary.

2. Ibid. In Ketchican, Ruth lived with a physician's family, doing their housework. The physician offered to pay her tuition to attend a business school in Seattle after graduation. Upon completing the course, Ruth was employed for a time by Veterans Post No. 1 in Seattle and later by the Bon Marche in Seattle.

3. Minutes, 60.

4. Byrum, interview.

5. Ibid.

6. Minutes, 65.

7. Ibid.

8. Ibid., 69.

9. Ibid., 75.

10. Griffin to Esther, October 22, 1946.

11. Frank Allen, interview.

12. Ibid.

13. In September and October 1947 Walter worked for the Giustina Brothers Lumber Company; from October to November, for the Razar Brothers Logging Company; and from November 1947 to January 1948, for the Gisle Robstad Logging Company, all of Eugene, Oregon. Then, from March to April 1948, when the family moved to Florence, he worked for the K & B Logging Company of Florence, and from April to May 1948 for the SFAC Logging Company of Reedsport. The family lived in Netarts and then Tillamook, Oregon. While there, in 1948 Walter worked for three companies: the Coos Bay Logging Company in May; the Western Logging Company of Siletz in September; and finally, the Prouty Lumber Company of Warrenton in November. Frank Allen, interview.

14. Social Security Administration to authors, July 11, 1996.

15. Edgar "Ed" Fitchen, interview by authors, May 25, 1995.
16. Frank Allen, interview.
17. Diary.

## CHAPTER 6

1. Frank Allen, interview.
2. F. A. Gross, acting superintendent, Western Washington Agency, Tulalip, to Mrs. Lloyd Martin, August 14, 1950.
3. Gross to Chairman John Silva, September 18, 1950. Gross also forwarded *Field Memorandum No. 157, Supplement No. 2 of Indian Claims Commission Act—Attorney Contracts* to the tribe. A copy of the *Field Memorandum* is in Esther's papers.
4. More recent research shows that the Stillaguamish had close ties with the Snoqualmies as well as the Snohomish, which at treaty time were, like the Stillaguamish, under the hegemony of the powerful Snoqualmie chief Patkanin.
5. Raymond H. Bitney, superintendent, Western Washington Agency, Tulalip, to Esther, November 17, 1950.
6. Minutes, 88.
7. Ibid., 90.
8. Minutes of Meetings, December 16, 1950. Minutes noted with a date instead of a page number are those minutes that are not in the Stillaguamish Indian Tribal Record ledger but are on loose sheets of paper in the Esther Ross Papers.
9. Frank Allen, interview. Esther, who never used cosmetics, had had to borrow the lipstick. The "lipstick map" is in Esther's papers.
10. Byrum, interview.
11. Ibid.
12. Frank Allen, interview.
13. Despite the marriage, Esther professed that she still "missed Walter in [my] heart." Diary.
14. The contract, approved on July 12, 1951, would be renewed on December 3, 1957, with Post and Gilbert. By December 7, 1964, only Post remained as the Stillaguamish attorney. He would represent the tribe until the conclusion of the claims process.
15. Warren Gilbert to Alvin Anderson, April 16, 1952. In the letter, Gilbert also asked for remittance of five hundred dollars for his services.
16. *Stillaguamish v. United States*, 15 ICC 1, deposition of Esther Ross, pp. 17–41.
17. Wayne Suttes to Esther, November 19, 1952.

18. Esther to Supt. Raymond Bitney, October 30, 1952.

19. Bitney to Esther, November 4, 1952.

20. Bitney to John Silva, December 11, 1952; the Indian Reorganization Act (IRA), also referred to as the Wheeler-Howard Act.

21. The constitution was approved by the BIA, January 31, 1953.

22. The morning of September 25, 1954, Joan had awakened to discover what appeared to be pans of spilled blood. Unassisted, Margaret had given birth to Dorothy, completing the birthing process before having Joan call for an ambulance to take her to the hospital. Interviewed as an adult, Joan said she had never been a child, had always been an adult. "I had to be," she recalled. "I had the responsibility." Joan Baker Benson, interview by authors, June 4, 1995.

23. Juvenile Court Order No. 3175, Snohomish County Courthouse, March 24, 1955; Arnold R. Zempel, prosecuting attorney, by Stuart C. French, deputy prosecuting attorney, Snohomish County, to the Rosses, March 31, 1955.

24. Benson, interview.

25. *Everett (Wash.) Daily Herald*, December 23, 1955. According to her son, Esther had hoped to get a used TV set and a piano as well as a washing machine from her appeal, but she got only the washing machine. Frank Allen, interview.

26. Benson, interview.

27. Ibid.

28. Margaret Greene, interview by authors, March 16, 1994; May 20 and July 13, 1995.

29. Frank Allen, interview.

30. *Stillaguamish v United States*, 15 ICC 1, p. 38.

31. *Stillaguamish Tribe of Indians, v United States*, No. 207, 22 Indian Claims Commission 361, pp. 361, 362, 366 (hereafter *Stillaguamish v United States*, 22 ICC 361).

32. Frank Allen, interview; *Stillaguamish v United States*, 22 ICC 361, pp. 361–62.

33. *Stillaguamish v United States*, 22 ICC 361, p. 366.

34. Esther wrote a letter to the *Seattle Post-Intelligencer* about the offer to the president and the response. It was published in "Northwest Today," a *Post-Intelligencer* Sunday magazine, April 10, 1966.

35. *Stillaguamish v United States*, 22 ICC 361, pp. 361, 362.

## CHAPTER 7

1. James Hovis, interview by authors, October 21, 1995.

2. Frank Allen, interview.

3. On October 13, 1965, seven other Puyallups were arrested. One was released and the others were given sixty-day suspended jail sentences. *Seattle Post-Intelligencer*, October 14 and 15, 1965.

4. Ibid., October 27, 1965.

5. Frank Allen, interview.

6. *Seattle Times*, December 11, 1966; *Arlington (Wash.) Times*, December 15, 1996. To this day, Indians celebrate annually their Point Elliott Treaty Day.

7. Frank Allen, interview.

8. Minutes, February 5, 1967.

9. Ibid. An undated letter with the February 5, 1967, minutes was sent to Supt. George Felshaw giving results of the election. Portions of the letter read very much like segments of the minutes.

10. Diary.

11. *Daily Olympian* (Olympia, Wash.), February 7, 1967.

12. Ibid. Esther's sign read: "Stillaguamish Indians are under Point Elliott Treaty. Take your Fish Hatchery's Out of Our rivers and Stop investing in our Tribal cemeterys. We Demand Now."

13. Ibid.

## CHAPTER 8

1. Juanita Jefferson, interview by authors, May 21 and June 17, 1998.

2. Bruseth, *Indian Stories*.

3. "Indian Problems and Their Solutions," Herbert C. Holdridge to editor, *Nevada State Journal* (Reno, Nev.), December 6, 1966.

4. "Criminal Induction of Indians into Armed Services," Holdridge to Gen. Louis B. Hershey, January 19, 1967; "Tax War!" Holdridge to Sheldon S. Cohen, "Outlaw Collector of Internal Revenue—Bandit and Pick-Pocket for the Wall Street—Vatican—LBJ Crime Ring," January 24, 1967. Lisa Seymour, archivist, Northeastern Nevada Museum and Northeastern Nevada Historical Society, Elko, to authors, August 21, 1995.

5. Frank Allen, interview; "Nemesis!" Holdridge to the United Press International, Associated Press, and "Seditious Press Generally," February 3, 1967.

6. "Action on Illegal Conscription of Indians and Others," Holdridge to the Indians of America, and Friends of the Indians, February 18, 1967. Lorraine Peterson of the Selective Service office in Elko, a favorite target of Holdridge's, was included on the list.

7. Holdridge to Frank and Esther, March 1, 1967.

8. The Constitutional Government of the United States v [twenty-nine named] Defendants: For Crimes of Kidnapping, Murder, and Treason.

9. Holdridge, "Commentary on the First Trial of the Superior Court, and Related Discussions, March 11-12, 1967." Holdridge's statement of visiting Indians having won at last a victory in his court would have raised the eyebrows of several attending. For instance, Andrea Woods, a Western Shoshone, remembered only the "big talk" of one she described as "a skinny fried chicken colonel." Notwithstanding Woods's description, Holdridge was a handsome man with the proud bearing of a true general. Andrea Woods, interview by authors, August 3, 1995.

10. Holdridge, "Nemesis!" and "Tax War!"

11. Diary.

12. Frank Allen, interview. Because the heavy headdress shifted uncomfortably on his head, Frank eventually give it to his son, Clyde Leo, who was living in Canada with his mother, Rosalee Leo, a Canadian Indian. Frank fathered the boy during a brief sojourn in Canada in the mid-sixties.

13. Holdridge to Esther, April 5, 1967.

14. Over the years Holdridge spent less time writing personal letters, sending instead copies of his releases to individuals and institutions with negative comments about these recipients of his mailings.

15. *Everett (Wash.) Herald*, Nov. 2, 1967; Frank Allen, interview. Impressed with her apparel, the Herald reporter commented that, unlike Esther, Indians cared so little for their Indianness that they failed to dress as Indians, making it impossible for whites to treat them as Indians, no matter how willing they might be to do so.

16. Holdridge to Gov. Daniel Evans, May 8, 1968.

17. American Friends Service Committee, *Uncommon Controversy*, 108, 110, 111.

18. Holdridge to Gov. Daniel Evans, May 8, 1968.

## CHAPTER 9

1. Frank's eleven-year-old stepdaughter, Barbara Miller, was the daughter of Frank's former wife, Mary Margaret Joseph. Frank raised the child as one of his own. David and Lois were born of Frank's marriage to Mary Margaret—David in 1958, Lois a few years later. By 1968, when he and Esther and the children joined the Poor People's Campaign, Frank had been separated from his wife for some six years and he had had a second son, Clyde, who lived in Canada and was affiliated with his mother's tribe. Eventually Frank would have another daughter, Sandra Martine, born on June 6, 1972, of Frank's marriage to Gloria Fay Grant, a

Musqueam Indian of Canada. Though Sandra was enrolled in her mother's tribe, she spent her childhood in Esther's home.

2. The Indian contingent of the Poor People's Campaign on May 31, 1968, issued a statement to the claims commission seeking redress for "fraud, deceit, confiscation and genocide" by the federal government. In the statement, they criticized instituting an "overly technical procedure which works only for the benefit of the Commission" to prolong federal jobs and benefit attorneys with high fees. The contingent decried being forced to show exclusive ownership of their claimed areas. The contingent also stated that Indians did not use surveyors to make boundaries and that "Areas between tribes were used in common." Charges were leveled at the commission for being "lily white," lacking Indian representation. "Statement to Indian Claims Commission, May 31, 1968."

3. *Washington Post*, June 1, 1968.

4. Frank Allen, interview. Because Frank had failed to load his camera, he asked a woman from Seattle who called herself "Princess Sunflower" to take the picture of Esther at Kennedy's grave. Sunflower promised to give Esther the picture, but she could not be found after the campaign.

5. T. W. Taylor, acting commissioner, BIA, to Esther, June 5, 1968.

6. Frank Allen, interview; *Time Magazine*, June 7, 1968, 28.

7. *Seattle Post-Intelligencer*, July 7, 1968.

## CHAPTER 10

1. Frank Allen, interview.

2. Ibid.

3. *Everett (Wash.) Herald*, September 12, 1968.

4. Ibid., September 13, 1968.

5. Holdridge to Esther, November 8, 1968. Holdridge had added John Silva and Frank Allen to the names listed on his stationery. Seventeen "chiefs" now served on his executive council. Women found no place in his officialdom. Subsequent letterheads listed an "Office of Negro Affairs," including a chief of staff and deputy chief of staff.

6. Holdridge to Esther, January 4, 1968.

7. The letter read: "Notice is hereby given that a general meeting of the Stillaguamish Tribe will be held at Kathleen Johnson's Route 2, Box 35A, Arlington, Washington on Sunday, December 28, 1969 [no time was given], to consider the following: 1. Ratification of prior resolution to accept $48,570 settlement of Indian Claims Commission against the United States. 2. To consider disposition of the $48,570, whether to hold for tribal

purpose or to distribute to individual members." Prior to this time, Esther had always mailed the notices of meetings.

8. Frank Allen, interview.

9. The resolution was labeled only "Resolution," without title or number, and dated December 28, 1969. The "prior resolutions" referred to are those that had been adopted at tribal meetings in March of 1965 and September of 1966.

10. Frank Allen, interview.

11. Esther to Felshaw, April 27, 1971.

12. Diary.

13. *Stillaguamish vUnited States,* 22 ICC 361, p. 371.

14. Photocopies of the checks are in Esther's files.

15. Esther to Jerome Kuykendall, January 27, 1970. Kuykendall had replaced John Vance as chair of the claims commission.

16. Frank Allen, interview. The Indian Reorganization Act, June 18, 1934, also cited above, was to develop Indian lands and resources, to extend to Indians the right to do business with other organizations, to establish tribal credit systems, to grant rights for home rule, and to provide education for Indians, among other purposes.

17. Acting associate commissioner, BIA, to Frank Allen, February 27, 1970.

18. Petition [February 28, 1970] to Disclaim All Actions of Attorney for Stillaguamish Tribes per Contract Disignated [sic] as Symbol 14-20-0500, Contract No. 2092, on date of July 12, 1967; Esther to Indian Claims Commission, October 22, 1970.

## CHAPTER 11

1. *Everett (Wash.) Herald,* November 29, 1968; David Getches, "Background Information on the Stillaguamish Tribe of Indians," 3, 4. Reporter Linda Bryant of the *Everett Herald* described the struggle over cemeteries as basically one between the Indian "soul" and the "practical reality of private ownership," arising from a conflict between the Indian concept of sacred communal ownership and that of the capitalistic view of private property. *Everett (Wash.) Herald,* April 18, 1976.

2. These tapes are in Esther's files.

3. *Arlington (Wash.) Times,* September 15, 1966.

4. Frank Allen, interview.

5. Sen. Henry Jackson to BIA, June 20, 1968; Charles P. Corke, deputy assistant commissioner, to Sen. Henry Jackson, July 15, 1968.

6. Steven "Bud" Lozar, interview by authors, March 15, 1994, and August 12, 1995.

7. John Bushman, acting superintendent, Western Washington Agency, to Dale Baldwin, Portland Area Office director, September 30, 1968; George Felshaw, superintendent, Western Washington Agency, to Baldwin, October 23, 1968.

8. Bushman to Baldwin, September 30, 1968.

9. Steven Lozar to Esther, November 5, 1968.

10. Lozar to Esther, November 29, 1976.

11. *Filipino Forum* (Seattle), July 14, 1969; Frank Allen, interview; Greene, interview, July 13, 1995.

12. George Ortez, interview by authors, July 23 and September 6, 1995; December 16, 1997.

13. Lozar, interview, March 15, 1994; *Seattle Times*, January 21, 1970; Frank Allen, interview.

14. *Arlington (Wash.) Times*, March 12, 1970.

15. A copy of Smith's will is in Esther's files; Diary.

16. The September 29 resolution amended the September 22 resolution by adding to it unrelated issues on recognition of Stillaguamish fishing rights and requested that the state give the tribe one of its fish hatcheries.

## CHAPTER 12

1. Frank Allen, interview; Benson, interview.

2. *Everett (Wash.) Herald*, November 2, 1967.

3. See Grace A. Franklin and Randall B. Ripley, *CETA Politics and Policy*; see also Indian Assistance Division, State of Washington, *Indian Economic Employment Assistance Program 1974–75 and 1975–76 Summary*; and U.S. Department of Labor, Employment and Training Administration, *Apprenticeship and CETA Technical Assistance Guide*. STOWW would eventually reach a membership of twenty-one tribes by 1974 when five tribes would leave the organization: Squaxin, Nisqually, Muckleshoot, Chehalis, and Skagit. Rudolph Ryser, interview by authors, May 26, 1992.

4. Charles "Chuck" McEvers, interview by authors, April 25, 1997.

5. William R. "Bill" Jeffries, interviews, April 18 and June 27, 1997; Linda Dombrowski, interviews by authors, March 23 and September 5, 1995. STOWW did not purport to isolate its tribal components but to unify them to stand up to the big tribes. STOWW's economic development program became their fisheries program during the genesis of the Boldt case.

6. Jeffries, interviews.

7. Leota George, interview by authors, May 10, 1997.

8. McEvers, interview.

9. Catherine Herrold Troeh to authors, January 9, 1994.

10. Diary; Frank Allen, interview; David Getches, interview by authors, July 3, 1995.

11. Terry V. Solomon, "Sound Defender: History of Fort Lawton," July 1970. Esther claimed that Solomon Allen had donated twenty acres to the government. Although Bernie Whitebear remembered Esther, he did not recall, some twenty-eight years after the Fort Lawton takeover, talking with her about any claim she had to Fort Lawton property. Whitebear did say the Duwamish, in whose territory the fort was located, were concerned about their right to its land. Bernie Whitebear, interview by authors, December 30, 1997. Esther always believed Whitebear failed her by not checking into a Solomon Allen connection to the Fort Lawton property. A decade after her death the family found evidence that it was not Solomon but his son, John Allen, who had owned land on the Fort Lawton site and who had sold it to the government.

12. Holdridge to Frank Allen, March 21, 1970.

13. *Seattle Post-Intelligencer*, March 8, 9, and 16, 1970. Malcolm McLeod, Gary Gass, and Alva Long represented the jailed protestors. According to Janet McCloud, Fonda's efforts on behalf of the Indians were discounted by those who believed she demonstrated only to enhance her public image. One Indian woman even whomped Fonda on the backside with the sign the woman was carrying.

14. Frank Allen, interview. The City of Seattle also operates a visitor and environmental center on the old fort grounds. A new center opened in the fall of 1997.

15. Governor's Indian Affairs Task Force, *Are You Listening, Neighbor?*, 1972; and Governor's Indian Affairs Task Force, *The People Speak: Will You Listen?*, 1973.

16. There were nine representatives of urban Indians and eight representing landless tribes. These eight, besides Esther, were Clifford Allen, Snohomish; Willard Dill, Duwamish; Margaret Greene, Samish; Kathleen Bishop, Snohomish; Philip LaCourse, Yakama-Colville; Pamela Root, Cree; and Virginia Ryan, Snohomish.

17. Robert Comenout, interview by authors, May 1, 1998. Regarding the Governor's Indian Advisory Council, Jeffries stated that its members pressed for adoption of programs to reverse the paternalistic federal government's heavy hand over the tribes. He also said the committee was successful enough to provide the initial spark in igniting adoption of the

Indian Self-Determination and Education Assistance Act (PL 93-638) signed into law on January 4, 1975. The law turned over to tribes broad administrative control and operations of Indian federal programs on reservations. It also passed down to Indians increased control over their own educational activities. Once in full operation, it released many Indian agency office personnel who until then had administered Indian policy and operations on reservations. With the law, Indians were able to plan and manage their own affairs. In Indian legislation the law was second in importance only to the Indian Reorganization Act of 1934. Senator Henry Jackson succinctly stated the significance of the law: "What this means to the Indian Community is that the heavy hand of the paternalism which had dominated the lives and affairs of Indian people so many years can now be broken."

## CHAPTER 13

1. Greene, interview, July 13, 1995. Hank Adams called Greene to tell her that while Indians were tearing up the BIA offices they came across some Samish records that he would send her, but Greene lacked money to pay their shipping costs.

2. Georgene Swenson, interview by authors, December 15, 1995, and January 3, 1996.

3. Dombrowski, interview, March 23, 1995.

4. Sam Stanley, interview by authors, November 26, 1996.

5. Charles "Chuck" Trimble to authors, July 11, 1996; Charles Trimble, interview by authors, September 12, 1995.

6. Trimble, interview; Frank Allen, interview; Dombrowski, interview, March 23, 1995; William "Bill" Black, interview by authors, January 10, 1994, and March 31 and July 11, 1995.

7. Indian groups experienced some difficulties, flourishing for a while, then waning as needs dictated. The Intertribal Council of American Indians (ICAI) and the Inter-tribal Council of Western Washington Indians (ICWW) were established to oppose termination of reservation tribes in the 1950s. They disbanded after the federal government no longer promoted terminating reservation tribes. Esther regularly attended those groups' meetings.

8. Later, when the Island Crossing property came up for sale, Esther suggested its purchase to accommodate an eleven-unit motel. She also suggested starting a tribal cannery near Florence.

9. Ramona Bennett, interview by authors, September 8, 1995.

10. Ibid.; Jack Kidder, interview by authors, October 10, 1995.

11. Mel Tonasket, interview by authors, June 3, 1995.

12. Wayne Williams, interview by authors, August 14, 1995, and February 28, 1997.

13. Esther was more accepting of this wedding than she was when Frank married Mary Margaret Joseph on August 25, 1956, in a ceremony performed by Rev. Joseph Dakin of St. Joseph's Parish in Ferndale, Washington. When Frank showed Esther that marriage certificate, she threw it to the floor, disgusted that Frank had married outside his own church.

## CHAPTER 14

1. Frank Allen, interview.
2. Getches, interview.
3. *Northwest Indian News* (Seattle), August 1979, 4. During about eighty years from its statehood in 1889, Washington regulated fishing of Indians who, in and out of courts, sought to obtain and protect their treaty rights to fish for personal and commercial purposes. They received a measure of justice in court cases prohibiting abuses by non-Indians. In 1905 in *United States v Winans* (198 U.S. 371), the Indians won their right to fish, in words of their treaties, in their "usual and accustomed places" without interference from non-Indian private and business interests. In 1942 Washington State was prohibited from licensing Indians to fish and from limiting them to fishing during seasons established for non-Indians. In *Tulee v Washington* (315 U.S. 681) the state was also prohibited from regulating Indian fishing for conservation purposes.

By mid-twentieth century there were in the Pacific Northwest two main areas of fishing confrontations between Indians and non-Indians—the lower Columbia River and the Puyallup and Nisqually Rivers in southern Puget Sound. Long a kingpin among Puyallup-Nisqually commercial fishers, Robert "Bob" Satiacum purchased Indian catches and peddled them at a profit. Indian fishing was a practice abetted by a time-honored aboriginal custom in which Indian families "owned" fishing sites along their rivers. The Indians won a major victory in 1957 when the Washington state supreme court ruled against the state in a suit brought against Satiacum. In their ruling, the justices upheld the status of the Puyallups as a tribe, even though they now lacked a reservation. They ruled that the Medicine Creek Treaty of December 26, 1954, was the supreme law of the land and superior to state police powers. Under this decision the Puyallups could fish within boundaries of their original reservation as could other tribes on their reservations in their "usual and accustomed places," as spelled out in *State of Washington v Robert Satiacum*. The treaty provision allowing Puyallup-Nisquallys to fish "in common with all citizens of the Territory," irrespective of state regulation, was merely a way of granting white fishing privileges at Indian off-reservation "usual and accustomed" places.

Satiacum continued his commercial ventures for a decade. Then, in January 1967, Indians, who had been taking large fish catches with nets, experienced a setback when the state supreme court ruled that the Washington State Department of Game could close rivers to net fishing for conservation purposes (*State of Washington, Department of Game v Puyallup Tribe*). In 1968 the U.S. Supreme Court, while upholding the right of the state to enforce fishing restrictions for conservation purposes, remanded the case to the state court to determine whether or not conservation was necessary. Backed by non-Indian sport and commercial fishers, the state continued trying to stop Indian net fishing. The court decision did *not* discontinue fishing with a hook and line. This was precisely what non-Indian fishers wanted. With this method of fishing, non-Indians had annual gross catches of steelhead trout, while Indian catches were meager. Washington State control of salmon harvests was under its Department of Fisheries, while the Department of Game controlled steelhead as a game fish. The two departments were separate entities at that time but merged on March 1, 1994, into the Department of Fish and Wildlife.

4. Puyallups long contested with the state in court cases involving Indian commercial fishing with nets, as prohibited by the state for both Indians and non-Indians, and before that, involving fishing "out of season" in noncompliance with rules set by the state. Finally, on September 18, 1970, the United States, on behalf of seven tribes, entered a suit against the Washington State Departments of Game and Fisheries [*United States v State of Washington* (384 F Supp 312)].

Among the seven tribes and their counsels in the suit were the Puyallups and Nisquallys, represented only by George Dysart and his assisting attorneys Stan Pitkin and Stuart F. Pierson, without their own counsel; the Skokomish and Muckleshoots, represented by David Getches, who was assisted by attorney John H. Stennhauser of Legal Services; the Hohs, represented by Lester Stritmatter; and the Makahs and Quileutes, represented by Alvin J. Ziontz. Of the defendants, the Department of Game and Carl Crouse were represented by Asst. Attorney General Joseph Larry Coniff; the Department of Fisheries and Thor Tollefson, by attorney Earl R. McGimpsey; the Washington Reef Net Owners Association, by the Association of Northwest Steelheaders, Inc., the Washington State Sportsmen's Council, Inc., and an amicus curiae from the Idaho Fish and Game Department, each with representation. The team for the State of Washington was Attorney General Slade Gorton and Edward B. Mackie, deputy attorney general.

A transplanted Montanan, George Boldt moved to Seattle, where, on July 27, 1953, Pres. Dwight Eisenhower appointed him to the U.S. district court judgeship for western Washington.

5. Frank Allen, interview; Getches, interview.

6. Esther's minutes of the March 20, 1971, meeting.

7. Members of the STOWW Fishing Advisory Committee were Cal Peters, Squaxin; Forrest Kinley, Lummi; Guy McMinds, Quinault; Gene Parker, Makah; Dale Johnson, Lower Elwah; and Charlie Peterson, Makah.

8. Culturally close, the Upper Skagits and Sauk-Suiattles early on were treated as one people. At one time they had received government services. Whether they had received them individually or collectively was no longer clear. STOWW's Linda Dombrowski states that it is forgotten how tribes initially receiving services found themselves later cut off. She likened the situation to poverty programs: "[First we're] going to help everyone and the next decade we can't remember why." In 1913 the Upper Skagit–Sauk-Suiattles were given an appropriation to purchase a small acreage for their common use as a cemetery plot. Later they were treated as a nonrecognized tribe since they had not complied with the requirement to organize under the 1934 IRA and draft an approved constitution. In the meantime, their members formed two separate organizations. Before *United States v Washington*, each of the two asked for acknowledgement in order to obtain annual BIA services. Receiving such services meant the federal government at some time had acknowledged the tribe as having treaty rights. Their trust status regarding cemetery land also entitled them to services. The stumbling block was whether or not they were two entities or one. With far less bother than Esther incurred, the government accepted them as two entities, requiring each to provide a constitution. Although they were not acknowledged, Judge Boldt had no problem permitting them to join in the case since they were entitled to treaty rights and had petitioned for recognition. The Sauk-Suiattle would be acknowledged by the federal government on June 2, 1973, just before the trial began, and the Upper Skagit would be recognized before a decision in the trial was rendered.

9. By trial time the seven intervening tribes and their counsels were the Squaxins, Sauk-Suiattles, and Stillaguamish represented by Getches and Stennhauser; the Lummis by Alvin J. Ziontz; the Quinaults by Michael Taylor, the Yakamas by James B. Hovis; and the Upper Skagits by William Stiles. One might question inclusion in the case of the Yakamas, a nation

of fourteen bands and tribes from east of the Cascade Mountains. Although not party to treaties signed in western Washington, one band in that area, the Taitnapams, had fishing rights west of the Cascade Mountains on Puget Sound. Relations between them and the Yakamas were probably forged through Klickitat Indians who had connections with both.

10. *United States et al. v State of Washington et al.*, No. 9213 (hereafter *United States v Washington*, 9213), deposition of Esther Ross, June 28, 1973. Judge George H. Boldt Papers, Washington State Historical Society, Tacoma. On August 1, 1973, when Getches sent Esther a copy of the transcription of the deposition on which to make corrections, she wrote on it that she had been elected chair by a vote of fifteen members of a "general council quorum."

11. *Sohappy v Smith* (U.S. District Court of Oregon, 68-409); *United States v State of Oregon* (U.S. District Court of Oregon, 68-513); Hovis, interview.

12. *Tacoma (Wash.) News Tribune*, August 23 and 25, 1973.

13. Ibid., August 27, 29, 30 and 31, 1973; Hovis, interview; *United States v Washington*, 9213, transcript of proceedings, September 10, 1973.

14. Greene, interview, July 13, 1995.

15. *Tacoma (Wash.) News Tribune*, September 4 and 5, 1973.

16. Ibid., September 9, 1973.

17. Ibid., September 10 and 11, 1973.

18. Esther's testimony is in *United States v Washington*, 9213, transcript of proceedings, 2707–24.

19. *Tacoma (Wash.) News Tribune*, September 11, 1973.

20. Ibid., September 12, 1973.

21. Ibid., September 13, 15, and 18, 1973.

22. Getches, interview.

23. *Tacoma (Wash.) News Tribune*, September 19, 1975.

## CHAPTER 15

1. The tribe would petition Congress, July 5, 1974, to purchase two pieces of land in the Arlington area to be put in trust status. It would ask the government to release its judgment money to pay for it. This was unworkable since the government would not pay judgment money in a lump sum to a nonrecognized tribe. Furthermore, it would not recognize a tribe lacking ownership of a trust status land base.

2. Diary.

3. Ibid.

4. Esther to Rogers C. B. Morton, January 19 and January 30, 1974.

5. Reaction in the non-Indian fishing community to the Boldt decision was one of anger. The decision was appealed, but not until July 2, 1979, would the U.S. Supreme Court uphold the judge's decision. Then began Phase II of the *United States v Washington* fishing rights case. Legal Services attorney Alan Stay faulted Gov. Dixie Lee Ray (who became Washington's governor in 1977) for asserting that Indians wanted a large measure of control of the state's fishery. The Native American Solidarity Committee stated that the "state of Washington was clearly given the authority to manage the fishery with the warning that if they do not comply with *U.S. v Washington*, the District court may enlist the aid of federal law-enforcement agents to carry out the ruling. It was the widespread defiance of *U.S. v Washington* by the state that warranted the Supreme Court review." That body noted that the decision brought about "the most concerted official and private effort to frustrate a decree of federal court witnessed in this century." James Heckman, director of the Northwest Indian Fisheries Commission (NWIFC), stated that the Supreme Court ruling was all the tribes wanted, hoping it meant law enforcement and protection of the fish. Robert Johnson of STOWW called the decision a historic victory. Dale Johnson of the NWIFC said the ruling vindicated the Indians' cause and hoped that it would bring an end to "resistence, recalcitrance, and misunderstanding." *Northwest Indian News* (Seattle), August 1979, 5; Native American Solidarity Committee, *To Fish in Common*, 38, 39.

6. Alan Stay, interview by authors, September 17, 1995. Recognized tribes intervening in the Boldt case following its decision were the Lower Elwahs, the Port Gamble Klallams, the Suquamish, Swinomish, Nooksacks, and Tulalips.

7. Frank Allen, interview.

8. Frank's announcements appeared on March 3, 1974, in the *Bellingham (Wash.) Herald* and the *Portland Oregonian*. His retraction appeared in the *Seattle Times* on March 6, 1974.

9. At the meeting on March 12, 1974, tribal members adopted a set of rules governing Stillaguamish who would fish their river. It noted that fishing gear, locations, and seasons would be promulgated annually. Those fishing must have an identification card "when fishing off reservation." (Undoubtedly the ordinance was copied from some other tribe.) No person could operate more than one fishing location; set nets must be placed to cover no more than a third of the distance across the river channel; unattended gear must be conspicuously marked to identify the owner; those who fished to sell commercially must pay a royalty of five

cents per pound to the tribe; and penalties for any violation would be levied by the Stillaguamish tribal council. See Ordinance for Fishing, March 12, 1974. Since the Stillaguamish were not fishers, there was never an adjudicable violation, and there was never an annual publication of the gear, locations, or seasons for fishing.

10. Resolutions were usually dated but not numbered.
11. Frank Allen, interview.
12. Bernie Gobin, interview by authors, June 27, 1997.
13. Getches was in contact with Charles R. Carey, one of Esther's attorneys involved with the Gus Smith estate. Getches wrote Carey, March 22, 1974, saying that it would be more difficult to get the land into trust status were it to be transferred to the tribe before its federal acknowledgement as a tribe. Were the Department of the Interior to act quickly on the tribe's petition to become recognized, the Smith estate should be probated after recognition for the tribe.
14. Petition of the Stillaguamish Tribe of Indians, to the Secretary of the Interior for Acknowledgement of Recognition as an Indian Tribe, April 5, 1974.
15. Diary.
16. Getches, "Background Information," 2.
17. Janet L. Parks, chief of the tribal enrollment section, BIA, to Esther, July 23, 1974.
18. Getches to Scott Keep, attorney-adviser, Indian Affairs, BIA, July 8, 1974; Keep to Getches, July 25, 1974.
19. Getches summarized and explained the course of the request for recognition. Much information from his letters is used to document occurrences. Getches to Sen. Henry M. Jackson, April 29, 1975; Getches to Louis Striegel, office of solicitor for the Interior Department, October 30, 1974.
20. Getches to Striegel, October 30, 1974.
21. Lloyd Meeds to Esther, August 13, 1974. While in Washington, D.C., Esther spent some time on August 5, 1974, at the National Archives researching tribal history under her issued card 508-752.
22. Don Smouse, interview by authors, July 17, 1995. Magnuson was especially bothered because the Indian lobbying was adverse to the interests of one of Magnuson's non-Indian constituents.
23. During the Nixon administration much federal block grant money was returned to the states. One program in which Indians participated was the Comprehensive Employment and Training ACT (CETA), passed by Congress in late 1973. Administered by the Department of Labor, CETA was part of the Comprehensive Manpower Program. While OEO

was primarily an economic development program, CETA was a work program for unemployed, unskilled minorities and the poor. The program provided training for many jobs under titles such as librarian assistants, custodians, plumbers, etc. STOWW funneled CETA funds to western Washington Indians. It also handled funds for the Office of Native American Programs (ONAP), another federally funded program specifically targeting Indians. The Stillaguamish benefited immensely from CETA in that it alleviated their burden of trying to function as a tribe lacking salaried positions for office help. Esther began receiving CETA funds in 1974; she was thus getting funding from both entitlements, OEO and CETA.

24. Rod Sayegusa, interview by authors, August 3, 1995.

## CHAPTER 16

1. Attorneys provided by STOWW for western Washington tribes were Frank LaFontaine, Phillip Katzen, Michael Taylor, Alan Stay, Frank Roman, and Cynthia Davenport. In 1976 nine offices of Legal Services in western Washington would be consolidated within Evergreen Legal Services. Beginning in the early 1990s those offices would be further consolidated in three state offices in Seattle, Spokane, and Tacoma. With a more recent name change it is now Columbia Legal Services.
2. Frank Allen, interview; Stay, interview.
3. Ryser, interview, May 10 and 26, 1997.
4. Stay, interview.
5. Michael Taylor to David Getches, March 21, 1974.
6. Sayegusa, interview.
7. Sampsel, interview.
8. Gov. Daniel Evans to Rogers C. B. Morton, April 18, 1974.
9. Linda Bryant, interview by authors, October 28, 1995.
10. Getches to Louis Striegel, October 20, 1974.
11. Ibid.
12. Ibid.; Getches, interview.
13. Trimble, interview.
14. Gary I. Adkinson to Esther, December 14, 1974. The Lodi, California, *News-Sentinel* on September 4, 1945, reported that Reid had died the previous day in Lodi at age seventy-three, having lived there for ten years. According to the paper, he was a retired salesman for a book and stationery business. The same paper on April 7, 1962, reported the death two days earlier of Mary Jane Reid at ninety-five. Born on August 12, 1866, Mary Jane had come to the United States in 1912.

15. U.S. Department of the Interior, Office of Hearings and Appeals, Indian Probate, in the matter of the estate of Arnold Ross deceased (hereafter Estate of Arnold Ross), Transcript of Proceedings before Robert C. Snashall, January 24, 1975. Arnold's first will, made January 30, 1958, in Everett, was composed of two sentences: "I give, devise, and bequeath all of the rest and residue of my estate, real, personal and mixed, to: Esther Ross, my wife. In witness thereof, I Arnold Ross, have hereunto set my hand, sealed, published and declared this to be my Last Will and Testament, this 30th day of January, in the year of our Lord one thousand nine hundred and fifty-eight."

16. Getches to Franklin Ducheneaux, counsel, Subcommittee on Indian Affairs, April 21, 1975; Getches to Sen. Henry Jackson, April 29, 1975.

17. Esther to "Congressmen and Senators," April 20, 1975.

18. Fitchen, interview. Marion married again twice after her divorce from Ed Fichten. She first married a Dick Travis and then Dick Byrum.

## CHAPTER 17

1. Port Angeles, Wash., *Daily News*, June 2, 1975.

2. The effort to have PL 280 repealed had begun earlier in the year when the tribes held a nationwide meeting in Denver on February 24–26, 1975. The subject of the meeting was legislation to dispense with federal jurisdiction over reservations by states.

3. The 1953 act mandated that five states (only Oregon in the Pacific Northwest) assume jurisdiction over criminal and civil cases arising on reservations. With government consent, other states, given limited optional jurisdiction on reservations, could oblige and bind themselves to assume criminal and civil jurisdiction over reservation Indians. In 1963 Washington State enacted legislation to assume certain police powers; however, states lacked federal funding for services on nontaxable trust lands. States with multiple reservations faced potential challenges to the constitutionality of the law for its uneven application to all Indians. In 1968, with the withdrawal from the termination program an amendment to the law permitted retrocession of jurisdiction for mandatory and optional states.

4. Lozar, interview, March 15, 1994.

5. Frank Allen, interview, Port Angeles (Wash.) *Daily News*, June 8, 1975. Other discussion centered around the Snyder Act of 1921; the Indian Reorganization Act of 1934; and the Self-Determination and Education Assistance Act, signed into law that very year (1975). Port Angeles (Wash.) *Daily News*, June 3 and 5, 1975.

6. Port Angeles (Wash.) *Daily News*, June 8, 1975.

7. *Everett (Wash.) Herald*, June 6, 1975.
8. Frank Allen, interview.
9. Sampsel, interview.
10. Frank Allen, interview.
11. Catherine Herrold Troeh, "Homer Settler," photocopy of an essay in possession of the authors.
12. Sampsel, interview.
13. Bryant, interview.
14. Ibid.
15. *Everett (Wash.) Herald*, June 12, 1975; *Skagit Valley Herald*, June 12, 1975.
16. Bryant, interview.
17. *Everett (Wash.) Herald*, June 13 and 14, 1975; *Northwest Passage*, June 16–30, 1975.
18. *Skagit Valley Herald*, June 13, 1975.
19. KING TV, June 12, 1975, and KIRO-KRKO audio tape 13.
20. *Bicentennial Wagon Train Pilgrimage*, 21. Scarcely had the wagon train rolled out of sight than in her continuing zeal to collect newspaper clippings, Esther contacted Scott Keep in Washington, D.C., asking him to send her a newspaper account from the *Washington Star* of the train episode. On June 24, he sent her a three-paragraph clipping from the Saturday, June 14, edition of the *Star*, telling of Stillaguamish leaders (without specific mention of Esther) who "waylaid" the caravan, demanding federal recognition and encouraging other tribes to "dramatize" their grievances.
21. Bryant, interview.
22. Sampsel, interview. Caught up in the bicentennial fever, Esther toyed with the idea of writing a history of her people, going so far as to inquire if the Interior Department's Bicentennial Coordinator Office would fund the publication. Through that office she was informed on November 29, 1975, that the BIA granted money to promote Indian awareness. She failed to follow through.
23. *Tacoma (Wash.) News Tribune*, June 22, 1975.
24. By 1978, ONAP took on a name change, Administration for Native Americans (ANA).
25. David Allen, interview by authors, April 21, 1997.
26. *Arlington (Wash.) Times*, July 9, 1975.

## CHAPTER 18

1. For more information on the struggle for recognition waged by these tribes, see Kathleen L. Bishop and Kenneth C. Hansen, "The Landless Tribes of Western Washington," *American Indian Journal*, May 1978.

2. James "Jim" Heckman, interview by authors, December 12, 1995. Heckman remembered Secretary Rogers Morton's now-famous remark on hearing results of the Boldt decision in 1974 that Indians won 50 percent of harvestable salmon. "Let's appeal it," he said, his memory having lapsed that he was supposedly on the Indian-government side in the case. Heckman said that federal funds furnished legal support for Indians; yet the government also knew that Washington State received financial assistance in its fight to oppose Indian fishing. With the Boldt case completed, the government asked Heckman to go to Alaska to participate in Alaska Native land claims work. Instead, he walked across the street to offices of NWIFC, taking a position with that organization.

NWIFC was newly organized at that point. It was a rollover of the work commenced with STOWW in 1970 when the Boldt case was getting underway. It was not an easy rollover, for it was accomplished by a STOWW faction that wanted management of Indian fisheries out of STOWW and into a separate entity. The move was headed by Hank Adams with assistance from Forrest L. "Dutch" Kinley, a Lummi, and Charlie Peterson, a Makah. They had begun planning before the Boldt decision was rendered. With the decision, with the Indians assured an equal harvest of salmon with non-Indians, the renegades took some money from STOWW to form NWIFC. They received BIA funding and money from the State Departments of Fisheries and Game in a formula established by Senators Warren Magnuson and Henry Jackson. The commission was to serve in a co-management role with the state's Department of Fisheries. The commission was composed of five commissioners, one from each of the five treaty tribes of 1854–55. The original commissioners were Dutch Kinley, Lummi; Charlie Peterson, Makah; Guy McMinds, Quinault; Cal Peters, Squaxin; and Dennis Allen, Skokomish. The first executive director was Jim Heckman. Today there are eight commissioners, one from each of the eight main drainageways. There is a large administrative staff to support an executive director and deputy director. The NWIFC is noted for its quality of work.

3. Charles Trimble to Morris Thompson, July 22, 1975.

4. Minutes, August 25, 1975. The *Wide Load* was at this time now dry-docked at Frank and Esther's home on the Lummi.

5. Kent Frizzell to Charles Trimble, September 22, 1975. Lewis Bell of Everett, attorney for the Tulalips, in an October 22, 1974, letter had suggested to Secretary Morton that the Interior Department could not extend recognition to an Indian tribe, that only Congress had that authority. Bell further noted that Tulalips did not favor Stillaguamish recognition, alleging they were not a tribe, but only a social or fraternal group. The Tulalips

called for a "full hearing" on the matter since all tribes of the Point Elliott treaty belonged to the Tulalip pursuant to the IRA.

There was considerable flux and scrambling with personnel changes during the period following President Nixon's August 8, 1974, resignation. At President Ford's request, Morton had remained during the first seven months on Ford's term, leaving Interior in March 1975. Stanley Hathaway then held the office briefly before Thomas S. Kleppe became secretary.

6. *Stillaguamish v Kleppe*.

7. *Indian Voice*, December 1975.

8. Estate of Arnold Ross, Supplemental Hearing, September 14, 1975. Attorney Michael Fitch was concerned about Esther's meager income since Arnold had left her destitute. Her monthly income at this time was about a hundred dollars from the Veterans Administration and ninety-four dollars from STOWW. Attorneys MacDonald, Hoague, and Bayless, to attorney Michael F. Fitch, September 11, 1975.

9. On October 3, 1975, Fitch sent a two-page letter to Esther preparing her for an adverse decision in the fight over the will. In the letter he included Dr. Watts's statement for time spent on the stand in September. Fitch also wanted Esther to know that he had been reviewing Indian law and that although some evidence had been put forth showing Arnold as having been incompetent at times, it was of no importance because "all Arnold had to know at the time he made the will was generally what property he owned, and who was close to him that he wanted to leave property to." Fitch continued, "Even if we show that Arnold acted incompetent at other times, we must have proof he was incompetent on the day he wrote the will in order to win." The judge had to make only one decision as to the validity of the will, Fitch said, and he suggested that, since it appeared the judge would rule the will valid, a settlement should be made out of court for a fifty-fifty split of the house and property or "risk ... losing everything if the judge upholds the will." Esther did not follow Fitch's suggestion to settle out of court. Fitch to Esther, October 3, 1975.

10. Estate of Arnold Ross, Supplemental Hearing, December 11, 1975.

11. Ibid.

12. Trimble, interview. The secretary of the interior scheduled an appearance for the mid-January NCAI meeting to discuss Congress's resolution for Stillaguamish recognition, but he failed to attend the meeting. *Indian Voice*, February 1976.

13. Ortez, interview, September 15, 1994; Kidder, interview. Frank remembered that his mother would much rather speak to politicians than write them. He remembered her telling him, "You can't get anything from writing, you gotta go and get it in person."

14. Malcolm McLeod, interview by authors, July 12, 1995.

15. Ken Hansen, interview by authors, May 26, 1995.

16. William Murdoch, interviews by authors, November 14, 1995, and May 10, 1996. The responsibility for the health care of Indians and Alaska Natives was transferred over from the Department of Interior to the U.S. Public Health Service, Department of Health, Education, and Welfare by an act of Congress in August 1954. By agreement between the Department of the Interior and the surgeon general, actual assumption of Indian health care took place on July 1, 1955. A subdivision was established within Health, Education, and Welfare to carry out the health care function. From then on that office was known as the Division of Indian Health. The U.S. Public Health Service was, and is, staffed by civil service (civilian) employees and also by commissioned officers in the U.S. Public Health Service. The commissioned officer grades are similar to commissioned grades in the U.S. Coast Guard and the U.S. Navy.

17. Estate of Arnold Ross, Order Approving Will and Decree of Distribution, February 13, 1976; Fitch to Esther, February 20, 1976.

18. The Tulalips cited the establishment of the Tulalip Reservation for Snohomish, Snoqualmie, Skykomish, and Stillaguamish tribes as successor to those party to the Point Elliot treaty and held themselves successor to all treaty rights, title, and interest of the Stillaguamish tribe and its individual members. The Tulalips cited Judge Boldt's affirmation that the Stillaguamish were "not recognized as organized tribes by the Federal Government . . . and that recognition of a tribe as a party to a treaty is a federal question in which state authorities and federal courts must follow the determination by the legislative or executive branch of the Federal Government."

19. *Stillaguamish v Kleppe*, Motion to Intervene as a Party Defendant; *Stillaguamish v Kleppe*, Memorandum of Points and Authorities in Opposition to Motion to Intervene.

## CHAPTER 19

1. *Everett (Wash.) Herald*, March 8, 1976.

2. *Washington Star*, March 6, 1976.

3. Morris Thompson, interview by authors, October 3, 1995; Scott Keep, interview by authors, September 6, 1995; *Indian Voice*, March 1976.

4. Frank Allen, interview.

5. LaDonna Harris, interview by authors, February 16, 1996.

6. Getches, interview; Getches to Wayne Chattin, April 6, 1976. Anthropologist Barbara Lane and others would give their depositions after Esther's visit to Boulder.

7. Getches, interview.
8. Thomas Kleppe to Esther, April 20, 1976.

## CHAPTER 20

1. Esther to Leo LaClair and Gary Johnson, May 3, 1976. Esther wrote Leo LaClair, May 12, 1976, that she was firing biologist Ron Constello.
2. Esther to STOWW, May 20, 1976.
3. Esther to Thomas Kleppe, June 22, 1976.
4. Esther to Festival of American Folklife Committee, July 21, 1976.
5. *Stillaguamish v Kleppe*, Amicus Brief. The 1974 version of the Stillaguamish Constitution was not an approved version.
6. As the case developed, it appeared that the principal issues were (1) whether the secretary's actions (or inaction) in effectively denying the Stillaguamish their status as a federally recognized tribe could withstand judicial scrutiny under the Administrative Procedure Act and (2) whether the secretary could make the decision needed to recognize Indian tribes.
7. Getches, interview.
8. Sampsel, interview.
9. Getches, interview.
10. Ibid.
11. *Stillaguamish v Kleppe*, Memorandum Order, September 24, 1976.
12. Kent Frizzell to David Getches, October 27, 1976. In reading that section of the Indian Reorganization Act (25 U.S.C. S 479), the acting secretary opined "that the benefits of the IRA are available to individual Indians of one-half or more Indian blood whether or not the tribe was administratively recognized as of the date of the act." Consequently, tribal members of that quantum would have to form a separate organization, requesting the Department of the Interior to take the land in trust for them, thus excluding others of the tribe, were such to happen.
13. Getches to Trimble, November 12, 1976.
14. From an unidentified and undated clipping in Esther's files.
15. Diary. Though Esther did not mention it here, she could not have forgotten how, when she and Arnold had custody of Margaret's four children, Margaret had not always released the children's funds from the Yakama agency for their care without threats from the welfare department.
16. Estate of Arnold Ross, Notice of Appeal, June 11, 1976, and Certification of Service, August 12, 1976.
17. Diary.
18. Dombrowski, interview, March 23, 1995. Sampsel, interview; Black, interview, July 11, 1995; McLeod, interview, July 12, 1995.

## CHAPTER 21

1. Steven Lozar to Esther, November 29, 1976.
2. Getches, interview.
3. Trimble, interview. The March 3, 1976, edition of the *Seattle Times* chronicled John Silva's passing on February 28, 1976, at age sixty-seven. Linda Bryant also covered it in the March 4 edition of the *Everett Herald*. Silva was buried in the Anderson Cemetery south of Stanwood. He had wished to be buried on his ancestral grounds in the Arlington-Oso area, but these had not been returned to the tribe.
4. Byrum, interview.
5. In a letter to Rudy Ryser six days after the dinner, Esther ruminated on the Indian head represented on the "buffalo nickel." She thought it was time for the government to issue a new fifty-cent piece, with that chief's head on one side and the American eagle on the obverse.
6. Getches to Esther, December 7, 1976. Esther, Frank, Rod Sayegusa, and others had presented Getches with a blanket in honor of his work on the tribe's behalf.
7. John W. Bush, acting superintendent, to Esther, November 23, 1976; Skip Skanen, executive director, ATNI, to Esther, November 26, 1976.
8. Estate of Arnold Ross, Appeal from an Order Denying Petition for Reopening. Affirmed and Dismissed, December 21, 1976.

## CHAPTER 22

1. Gregory Austin, BIA solicitor, to David Getches, January 14, 1977. When William A. Gershuny, acting associate solicitor in the Division of Indian Affairs, received a copy of the November 1, 1976, *Everett Herald* with a story that the tribe had been recognized, he wrote reporter Wayne Kruse. Two introductory paragraphs stated his belief that the article was inaccurate in concluding that the acting secretary's October 27 letter to Getches meant that the tribe was being "recognized" by the letter. Gershuny wrote, "The Stillaguamish Tribe and I would like to clarify this point." The remaining three paragraphs of his letter contained the same wording as Austin's letter. William A. Gershuny to Wayne Kruse. Kruse sent a copy of the letter to the Everett agency. That letter and Gregory H. Austin's to Getches carried identical messages. Gershuny himself sent virtually the same letter to Robert Johnson, editor of STOWW's *Indian Voice*. Johnson sent a copy of the letter on January 28, 1977, to Alan Stay, Thomas Schlosser, Rudy Ryser, and Frank Wright, adding "We should all study the attached letter which is a word game . . . re the Stillaguamish Recognition. I think we should lean on those guys in the *Indian Voice* . . . and in other media outlets."

The identical message from various individuals in the Interior Department was this: Kent Frizzell's letter of October 27, 1976, did not extend "federal recognition" to the Stillaguamish tribe as that phrase had frequently been used in the past. What the letter did do was to make a determination that the Stillaguamish tribe was entitled to exercise treaty fishing rights and that therefore the department had a trust responsibility with respect to the protection of those rights. The letter also concluded that the Stillaguamish tribe was "recognized as eligible" for federal Indian services under the Indian Financing and the Indian Self-Determination and Education Assistance Acts *based on our interpretation of those acts*. The specific implications of that determination under existing statutory law were also discussed.

The term "recognition" as applied to Indian tribes has never been adequately defined in a legal sense. What that term means at this time in history is open to speculation. In more recent years, it has often been used to mean that a group of Indians was eligible for the full range of Bureau of Indian Affairs services in the broadest sense of the word "services."

2. In September 1977, Esther would receive a letter from Jessie Carney Smith, librarian at Fisk University in Nashville, Tennessee, advising her she'd been chosen for inclusion in a forthcoming publication, *Directory of Significant Twentieth Century American Minority Women*. The volume would profile a thousand black, Indian, Hispanic, and Asian-American women of achievement. Smith asked Esther to write a brief biographical sketch of herself, expressing her views on her area of interest. There was an October 10 deadline. Esther did not respond to the invitation. The publication scheduled for the next year did not materialize.

3. At this time, the Seattle Indian Health Board Clinic served urban Indians. By contrast, those on reservations were served by Indian Health Service physicians.

4. Medical records of Esther Ross, St. Luke's General Hospital, Bellingham, Wash., February 15, 1977. Hereafter Medical records, St. Luke's. Today the facility is known as St. Joseph Hospital.

5. Ibid.; Frank Allen, interview.

6. Swenson, interview, January 3, 1996.

7. "Stillaguamish Futures: Plan for Restoration, Phase I," June 6, 1977.

8. Peter Three Stars, interview by authors, February 27, 1994.

9. Frank Allen, interview.

10. Greene, interview, May 20 and July 13, 1995. Despite legal reverses, the Samish finally received federal recognition in 1995.

11. Greene, interview, July 13, 1995.

12. Ibid.; Cecelia Myrick, interview by authors, November 11, 1995.

13. Greene, interview, May 20, 1995.

14. Medical Records, Esther Ross, Lummi Medical Clinic, Bellingham, Washington (hereafter Medical Records, Lummi Clinic), August 19, 1977.
15. Cynthia Davenport to Esther, August 25 and September 14, 1977.
16. Frank Allen, interview.
17. Ibid.
18. Ibid.
19. Diary.
20. Valda Orr, interview by authors, August 21, 1995; minutes, November 7, 1977.
21. Dixie Lee Ray to Esther, January 17, 1978; *Everett (Wash.) Herald*, November 1977.

## CHAPTER 23

1. Resolutions 32-78 and 29-78, January 16, 1978.
2. Resolutions 33-78 and 34-78, January 16, 1978.
3. Resolution 39-78, January 30, 1978. On May 1, 1978, at a regular meeting the tribe passed a resolution to use a different numbering system for their resolutions to conform to that of other BIA agencies. This resolution was 1978-1.
4. Frank Allen, interview; Greene, interview, July 13, 1995.
5. Peter Three Stars to Llewellyn Goodridge, January 30, 1978.
6. Three Stars to Goodridge, February 6, 1978.
7. Orr, interview.
8. Myrick, interview.
9. Frank Allen, interview. Esther's extra-tribal support systems were beginning to wane. She sought aid from Native American Rights Fund officials in trimming the tribal enrollments. Jeanne S. Whiteing of NARF responded, advising Esther that NARF had a policy of noninvolvement in intratribal conflicts. Whiteing to Esther, February 16, 1978.
10. Fitchen, interview.
11. Notes made by Winifred Blodgett, National Resources Branch, Western Washington Agency, February 22, 1978; Esther to Peter Three Stars, February 21, 1978.
12. Esther to Three Stars, February 21, 1978.
13. Winifred Blodgett, notes, February 22, 1978. Taking notes of her conversations with Esther and Frank in the agency office, Blodgett wrote that Frank had told her that if Three Stars did not give Esther back her power, she (Esther) and Frank would "begin an active campaign to have him removed." As for the check Esther had written herself for a September 1977 invoice, and which the tribe wanted returned, Blodgett told her to give it to either Bill Black or James Sovak, Jr., of the agency's tribal

operations, and were they not in the office, to return it to her. Since Black was there, he received the check.

14. The articulate Rudy Ryser played a major role in the Nashville meeting. And it was he and others who, at Esther's request, provided funds for her and David to pay for their room and board in Nashville and for their return trip home. The one performer Esther wanted to see in Nashville was Minnie Pearl. Pearl was not performing at the time so Esther and David went to a Johnny Cash concert.

15. Shirley Saulnier to Llewellyn Goodridge, March 20, 1978; minutes, April 21, 1978.

16. Frank Allen, interview.

## CHAPTER 24

1. Memorandum of Stillaguamish Tribal Council, May 26, 1978.

2. Resolution 78-3, April 21, 1978.

3. Resolution 78-17, July 17, 1978.

4. "Resolution 1," August 24, 1978. The ATNI meeting was held from August 22 through 25.

5. Peter Three Stars to Esther, September 15, 1978.

6. Resolutions 78-13 and 78-14, June 16, 1978; 78-18, July 17, 1978; 78-19, 78-21, 78-25, and 78-22, July 25, 1978; 78-17, July 17, 1978; and 78-24, July 25, 1978.

7. Being out of money was a common enough occurrence for Esther. However, there were occasions when she amazed her family by pulling a rabbit from a hat. She once pulled a hundred-dollar bill from the inside of her blouse early one morning in Bellingham when her family needed breakfast and could pool no more than a dollar among them.

8. Sovak also responded to Esther's charge in her November letter to Gerard that "the present bookkeeper [Miriam Levin] . . . has a criminal history of grand theft and is presently on probation." The Bureau of Indian Affairs was aware of the situation and was following it closely, Sovak said. Levin had pleaded guilty, February 7, 1974, to grand larceny by embezzlement from her place of employment at that time and to forgery in the first degree. She was sentenced on October 3, 1974. *State of Washington v Miriam Levin*, No. 8465.

9. Three Stars to Esther, March 3, 1979.

10. M. E. Seneca, Jr., acting deputy commissioner, BIA, to Esther, May 4, 1979.

11. Ibid.

## CHAPTER 25

1. David P. Weston to Leo LaClair, May 24, 1974.

2. Esther to David Getches and Barbara Lane, January 2, 1974.

3. Resolutions 79-45, 79-50, 79-55, 79-52, 79-51, 79-47, 79-58, 79-47 and 79-57, August 23, 1979.

4. *Stillaguamish Tribe v Frank Allen, Esther Ross, and David Allen*, No. 79-CA-167; Esther to Three Stars, August 17, 1979.

5. A final draft of the new constitution to meet the tribe's and BIA requirements was finally adopted by the Stillaguamish on June 18, 1986. The BIA approved it on August 28. Under the 1986 constitution the tribal chair and other officers are elected annually from the six-person board of directors (the council) for three-year terms. A quorum of four is required to consider and act upon tribal business. There is no provision for an audit committee of tribal membership; however, the treasurer's books and records are audited annually by an outside auditor. The Indian blood quantum qualification for membership was not changed from the 1953 constitution. Compared with that document, the new one contains several sophisticated measures and checks and balances.

6. *Indian Voice*, November 1979. Charlie had specified an Indian Shaker funeral, which was "quite ceremonial," he told attorney Cynthia Davenport. "The Indians would gather at the person's house and ring bells and light candles before they went to the Cemetery." Cynthia Davenport to Esther, January 11, 1979.

7. Steven Lozar to the Chair of the Stillaguamish Tribe, November 1, 1979. Frank threatened to sue Lozar for his failure to acquire an Indian burial ground for the tribe.

8. Peter Three Stars to the council, November 9, 1979. As of July 11, 1979, the Western Washington Agency was divided into the two agencies—Everett became the Puget Sound Agency and the Olympic Peninsula Agency was headquartered at Hoquiam. Three Stars was now superintendent of the Puget Sound Agency.

9. Llewellyn Goodridge to Three Stars, January 24 and February 4, 1980; Three Stars to Goodridge, February 14, 1980.

10. Three Stars to the council, May 21, 1980.

11. Stillaguamish Indian Tribe Election Ordinance, 1980. The election committee included Dolly Brasfield, Jerry Martin, Gail Abel, Ralph Smith, and LaVaun Tatro. They were called to attend a council meeting on August 15, 1980. Lew Goodridge to "Dear Member," n.d.

12. Notes in longhand, signed "GG," August 12, 1980.

13. Three Stars to Esther, August 20, 1980.

14. Esther Ross and Frank Allen to Three Stars, August 22, 1980. In fact, Valda Orr said Esther was treated "as a joke." Valda Orr Elixman, interview by authors, August 21, 1995.

NOTES TO PAGES 222–27

15. Three Stars to Esther, September 26, 1980.

16. Three Stars to the council, September 11, 1980.

17. Esther to Three Stars, September 22, 1980; Three Stars to Esther, September 26, 1980.

18. Goodridge responded to Esther's request to attend the NCAI meeting in Spokane by calling for a 10 a.m. October 15 meeting to choose a tribal delegate. However, no record shows the meeting was held, and Esther's request was not granted.

19. Note dated, September 24, 1980, in longhand on memorandum from Patricia Rudd to the superintendent, dated September 23, 1980. Presumably the superintendent made a note on the memorandum and returned it to Rudd. It is initialed but the initials are not legible.

20. Hans Walker, Jr., Interior Department, to the BIA, October 1, 1980.

21. Patricia A. James to Frank Allen, May 7, 1980.

22. Eugene Crawford to Esther, September 11, 1980.

## CHAPTER 26

1. The Boldt decision, February 12, 1974, settled the conflict between net-fishing Indians and sportfishers by mandating a fifty-fifty division of annual harvests. With Phase I implementing the Boldt decision for the Indians, there began intertribal conflicts over fishing sites. Boldt specified that tribes had to fish in their aboriginal usual and accustomed places and not outside them unless invited there by other tribes to fish in these host territories. Tribes under the Point Elliott treaty were assigned to one of four reservations: Tulalip, Lummi, Swinomish, and Suquamish (also referred to as Fort Kitsap and Port Madison). Portions of these tribes such as the Upper Skagits, Stillaguamish, Snohomish, and Snoqualmies, were assigned to the Tulalip, but did not go. In the meantime, individuals within these tribes, particularly the Stillaguamish, were becoming dispersed, dispossessed, and amalgamated within the surrounding Euro-American culture. The Tulalips claimed fishing areas of tribes like the Stillaguamish that had been dispossessed by the Point Elliott treaty and assigned to the Tulalip Reservation. With resurgence of tribal affiliations a century following the treaty, these dispossessed tribes could once again claim their own fishing territories. The Stillaguamish and other tribes strove for recognition apart from the Tulalips, believing their fishing areas belonged to themselves. Because of this, Lummis and Tulalips opposed recognition of the "maverick" tribes. Thus it was that Phase I of the Boldt implementation led to intertribal turf wars.

The Stillaguamish claimed the Stillaguamish River and saltwater fishing in the dome of Port Susan. While the tribe waited in limbo between the Boldt decision affirming their treaty rights to fish and the time they received recognition in October 1976, they had no financial means nor governmental assistance to establish a fishing program. They intended to shut the Tulalips out of Port Susan. During this time the State Department of Game, vigilant on behalf of steelhead fishing, kept tabs on the tribes. With the Stillaguamish seeking to claim upper Port Susan, attorney Alan Stay contacted anthropologist Barbara Lane, who affirmed the tribe's rights, as in aboriginal times, to fish the salt waters of Port Susan. In response to communications sent by Esther, Stay advised Michael D. Shockman, executive director of the Department of Game in Olympia, that Stillaguamish did have fishing rights not only in their river but in Port Susan north of a line drawn west from Kayak Point (at McKee's Beach ten miles south of Stanwood) to Camano Island. (Stay to Shockman, December 30, 1974.) That same day, Stay also wrote Esther that her Stillaguamish were justified in fishing in northern portions of Port Susan.

Tribes were in and out of the U.S. District Court for Western Washington in Tacoma, trying to settle their differences in these fishing matters. (Civil Case No. 9213) In 1978 attorney Cynthia Davenport filed a lawsuit for the Stillaguamish, seeking to extend their usual and accustomed fishing places to include *all* of Port Susan. (Davenport to Mack J. T. Barnette, June 5, 1978) It was "unconscionable," David Getches observed, for larger tribes "to muscle out small tribes like Stillaguamish." Judge Boldt had made it "crystal clear the Tulalip Tribe's objection to Stillaguamish fishing . . . [was] totally unfounded," Getches said. (Getches to Rod Sayegusa, April 6, 1976)

On May 1, 1979, Cynthia Davenport sent a memorandum to the tribe:

> You will notice that the pleadings request the Tribe's usual and accustomed fishing grounds be extended into all of Port Susan, not just the northern portion. I felt that since [Barbara Lane's] anthropological evidence shows there were Stillaguamish villages on Port Susan, with no mention that the Tribe limited its fishing to the northern portion of that body of water, there was no reason why the Tribe should not include all of Port Susan in its request. This will also allow the tribe to have a fallback position of extending only into northern Port Susan if the other Tribes in the area strenuously object or if it appears the Court will not give you all that you have asked for.

I urge you to make every effort to come to some agreement regarding joint management of lower Skagit Bay and Port Susan with the appropriate tribes. I cannot stress too strongly the importance of reaching such an agreement as quickly as possible. It will minimize any intertribal conflict being aired in open court and will facilitate a favorable decision for the Tribe. If I can be of any help in obtaining such an agreement, please let me know.

The Stillaguamish faced opposition to their Port Susan fishing from other quarters—namely, the Sauk-Suiattles and Upper Skagits. On June 1, 1979, Stay, Davenport, and Russell W. Busch, all involved in the Native American Project of Evergreen Legal Services, sent a letter to the Sauk-Suiattles, Skagits, and Stillaguamish stating that since they (these three attorneys) represented each of the three tribes there was a potential conflict of interest; they would have to withdraw since they could not represent parties on both sides of a dispute. They advised the three tribes to get together to discuss the issue, suggesting that accommodation and compromise among the tribes would be the ideal way of resolving disputes concerning Port Susan fishing. The three attorneys wrote again in March 18, 1980, that since there appeared to be coordination among the tribes, they would like to schedule a meeting with all concerned. This did resolve the problem among the smaller tribes but not that between the Stillaguamish and the Tulalips, who had fishing rights in lower Port Susan that kept the Stillaguamish from fishing below the line from Kayak Point to Camano Island. Still wanting fishing rights in upper Port Susan as well, Tulalip fisheries officials began negotiations with Stillaguamish fisheries manager Lew Goodridge. The result led to an agreement between the two tribes by which the Tulalips would offer their expertise to the Stillaguamish in exchange for fishing rights in upper Port Susan and a small percentage of the Tulalip salmon catch. Esther criticized this arrangement, saying that it gave an unfair advantage to the Tulalips with their superior expertise and equipment and that the percentage of salmon allowed the Stillaguamish was unjustly small. She accused Goodridge of selling out to the Tulalips. At this point, however, Esther was criticizing everything the tribe did, and Goodridge's agreement with the Tulalip was an easy mark for complaint. It would be some dozen years before the Stillaguamish would have a workable fishing program of their own.

2. Bennett, interview; notes made by Winifred Blodgett at the agency, February 22, 1978.

3. Frank Allen, interview; Smouse, interview.

4. Black, interview, July 11, 1995.

5. Michael "Mike" Grayum, interview by authors, December 11, 1995, and February 20, 1996.

6. Bennett, interview.

7. Diary.

8. Marion had a week to answer her summons of May 29 to appear in court in Seattle on June 5. An attorney she contacted demanded seven hundred dollars up front before even talking with her.

9. The Last Will and Testament of Esther Ross. On leaving her office as chair, Esther continued refusing to release her papers to the tribe, while trying to place them in some academic depository. On her behalf, David Getches, professor at the University of Colorado Law School, wrote a December 11, 1979, letter to the National Archives in Washington, D.C. These archives referred him to branch archives at the Sand Point Naval Station outside Seattle. The D.C. facility did not want the papers unless they were catalogued and indexed. After Eugene Crawford of the National Indian Lutheran Board refused Esther's request for funds to sort and index the papers, they were offered to the Center for Pacific Northwest Studies at Western Washington University in Bellingham, but when Esther learned the university would not keep and store clipped newspaper articles, she withdrew her offer. The agency superintendent sought to satisfy the tribe's wish for the papers by permitting it to photocopy those documents it wanted. On a Canon copier STOWW had loaned Esther for her work at the Lummi house, Ardelle Preston copied the papers the tribe specified.

10. *Margaret Ross Baker v Esther Ross*, et al., No. 81-CA-593, Judgment Order, July 28, 1981.

11. McCloud, interview.

12. Medical records, Lummi Clinic, April 13, 1982.

13. *Bellingham (Wash.) Herald*, May 29, 1982.

14. Arriving first in Oregon, Allen took up a land claim at Hillsboro outside Portland. He then went south to Sutter's Mill near Sacramento, seeking gold. On returning to Hillsboro with $140,000 in gold dust and nuggets, he discovered that a squatter had taken his land. Then in 1883 he went north to take up 160 acres in Marietta. Since that place was at the mouth of the Nooksack River on Bellingham Bay, it became a station for boats plying the river upstream to communities like Ferndale. Unable to shake the gold fever, he moved farther north into Canadian goldfields. On returning from them by boat, he was accompanied by the lower Thompson River Spuzzum band Indian chief, the chief's wife, and his daughter Mary. The chief and his wife drowned in a boating accident and

Solomon lost the gold he had mined. The union he entered with the chief's daughter Mary at Yale, British Columbia, was solemnized on his return to American territory by Rev. Jean Baptiste Brouillet. One of their fifteen children was Walter Allen's father, Fred. In 1882 Solomon changed the name of the town from Lummi to Marietta.

15. Frank also asked the NILB for money to erect a monument to Solomon Allen at Marietta. The board turned down that request. He next visited Jacob E. Thomas of the State Historical Preservation Office to try to get Marietta listed on the National Register as a historical site. Office documentation by Jacob E. Thomas of a visit by Superintendent Three Stars and Frank, November 11, 1982.

16. By December 28, 1969, the $48,570 claims award had accrued to $139,222.26. After paying attorneys fees of 10 percent, or $13,922.23, and the BIA $12,366.53 for a May 1981 overexpenditure on its fisheries program, the tribe received an initial allotment of about $70,000. With that money it purchased 3.5 acres adjacent to the existing twenty acres it already owned.

## CHAPTER 27

1. Madge Slaughter was the granddaughter of Lt. William A. Slaughter, killed by Indians in the 1855 Puget Sound War.
2. Bill Black to Frank Allen, September 8, 1984.
3. Heckman, interview.
4. Esther to Mike Grayum, December 11, 1984.
5. Esther's fear of Catholicism had left her with misgivings in the fall of 1983 when the United States Congress approved legislation to repeal an 1867 law prohibiting expenditures of federal funds for a diplomatic mission at the Vatican. She expressed her concern to Sen. Daniel Evans. He responded on March 15, 1984, attempting to calm her fears by assuring her no threat was posed to the United States and its Constitution.
6. Medical records, Lummi Clinic.
7. Ibid.
8. Ibid.
9. Ibid.
10. Ibid.; medical records, Sehome Park Care Center.
11. Frank bargained for the Oldsmobile with Jesse James Auto Sales in Tukwila, Washington.
12. Medical records, Sehome Park Care Center.
13. **Guardianship of Esther Ross, An alleged incompetent/disabled person**, No. 88 4 00216 2, Guardian Petition July 19, 1988; Motion and

Order Appointing Guardian *ad litem*, July 22, 1988 (hereafter Guardianship of Esther Ross); Medical records, Sehome Park Care Center.

14. Guardianship of Esther Ross, Note for Hearing on Guardianship Petition, July 26, 1988.

15. Frank Allen, interview.

16. Sandra, then a fourteen-year-old student at the Bakerview Adventist School, raised $1,057.65 in a basketball shoot-out for the Easter Seal Society, having shot fifty-four baskets in three minute. Frank was among the top fund-raising coordinators in the 1986 Washington State Shoot-Out. Sandra's grand prize award was a trip for three to Disneyland. Frank's was tickets to a Seattle SuperSonic game and overnight accommodations at Seattle's Sheraton Hotel. Both he and Sandra were honored guests at a banquet hosted by Seattle SuperSonic Al Wood, honorary chairman of the event. More than 185 students in the state raised eleven thousand dollars for the Easter Seal Society that year.

17. Doug Venn, interview by authors, February 27, 1997.

18. Getches to Frank Allen, August 4, 1988, and September 29, 1993.

19. Susan Shown Harjo to Frank Allen, August 5, 1988.

## CHAPTER 28

1. Gobin, interview, February 28, 1997.
2. Bryant, interview.
3. McLeod, interview, July 12, 1995.
4. *Bellingham (Wash.) Herald*, December 23, 1991.
5. Frank complained that some of his own family members were refused enrollment. Tribal chair Gail Greger, who followed her father, Llewellyn Goodridge, and Marie MacCurdy, leader of the Stillaguamish, held that as a sovereign group the tribe could enroll non-Indians. "There is no blood limit for Stillaguamish membership," said Greger in 1994. Gail Greger, interview by authors, July 19, 1994. The constitution, however, required a one-sixteenth blood quantum for membership. Goodridge resigned as fisheries manager on September 30, 1988, two months after Esther's death.
6. *Bellingham (Wash.) Herald*, July 28, 1990; Frank Allen, interview. In 1980 Frank had wanted to give up his Stillaguamish tribal membership, and he applied for membership in the Lummi tribe. On June 13, 1980, attorney Howard L. Graham of Evergreen Legal Services wrote Frank that the Lummi Indian Business Council had rejected his application for enrollment in the Lummi tribe. Note that Frank was only one-eighth Stil-

laguamish. He himself would not have qualified for enrollment in the "Lower Stillaguamish Indian Nation."

7. Getches to Frank Allen, January 28, 1991.

8. Linda Dombrowski in an interview with the authors reported on Greger's remarks to NCAI delegates. Dombrowski, interview, March 23, 1995. *Bellingham (Wash.) Herald*, December 23, 1991.

9. *Seattle Post-Intelligencer*, January 15, 1992; *Bellingham (Wash.) Herald*, December 23, 1991.

10. Smouse, interview; Patricia "Pat" Rudd, interview by authors, November 7, 1995.

11. Black, interview, July 11, 1995.

12. Greene, interview, July 13, 1995.

# BIBLIOGRAPHY

Because Esther Ross may be termed a contemporary, there is abundant information about her from numerous individuals, including those in both the public and the private sector. Yet Esther herself provides much information. The Esther Ross Papers at the Eastern Washington State Historical Society in Spokane comprise an amazing number of letters, notes, reports, clippings, and a variety of documents and general family and work memorabilia collected over her lifetime. Included in this array is her loosely assembled diary; entries made at odd times on undated pieces of paper give glimpses into her thoughts and provide memories of events. There also are records of abundant interviews and conversations with the one nearest her—her son, Frank Allen. With a keen memory Frank recalls major and minute incidents in his mother's career. Though Frank is unable to read or write, official records confirm his remarkable memory. Our conversations with Frank Allen took place over seven years in some eighty-six interviews, some lasting days at a time, others in lengthy telephone calls. It is from Esther's papers, from Frank's memories, and from some one hundred other sources, including interviews with those who knew and worked with Esther Ross, that we have traced her life story. All unpublished documents cited here are in the Esther Ross Papers unless otherwise indicated. The assorted articles, letters, and "court records" of Herbert Holdridge are also in the Esther Ross Papers, placed there through the courtesy of Lisa Seymour of the Northeastern Nevada Historical Society, Elko.

## GOVERNMENT DOCUMENTS

### Federal Government

Indian Financing Act, 25 U.S.C. S 1451 et seq.

Indian Reorganization Act of 1934 (Wheeler-Howard Act). Public Law 383, Chap 576.

Indian Self-Determination and Education Assistance Act of 1975. Public Law 93-638, 25 U.S.C. S 450b.

Johnson-O'Malley Act, 25 U.S.C. S 452 et seq.

Limits of State Jurisdiction over Reservation Indians. Public Law 280 Act of August 15, 1953, 67 Stat 588. Revisions August 24, 1954, Chap 910 68 Stat 795 Sec 1; August 8, 1958 Public law 85-615, Sec 1, 72 Stat 545; November 25, 1970 Public Law 91-253 Secs 1 and 2, 84 Stat 1358.

Roblin, Charles E. Schedule of Unenrolled Indians, Stillaguamish Tribe, January 1, 1919.

Snyder Act of 1921, 25 U.S.C. S 13.

*Duwamish et al. v United States*, 3 Stat 886. U.S. Court of Claims, March 5, 1934, to November 4, 1934, Vol. 79, CtCls, 530–613.

*Sohappy v Smith*, No. 68-409. U.S. District Court for District of Oregon.

*Stillaguamish Tribe of Indians v Thomas S. Kleppe et al.,* Civil No. 75-1718. U.S. District Court for District of Columbia.

*Stillaguamish Tribe of Indians v Unites States*, No. 207, 15 Indian Claims Commission, 1.

*Stillaguamish Tribe of Indians v Unites States*, No. 207, 22 Indian Claims Commission, 361.

*Tulee v Washington* 315 U.S. 681.

*United States v State of Oregon*, No. 68-513, U.S. District Court for District of Oregon.

*United States v State of Washington* 384 F Supp 312.

*United States v State of Washington* 520 F 2d 676, 9th Circuit, 1975.

*United States et al. v State of Washington et al.*, No. 9213. U.S. District Court for District of Western Washington, Tacoma. In the Judge George H. Boldt Papers, Washington State Historical Society, Tacoma.

*Unites States v Winans* 198 U.S. 371.

U.S. Department of Interior, Office of Hearings and Appeals, Indian Probate. In the Matter of the Estate of Arnold Ross, Deceased, No. 130-5768. Western Washington Indian Agency, Probate No. IP PO 148L 75-52.

### State Government

Guardianship of Esther Ross, an alleged incompetent/disabled person, No. 88-4-00216-2. Superior Court, Whatcom County.

*State of Washington v Miriam Levin*, No. 8465. Superior Court, Whatcom County.
*State of Washington v Robert Satiacum* 50 Wn 2d 513, 314 P 2d 400.
*State of Washington, Department of Game v Puyallup Tribe* 70 Wn 2d 245, 422 P 2d 754.

### Tribal Government

*Margaret Ross Baker v Esther Ross et al.*, No. 81-CA-593, Judgment Order, July 28, 1981. In the Lummi Tribal Court for the Lummi Indian Reservation, State of Washington.
*Stillaguamish Tribe v Frank Allen, Esther Ross, and David Allen*, No. 79-CA-167. In the Lummi Tribal Court for the Lummi Indian Reservation, State of Washington.

### BOOKS, PAMPHLETS, AND ARTICLES

American Friends Service Committee. *Uncommon Controversy*. Seattle: University of Washington Press, Seattle, 1970.
*Bicentennial Wagon Train Pilgrimage*. Kenosha, Wis.: Jern Publishers, 1977.
Bishop, Kathleen L., and Kenneth Hansen. "The Landless Tribes of Western Washington." *American Indian Journal*, May 1978.
Blanchet, F. N. *Notices and Voyages of the Famed Quebec Mission to the Pacific Northwest, Being the Correspondence, Notices, etc., of Fathers Blanchet and Demers, Together with Those of Fathers Bolduc and Langlois . . . 1838 to 1847*. Carl Landerholm, ed. Portland: Oregon Historical Society, 1956.
Bruseth, Nels. *Indian Stories and Legends of the Stillaguamish, Sauks, and Allied Tribes*. Arlington, Wash.: *Arlington Times* Press, 1926.
Essex, Alice. *The Stanwood Story*, vol. 1. Stanwood, Wash.: *Stanwood News*, 1971.
Franklin, Grace A., and Randall B. Ripley. *CETA Politics and Policy, 1973–1982*. Knoxville: University of Tennessee Press, 1984.
Governor's Indian Affairs Task Force. *Are You Listening, Neighbor?* Olympia: State of Washington, 1972.
———. *The People Speak: Will You Listen?* Olympia: State of Washington, 1973.
Hancock, Samuel. *The Narrative of Samuel Hancock, 1845–1860*. New York: R.M. McBride, 1927.
Indian Assistance Division, State of Washington. *Indian Economic Employment Assistance Program 1974–75 and 1975–76 Summary Progress Report*. Olympia: Washington State, February 1977.
Murdock, George. *Ethnographic Bibliography of North America*. New Haven, Conn.: Yale University Press, 1941.

Native American Solidarity Committee. *To Fish in Common*, 2d ed. n.p., December 1979.
Ruby, Robert H., and John A. Brown. *A Guide to the Indian Tribes of the Pacific Northwest*. Norman: University of Oklahoma Press, 1986, 1992.
———. *Indian Slavery in the Pacific Northwest*. Spokane, Wash.: Arthur Clark, 1993.
———. *John Slocum and the Indian Shaker Church*. Norman: University of Oklahoma Press, 1996.
Solomon, Terry V. *Sound Defender: History of Fort Lawton*. n.p., July 1970.
U.S. Department of Labor, Employment and Training Administration. *Apprenticeship and CETA Technical Assistance Guide*. Washington, D.C.: Department of Labor, 1979.

## NEWSPAPERS AND NEWSMAGAZINES

*Arlington (Wash.) Times*, 1925, 1926, 1930, 1970, 1975.
*Bellingham (Wash.) Herald*, 1974, 1975, 1983, 1984, 1988, 1990, 1991.
*Daily News* (Port Angeles, Wash.), 1975.
*Daily Olympian* (Olympia, Wash.), 1967, 1973.
*Everett (Wash.) Daily Herald*, 1955.
*Everett (Wash.) Herald*, 1967, 1968, 1975, 1976, 1977, 1988, 1991.
*Filipino Forum* (Seattle), 1969.
*Hayward (Calif.) Journal*, 1914.
*Indian Voice*, 1975, 1976, 1979.
*Lodi (Calif.) News-Sentinel*, 1945, 1962.
*Minneapolis Tribune*, 1968.
*Nevada State Journal* (Reno), 1966.
*Northwest Indian News* (Seattle), 1975, 1978, 1979.
*Northwest Passage*, June 16–June 30, 1975.
*Portland Oregonian*, 1974.
*St. Paul Pioneer Press*, 1968.
*Seattle Post-Intelligencer*, 1965, 1968, 1970, 1972, 1992.
*Seattle Times*, 1966, 1970, 1974, 1976.
*Skagit Valley Herald* (Mount Vernon, Wash.), 1975.
*Stanwood (Wash.) Tidings*, 1913.
*Tacoma (Wash.) News Tribune*, 1973, 1975, 1977.
*Time Magazine*, June 7, 1968.
*Toledo (Ohio) Blade*, 1968.
*Washington Post*, 1968.
*Washington Star*, 1975, 1976.

## INTERVIEWS BY AUTHORS

The transcriptions of these interviews are in the Esther Ross Papers in the Eastern Washington State Historical Society. Also in that collection are transcriptions of other interviews at other times with persons listed above but not cited here because direct quotes from them were not used. And there are many other interviewees who are not listed here because, while information was drawn from them, they are not directly quoted in the text.

Allen, David. April 21, 1997.
Allen, Frank. Multiple conversations, June 22, 1993, to July 2, 2000.
Bennett, Ramona. September 8, 1995.
Benson, Joan Baker. June 4, 1995.
Black, William A. "Bill." January 10, 1994; March 31 and July 11, 1995.
Bryant, Linda. October 28, 1995.
Byrum, Marion L. Carlton. June 11, 1995.
Comenout, Robert. May 1, 1998.
Dombrowski, Linda. March 23 and September 5, 1995.
Elixman, Valda Orr. *See* Orr, Valda.
Fitchen, Edgar "Ed." May 25, 1995.
George, Leota (Mrs. Roy). May 10, 1997.
Getches, David H. July 3, 1995.
Gobin, Bernie. February 28 and June 27, 1997.
Grayum, Michael C. "Mike." December 11, 1995; February 20, 1996.
Greene, Margaret. March 16, 1994; May 20 and July 13, 1995.
Greger, Gail. July 19, 1994.
Hansen, Kenneth C. May 26, 1995.
Harris, LaDonna. February 16, 1996.
Heckman, James "Jim." December 12, 1995.
Holly, Michael "Mike." May 30, 1995.
Hovis, James. October 21, 1995.
Jefferson, Juanita. May 21 and June 17, 1998.
Jeffries, William R. "Bill." April 18 and June 27, 1997.
Keep, Scott. September 6, 1995.
Kidder, Jack. October 10, 1995.
Lozar, Steven A. "Bud." March 15, 1994; August 12, 1995.
McCloud, Janet. March 17, 1995.
McEvers, Charles "Chuck." April 25, 1997.
McLeod, Malcolm. June 27 and July 12, 1995.
Meeds, Lloyd. November 21, 1995.

Murdoch, William A. November 14, 1995; May 10, 1996.
Myrick, Cecilia. November 11, 1995.
Orr, Valda. August 21, 1995.
Ortez, George. September 15, 1994; July 23 and September 6, 1995; December 16, 1997.
Rudd, Patricia "Pat." November 7, 1995.
Ryser, Rudolph "Rudy." May 10 and 26, 1997.
Sampsel, Roy H. July 17, 1994.
Sayegusa, Rod. August 3, 1995.
Smouse, Don. July 17, 1995.
Stanley, Sam. November 26, 1996.
Stay, Alan. September 17, 1995.
Swenson, Georgene. December 15, 1995; January 3, 1996.
Thompson, Morris. October 3, 1995.
Three Stars, Peter. February 27, 1994.
Tonasket, Mel. June 3, 1995.
Trimble, Charles "Chuck." September 12, 1995.
Venn, Douglas "Doug." February 27, 1997.
Whitebear, Bernie. December 30, 1997.
Williams, Wayne. August 14, 1995; February 28, 1997.
Woods, Andrea. August 3, 1995.

## LETTERS TO AUTHORS

Murdoch, William A. March 7, 1994.
Seymour, Lisa. August 21, 1995.
Social Security Administration. July 11, 1996.
Trimble, Charles "Chuck." July 11, 1996.
Troeh, Catherine Herrold. January 9, 1994.

## UNPUBLISHED MATERIALS

Getches, Davis. "Background Information on the Stillaguamish Tribe of Indians," April 1976. Photocopy in possession of authors.
Holdridge, Herbert. Assorted Letters and News Releases.
———. Tribal Proceedings, The Constitutional Government of the United States v Defendants [29 names]: For Crimes of Kidnapping, Murder, and Treason. Wells, Nev., March 11, 1967.
Indian Contingent of the Poor People's Campaign. "Statement to Indian Claims Commission, May 31, 1968." Photocopy in possession of authors.
Medical records of Esther Ross. Lummi Indian Medical Clinic, Bellingham, Wash., January 3, 1976, August 19, 1977; April 13, 1982; St. Luke's

General Hospital, Bellingham, Wash., February 15, 1977; Sehome Park Care Center, Bellingham, Wash., May 17, 1988. Photocopies in possession of authors.

"Stillaguamish Futures: Plan for Restoration, Phase I." June 6, 1977. Photocopy in possession of authors.

Troeh, Catherine Herrold. "Homer Settler," n.d. Photocopy in possession of authors.

# Index

Abel, Gail. *See* Greger, Gail
Aberdeen, Wash., 39
Abernathy, Ralph, 74, 76, 84, 98
Adams, George, 243
Adams, Hank, 61, 74–78, 84, 93, 103, 106, 109, 116, 154, 266n.1, 276n.2
Adkinson, Gary E., 141
Administration for Native Americans, 275n. 24
Adult Protective Services (APS), 238, 240
Affiliated Tribes of Northwest Indians (ATNI), 106, 107, 145–47, 184, 210, 217
Agnew, Spiro, 236
Alaska, 132, 276n.2
Alaska Native Land Claims, 276n.2
Albertson's Food Stores, 232
Alcatraz Island, 99, 147
Alcohol use and abuse, 21, 48, 54, 94, 96, 108, 160, 178, 229
Aleut Indians, 172
Alexander, Gertrude (Charlie Smith's sister), 219
Allen, Agnes (Esther's sister-in-law), 31
Allen, Clifford G. (Snohomish Indian), 167, 265n.16
Allen, David (Esther's grandson), 74, 95, 96, 98, 108, 127, 141, 170, 181, 187, 205, 218, 224, 234, 261n.1
Allen, Earl E., 94, 125
Allen, Esther Ruth. *See* Ross, Esther
Allen, Frank Ellsworth (Esther's son), 29, 30, 32, 34, 35, 37, 256–57; became chief, 246; fired for demonstrating, 60; lobbying for his mother in Washington D.C., 84; marriage, first, 261n.1, 267n.13; marriage, second, 108, 261–62n.1; runs for governor, 247–48; tribal offices held, appointments, business ventures, 61, 79, 133, 135, 189, 236; writes President Johnson, 56
Allen, Fred (Walter's father), 288–89n.14
Allen, Gloria Fay (Frank's second wife), 108, 261n.1
Allen, John (Walter's uncle), 265n.11
Allen, Lois (Esther's granddaughter), 74, 108, 261n.1
Allen, Mary (Solomon Allen's wife), 289n.14
Allen, Mary Margaret (Frank's first wife), 261n.1, 267n.13
Allen, Sandra Martine (Esther's granddaughter), 108, 189, 194, 211, 234, 240, 242, 243, 246, 261n.1, 262n.1
Allen, Solomon (Walter's grandfather), 100, 232, 265n.11, 288–89n.14
Allen, Walter Frederick (Esther's second husband), 29, 32–35, 37, 100, 236, 250; death, 40; marriage to Esther, 32; occupations, 33, 35, 37, 39, 40, 257n.13
Allen Bus Line, 236
American Friends Service Committee, 97
American Indian Movement (AIM), 99, 147, 149
American Revolution Bicentennial Administration, 168
Americans for Indian Opportunity (AIO), 167
Anderson, Alvin, 46, 49

# INDEX

Anderson, Wallace ("Mad Bear") (Tuscarora Indian), 59, 60, 61, 67, 73, 219
Anderson Cemetery, 280n.3
Andrew, Joseph (Skokomish Indian), 122
Andrus, Cecil, 205
Animals, pets, 34, 35, 235
Arctic Fur Co., 42
Arkinson, Peter, 142
Arlington, Wash., 5, 18, 20, 22, 23, 27, 44, 62, 80, 106, 155, 179
Arlington National Cemetery, 76
Association of Northwest Steelheaders, Inc., 268n.4
Athabascan Indians, 172
Atkins, Lee, 90
Auburn, Calif., 194
Austin, Gregory H., 280n.1
Automobiles: Buick Skylark, 79; Chevrolet, 47, 48; Ford, 26, 47, 190, 202; Graham Paige, 39, 40, 41, 42; Jeep Waggoner, 190; Oldsmobile, 240, 289n.11; Plymouth, 141, 236; Reo, 34; Volkswagon, 143, 190; White truck, 32

Backstrom, Henry, 62
Baker, Donald (Esther's stepgrandson), 160, 178
Baker, Dorothy (Esther's stepgranddaughter), 52, 95, 124, 125, 130, 142, 148, 159, 161, 259n.22
Baker, Joan. *See* Benson, Joan Baker
Baker, Margaret (Esther's stepdaughter), 52–54, 142, 159, 178, 179, 184, 192, 230, 259n.22, 279n.15
Baker, Suzie (Esther's stepgranddaughter), 52
Baker, Walter (Margaret Baker's husband), 52
Balderroma, Hank (Esther's temporary guardian), 242
Barnette, Mack J. T., 286n.1
Bartholome, Shirley, 147
Bechthold, Etta, 194
Bell, Lewis A., 276–77n.5
Bell, Mary Jane. *See* Reid, Mary Jane Bell Chamberlain
Bellingham, Wash., 95, 98, 99, 108, 141, 228, 235, 236, 254n.1
Bellingham Bay, 288n.14
Belloni, Robert C., 116
Bennett, Ramona (Puyallup Indian), 61, 101, 106, 107, 116, 117, 159, 243, 249
Bennett, Robert, 96, 229

Bennickson, Marianne, 194
Benson, Joan Baker (Esther's stepgranddaughter), 52–54, 259nn.22, 24, 26
Betsey. *See* Silva, Betsey
Bicentennial Coordiantion Office of the Interior Department, 275n.22
Bicentennial Pony Express, 171
Bicentennial Wagon Train, 146–54, 166
Bishop, Kathleen (Snohomish Indian), 167, 172, 173, 181, 249, 265n.16
Bitney, Raymond H., 45, 50, 51
Black, William Arthur ("Bill"), 105, 179, 189, 194, 201, 203, 206, 209, 217, 220, 228, 244, 249, 250, 282–83n.13
Blaine, Wash., 146
Blanchet, Rev. F. N., 255n.12
Blodgett, Winifred ("Win"), 194, 205, 206, 282n.13
Blue Spruce, George, 155
Boats: loaned by Robert Satiacum, 127; *Smoker Craft*, 187, 217, 224; *Tuna*, 35; *Wide Load*, 137, 138, 158, 187, 217, 276n.4
Boldt, George Hugo, 110, 113, 116, 118, 120–23, 203, 227, 244, 269n.4, 286n.1
Boldt Decision, 126, 128, 133, 142, 143, 155, 176–85, 215, 226, 236, 271n.5, 276n.2; implementation, 285–87n.1; the trial, 116–23
Bon Marche, 257n.2
Bonneville Power Administration, 139
Boome, Charlie (Upper Skagit Indian), 45
Boudler, Colo., 109, 159, 167, 169, 177, 181, 184
Brando, Marlon, 73
Brasfield, Dolly (Stillaguamish Indian), 284n.11
Brenner, Cecil, 212
Bridges, Al (Nisqually Indian), 75
Broadhead, W. Sherwin, 188
Brouillet, Rev. Jean Baptiste, 288–89n.14
Brum, J., 253–54n.7
Bruseth, Nels, 64
Bryant, Linda, 139, 140, 149–53, 235, 246, 263n.1
Bryant, Wash., 233
Bureau of Indian Affairs (BIA). *See* Department of the Interior
Bureau of Land Management, 57
Burials, 21, 83, 87–91, 102, 131, 215, 218, 219, 263n.1, 284n.6
Busch, Russell W., 287n.1
Bushman, John W., 90

# INDEX

Byrum, Dick, 243
Byrum, Marion (Esther's daughter), 29, 30–33, 37, 144, 182, 229, 230, 243, 250, 256n.10, 274n.18, 288n.9

Cagey, Bill, 243
Cagey, Sam (Lummi Indian), 240, 242
Camano Island, 122, 148, 286n.1
Cardinet, George, 151
Carey, Charles E., 93
Carlton, Esther. *See* Ross, Esther
Carlton, Fletcher Valentine (Esther's first husband), 9, 11, 29, 30, 31, 249, 256n.10; marriage, 10; death, 47
Carlton, Marion Lavina. *See* Byrum, Marion
Carpenter, Craig, 64
Carter, Jimmy, 184, 186
Cascade District Court, 80
Cascade mountains, 19, 53, 149, 270n.9
Cash, Johnny, 283n.14
Cedarville, Calif., 64
Celebrations: achievement of recognition, 180–84, 188; Festival of American Folklife, 172, 173; Fourth of July, 27, 114
Cemeteries. *See* Burials
Chaddus (Stillaguamish Indian) (Esther's great-grandfather), 3, 15, 183, 246
Chamberlain, Mary Jane. *See* Reid, Mary Jane Bell Chamberlain
Chambers, Reid P., 132
Chattin, Wayne, 168, 169
Chehalis Indians, 264n.3
Cherokee Memorial Park Cemetery, 141, 142
Chicago, Ill., 85
Churches: Assemblies of God, 84; Indian Shaker Church, 219, 284n.6; Methodist, 75; Presbyterian, 32; Roman Catholic, 20, 255n.13, 267n.13, 289n.5; Seventh Day Adventist, 3, 32, 33, 34, 54, 96, 191, 232, 237, 242, 243, 254n.8, 284n.6
Claims, 27, 37, 44, 46, 50, 80–86; awards, 80, 82–85, 131, 289n.7, 289n.16; Court of Claims, 28; *Duwamish et al.*, 13, 23, 25, 28, 29, 39, 48, 49; Indian Claims Commission, 36, 38, 43, 46, 55, 62, 85, 137, 210, 262n.7
Clallam Indians, 15
Clark, Don, 168
Clark, George, 155

Clark, Ramsey, 55
Claxton, Mildred, 225
Clear Lake, Wash., 33
Cohen, Felix, 149
Columbia legal Services. *See* Evergreen Legal Services
Columbia River, 110, 232
Colville Indians, 97, 107
Comenout, Robert, 102, 167, 172, 173
Community Action Project Director's Association, 64
Comprehensive Employment and Training Act (CETA), 133, 134, 138, 143, 170, 199, 272–73n.23
Comprehensive Manpower Program, 272n.23
Concrete, Wash., 38
Confederated Tribes of the Siletz Indians of Oregon, 172
Confederated Tribes of the Warm Springs Reservation of Oregon, 172
Coniff, Joseph Lawrence ("Larry"), 117, 268n.4
Constitutional Government of the United States, 65, 69, 177
Constitutions and by-laws, 28, 51, 59, 121, 127–28, 131, 153, 173, 175, 193, 210, 216, 217, 220, 247, 259n.21, 279n.5, 284n.5
Cooper, Al (Snohomish Indian), 98
Cooper, Kenneth, 159, 160
Cooper, Willifred, 159, 160
Coos Bay Logging Co., 257n.13
Coquille, Oreg., 40
Costello, Ron, 279n.1
Covington, Lucy (Colville Indian), 101, 249
Crawford, Eugene, 186, 187, 224, 232, 288n.9
Crouse, Carl, 268n.4
Crow Agency, 180

Dakin, Rev. Joseph, 267n.13
Dallas, Tex., 192, 195
Darrington, Wash., 18, 47, 79, 121
da Silviera, Joao. *See* Silva, John, Sr., (Esther's grandfather)
Davenport, Cynthia, 136, 179, 188, 220, 224, 273n.1, 286–87n.1
Dawes Indian Severalty Act, 57
Daybreak Star Indian Cultural-Education Center and Arts Center, 101
Decker, Craig A., 55
Deer Creek (tributary of North Fork of Stillaguamish River), 79

Denver, Colo., 168
Department of Health, Education and Welfare (HEW), 155, 278n.16
Department of the Interior, 22, 25, 45, 54, 55, 56, 83, 90, 94, 110, 132, 134, 142, 147, 148, 151, 154, 175, 176, 185, 199, 204, 206, 211, 213, 214, 220, 222, 224, 249
Department of Justice, 62, 77
Department of Labor, 272n.23
Department of Social and Health Services (DSHS), 238, 239, 241
Diefendorf, Mark, 193
Diehl Ford Inc., 190
Dill, William (Duwamish Indian), 265n.16
Diseases, 20
Disneyland, 240, 290n.16
Dombrowski, Linda, 104, 105, 179, 247, 248, 250
Dorsey, James ("Jimmy") (Stillaguamish Indian), 15, 23–26, 38, 49, 80, 91, 118, 125
Dorsey, Susan, 15
Duchene, Greg, 107
Dunbar, Bill, 40, 41, 47
Dunbar, Ernest ("Sparky") (Bill Dunbar's son), 47, 129
*Duwamish et al. See* Claims
Duwamish Indians, 265n.11
Dysart, George D., 110, 112–16, 268n.4

East Stanwood, 32
Eikenberry, Kenneth O., 240, 241
Eisenhower, Dwight D., 269n.4
Elefson, Erland, 93
Elixman, Valda, 189, 199–202, 205, 236
Elko, Nev., 65, 260n.6
Ellis Island, 99
Enick, Evelyn Kanim (Snoqualmie Indian), 249
Eugene, Oreg., 257n.13
Eureka, Calif., 8, 9
Evans, Daniel ("Dan"), 70, 71, 79, 92, 97, 137, 173, 231, 232, 243, 289n.5
Everett, Wash., 19, 29, 30, 37, 60, 71, 80, 83, 98, 106, 201, 212, 222, 254n.1
Everett Agency. *See* Western Washington Agency
Evergreen Legal Services, 109, 110, 126, 130, 136, 137, 273n.1
Evergreen State College, 113, 190
Everson, Wash., 84

Falk, Frank, 89, 92
Farring, Robert, 214

Felshaw, George M., 83, 89, 160
Ferndale, Wash., 242
Festival of American Foklife. *See* Celebrations
Finkbonner, Charles D., 217, 224, 230, 264n.5
Fireside Tavern, 52
Fish and fishing, 62, 79–81, 127, 164, 166, 167, 186, 269n.7; in the court, 109–21; fish-ins, 54, 59, 71, 79, 99; hatcheries, 63, 211, 226, 227, 233, 264n.16; history of state and federal control, 267–68nn.3,4; post-Boldt decision intervention, 215, 218, 271n.6; Stillaguamish Fisheries Management Program, 189, 194; Stillaguamish fishing rights, 54, 57, 110, 126–28, 137, 179, 204, 227, 264n.16; tribal fishing ordinance, 128, 158, 171–72n.9. *See also* Boldt Decision; Claims
Fisher Brothers Furniture Store, 41
Fisk University, 281n.2
Fitch, Michael F., 130, 159, 164, 277nn.8,9
Fitchen, Edgar ("Ed"), 41, 43, 47, 143, 189, 203
Fitchen, Lloyd, 47
Fitchen, Marion. *See* Byrum, Marion
Florence, Oreg., 257n.13
Florence, Wash., 5
Fonda, Jane, 101, 265n.13
Food preparation, 20
Ford, Gerald R., 132, 166, 277n.5
Fort Lawton, 99, 100, 147, 265nn.11,14
Fort Lewis, 101
Frank, Bill, Jr. (Nisqually Indian), 122
Frank's Landing, 74, 84
French, Stuart C., 249n.23
Frizzell, Kent, 158, 175–78, 185, 189
Fujii, Massao, 91
Funderberg, Chuck, 148

Gabb, Sandra, 205
Gass, Gary, 265n.13
Genschow, William, 159, 160, 161
George, Ike, 158
George, Leota, 98
George, Roy S. (Nooksack Indian), 97
George, Ted J. (Clallam Indian), 97
Gerard, Forrest J., 107, 181, 205, 211, 212
Gershuny, William A., 280n.1
Getches, David H., 109–16, 119–23, 129, 132, 136, 140–42, 157–59, 164, 168, 169, 173–78, 181–88, 203, 217, 243, 247, 249, 250, 268–69n.4, 269n.9, 286–87n.1

## INDEX

Gilbert, Warren J., 48, 49, 83, 258nn.14,15
Gilbert and Bennister, 48
Gisle Robstad Logging Co., 257n.13
Giustina Brothers Lumber Co., 257n.13
Gobin, Bernard ("Bernie") (Tulalip Indian), 129, 246
Gobin, Tommy, 243
Goodridge, Edward, 28, 38, 170, 224
Goodridge, Gardner, 21
Goodridge, Kathleen. *See* Johnson, Kathleen
Goodridge, Llewellyn ("Lew"), 38, 115, 170, 181, 191, 193–95, 199–202, 205, 206, 208, 211, 212, 215, 220–23, 226, 227, 243, 287n.1
Goodridge, Ruth, 44
Goosberry Fire Department, 238
Gooseberry Point, 236
Gorton, Slade, 269n.4
Governor's Indian Advisory Committee (GIAC), 96, 97, 101, 102
Governor's Indian Advisory Council, 97, 106, 139, 182, 265n.17
Graham, Howard L., 290n.6
Granite Falls, Wash., 205
Grant, Gloria Fay. *See* Allen, Gloria Fay
Grayum, Michael M. ("Mike"), 157, 228, 237, 243
Green, June L., 173–75
Greene, Margaret (Samish Indian), 54, 103, 183, 189, 191, 192, 198, 199, 202, 230, 238, 240, 242, 243, 248, 249, 265n.16, 266n.1
Green Parrot Theatre, 99
Greger, Gail (Stillaguamish Indian), 200, 248, 284n.11
Gregory, Dick, 60, 61, 71, 73
Griffin, Arthur E., 13, 23, 25–30, 38
Gross, F. A., 44, 45, 50
Gusman, Louis, 80

Haida Indians, 172
Haley, R. Bruce, 238
Hancock, Samuel, 20
Hansen, Kenneth ("Ken") (Samish Indian), 83, 162, 187, 188
Harbor Island, 59
Harjo, Susan Shown, 244
Harlow Pass, 79
Harris, LaDonna, 167
Harvey, Jackson, 183
Harvey, Paul (Jackson Harvey's son), 83, 148, 183
Hatch, Clarence, 243

Hathaway, Stanley K., 150, 277n.5
Haveman, Dale E., 238–41
Hayward, Calif., 3, 4, 253n.7
Hazel, Wash., 87, 89, 219
Health and Medical Facilities: Indian Health Board Clinic, 187, 281n.3; Indian Health Service, 238, 281n.3; Loma Linda Adventist Hospital, 40; Lummi Indian Health Clinic, 188, 192, 232, 238; Old Marine Hospital, Seattle, Wash., 163, 187; Public Health Services Hospital, Seattle, Wash., 187; Puget Sound Health Board, 217; St. Joseph Hospital, Bellingham, Wash., 281n.4; St. Luke's Hospital, Bellingham, Wash., 187, 239; Sehome Park Care Center, Bellingham, Wash., 239, 240; Veterans Administration Hospital, Seattle, Wash., 125
Hebo, Oreg., 41
Heckman, James L. ("Jim"), 157, 186, 207, 236, 271n.5, 276n.2
Helligso, M. N., 253n.3
Helms, Richard, 67
Hermes, Bill, 80
Hillaire, Miriam Levin, 189, 202, 217, 220, 283n.8
Hillsboro, Oreg., 288n.14
Hinton Motors, 190
Hoag, Richard, 91
Hoh Indians, 268n.4
Holdridge, Dorothy, 81
Holdridge, Herbert C., 64–71, 73, 81, 100, 261n.9, 262n.5
Hoover, J. Edgar, 67
Hoquiam, Wash., 93, 284n.8
Horrowitz, Don, 80
Hoshy, Gwen, 239
Hospitals. *See* Health and Medical Facilities
Housing Improvement Program (HIP), 227
Housing and Urban Development (HUD), 233
Hovis, James B., 102
Human Affairs Council, 102
Humphrey, Hubert H., 81

Idaho Fish and Game Department, 268n.4
Indian Affairs Task Force, 101
Indian Claims Commission. *See* Claims
Indian Financing Act, 176

Indian Health Care Improvement Act, 184
Indian Reorganization Act (IRA), 51, 84, 85, 130, 177, 217, 224, 263n.16, 266n.17, 269n.8, 274n.5, 279n.12
Indian Self-Determination and Education Assistance Act, 176, 274n.5
Interior Board of Indian Appeals, Office of Hearings and Appeals, 179, 184
Intertribal Council of American Indians (ICAI), 266n.7
Inter-tribal Council of Western Washington Indians (ICWW), 64, 266n.7
Iroquois Indians, 219
Island Crossing (location Stillaguamish tribal office), 106, 148, 151, 157, 202, 205, 216, 266n.8
Issaquah, Wash., 137

J. C. Penny Co., 41
Jackson, Henry W., 29, 35, 37, 76, 79, 84, 90, 107, 130, 134, 142, 143, 266n.17, 276n.2
Jackson, Marie (Henry Jackson's mother), 29
Jackson, Peter (Henry Jackson's father), 29
James, Patricia A., 224
Jefferson, Juanita (Lummi Indian), 64
Jeffries, William R. ("Bill"), 97, 101, 102, 265n.17
Jesse James Auto Sales, 289n.11
Jim, Robert (Yakama Indian), 96, 116
Jim, Roger (Yakama Indian), 210, 243
Jim Creek (Stillaguamish South Fork tributary), 29, 32, 37
Johnson, Angelina ("Augua") (Esther's mother), 3, 5, 10, 11, 13, 29, 32, 141, 194, 195, 235, 253n.7, 254n.8; death, 33; marriage, 66, 253n.1
Johnson, Charles, 63
Johnson, Christian Voreg (Esther's father), 3, 253n.1
Johnson, Dale (Squaxin Indian), 269n.7, 271n.5
Johnson, Esther. See Ross, Esther
Johnson, Gary, 170
Johnson, Kathleen ("Kate"), 38, 43–45, 52, 57, 61, 82, 91, 191, 199, 202, 223, 262n.7
Johnson, Lady Bird, 69
Johnson, Lyndon B., 56, 65, 67, 76, 81, 96
Johnson, Margaret Ruth (Esther's daughter), 9, 11, 29–33, 37, 98, 182, 229, 230

Johnson, Robert, 280n.1
Johnson-O'Malley Act, 146, 176, 177
Jones, Nancy, 129
Jorgenson, Art, 159
Joseph, Mary Margaret. See Allen, Mary Margaret

K & B Logging Co., 257n.13
Kannan (Snoqualmie Indian), 27
Katzen, Phillip, 273n.1
Kavanaugh, S. J., 23, 24
Kayak Point, 286n.1
Keep, Scott, 106, 131, 132, 224, 249, 275n.20
Kennedy, Edward, 81
Kennedy, John, 76, 77, 262n.4
Kennedy, Robert, 78
Kerry, Charles, 188
Ketchikan, Alaska, 35, 257n.2
Kidder, Jack (Snohomish Indian), 107, 162
Kikiallus (Kikkialis) Indians, 19, 24, 50, 61, 122
King, Martin Luther, Jr., 74
Kinley, Forrest L. ("Dutch") (Lummi Indian), 269n.7, 276n.2
Kleppe, Thomas S., 158, 166–69, 171, 277n.5
Klickitat Indians, 19, 270n.9
Knight, Vale and Gregory, 193
Krenzke, Theodore C., 211
Kruse, Wayne, 280n.1
Kutenai Indians, 147
Kuykendall, Jerome K., 84, 263n.15

LaClair, Leo J., 170, 217
LaCourse, Philip, 265n.16
LaFontaine, Frank, 273n.1
Lane, Barbara, 118, 217, 243, 246, 255n.1, 278n.6
Lane, Vernon, 243
Laramie, Wyo., 146
Lasater, J. E., 117
Legal Services. See Evergreen Legal Services
LeMay, Curtis, 69
Leo, Clyde (Esther's grandson), 246, 261
Leo, Rosalee (Clyde Leo's mother), 261
Levin, Miriam. See Hillaire, Miriam Levin
Lipman and Wolfe and Company, 29
Lipstick map, 47, 55
Little, Vincent, 57, 89, 205, 212
Lodi, Calif., 141, 144

Long, Alva C., 265n.13
Los Angeles, Calif., 39
Lovejoy, Ella, 257n.10
Lower Elwah Indians, 145, 271n.6
Lower Stillaguamish Indian Nation, 247, 291n.6
Lozar, Steven A. ("Bud"), 90, 91, 93, 145, 146, 180, 189, 215, 219
Luesson, Francia, 241
Lummi Indians, 59, 113, 120, 128, 147
Lynden State & Charter Lines Inc., 236
Lyons, John (Kikiallus Indian), 24

McCloud, Janet, 59, 61–63, 68, 69, 103, 231, 243, 249, 265n.13
MacCurdy, Joe, 205, 217
MacCurdy, Marie Antoinette, 80, 83, 93–94, 193–95, 199, 200, 202, 205, 208, 216, 217, 221, 223, 224, 227, 233
McEvers, Charles L. ("Chuck"), 97, 98
McGimpsey, Earl L., 115, 119, 120, 121, 122, 268n.4
McKee's Beach, 286n.1
Mackie, Edward B., 269n.4
McLeod, Malcolm S., 48, 73, 83, 85, 119, 127, 162, 179, 206, 229, 230, 246, 265n.13
McMinds, Guy (Quinoult Indian), 112, 269n.7
McMinimee, Warren A., 40, 41
MacNamara, Inez, 125, 161
Mad Bear. *See* Anderson, Wallace
Madison, Wis., 75
Maglessen, Harold, 148
Magnuson, Warren G., 133, 272n.22, 276n.2
Makah Indians, 145, 268n.4
Marietta, Wash., 232, 236; change of name, 289n.14
Martin, Gail. *See* Greger, Gail
Martin, Karen K., 256n.10
Martin, Kathleen. *See* Johnson, Kathleen
Martin, Terry, 202
Marysville, Wash., 16
Mayberry, Carol, 61
Maywood Logging Company, 34
Meeds, Lloyd, 132, 134
Meshorer, Hank, 168
Methow Indians, 19
Metlakatla Indians, 35
Meyer, D. C., 43, 44
Miller, Barbara, (Frank Allen's stepdaughter), 74, 261n.1
Miller, Donald B., 165

Milltown, Wash., 79, 89, 121, 235
Minneapolis-St. Paul, Minn., 75
Mission, B.C., Canada, 235
Missoula, Mont., 115
Moclips, Wash., 39
Mohr, Carrie, 254n.8
Mohr, Fred, 254n.8
Moles Funeral Home, 242
Moos, Donald W., 186
Morton, Rogers C. B., 125, 132, 139, 141, 150, 158, 276n.2, 277n.5
Mount Higgins, Wash., 79
Mount Vernon, Wash., 33, 38, 48, 148, 149
Muckleshoot Indians, 57, 110, 264n.3
Mukilteo, Wash., 15
Murdoch, William A., 163, 192
Murdock, George P., 45
Musqueam Indians, 108, 202n.1
Myrick, Cecelia, 202, 203, 206, 209

Nashville, Tenn., 205, 281n.2, 283n.14
National American Indian Association, 106
National Archives & Records Administration, Pacific Northwest Regional Archives, 288n.9
National Congress of American Indians (NCAI), 84, 92, 104, 106, 131, 134, 141, 142, 146, 157–59, 162, 172, 174, 177, 181, 192, 205, 211, 244, 247, 248
National Easter Seal Society. *See* Washington State Easter Seal Society
National Indian Lutheran Board, 187, 224, 225, 232
National Tribal Chairmans Association (NTCA), 96, 128, 131, 146
Native Amrican Rights Rund (NARF), 109, 159, 168, 173, 177, 249, 282n.9
Native American Solidarity Committee, 271n.5
Navajo Indians, 97
Netarts, Oreg., 40, 257n.13
Neyens, Antone A., 84
Nez Perce Indians, 97
Ninth Circuit Court of Appeals, 176
Nisqually Indians, 110, 264n.3
Nisqually River, 59, 74, 117, 127
Nixon, Richard, 81, 132, 277n.5
Nooksack Indians, 57, 271n.6
Nooksack River, 119, 288n.14
North American Trail Ride Conference, 151
Northwestern Federation of American Indians, 23, 256

Northwest Indian Fisheries Commission (NWIFC), 157, 186, 202, 205, 215, 228, 236, 237, 271n.5, 276n.2
Northwest Power Planning Council, 231
Norway and Norweigians, 4
Norwood, J. L., 56, 62

Oakland, Calif., 3, 11, 254n.8, 256–57n.10
Office of Economic Opportunity (OEO), 96, 106, 128, 133, 272–73n.23
Office of Management and Budget (OMB), 132
Office of Native American Programs (ONAP), 155, 170, 171, 273n.23; name change, 275n.24
Olfert, Rev. Wesley, 243
Olympia, Wash., 62, 66, 79, 113, 166
Olympic Peninsula Agency, 284n.8
Oman, Shirley, 68, 217, 223, 224
Oregon State Fish Commission, 116
Orr, Valda. *See* Elixman, Valda
Ortez, George H., 92, 162
Oso, Wash., 80, 87, 89, 93, 210
Ostlund, Jon E., 159, 192

Pacific Beach, 39
Paiute Indians, 65
Parker, Gene (Makah Indian), 269n.7
Parks, Janet L., 272n.17
Patkanin (Snoqualmie Indian), 15, 258n.4
Patrick, Wesley, 28, 38, 87, 91, 116, 125
Paul, Roy, 159, 160
Pearl, Minnie, 283n.14
Peltier, Leonard, 101
Percival, Ed (Snoqualmie Indian), 24, 28
Perkins, Louise, 131
Pertram, Gary, 213
Peters, Cal (Squaxin Indian), 118, 269n.7, 276n.2
Peterson, Charlie (Makah Indian), 269n.7, 276n.2
Peterson, Dora I., 10, 254n.8
Peterson, Lorraine, 65, 260n.6
Pierson, Stuart F., 268n.4
Pitkin, Stan, 268n.4
Placid, Rose Mary, 159, 160
Poor Peoples Campaign, 74–78, 90, 115, 247, 261n.1
Pope Paul VI, 69
Popwell, R. L., 30
Port Angeles, Wash., 145–48
Port Gamble Klallam Indians, 271n.6
Portland, Oreg., 29, 41, 106, 159, 184

Portland Area Office, BIA, 51, 57, 89, 90, 132, 138, 149, 204, 205, 212
Portland Office of Hearings and Appeals of the Department of the Interior, 142
Port Susan, 50, 226, 227, 286–87n.1
Portuguese immigrants, 20
Post, Frederick W., 48, 55–57, 61, 62, 82, 83, 85, 258n.14
Preston, Ardelle, 191, 192, 288n.9
Princess Sunflower, 262n.4
Prouse, Charles, 254n.8
Prouty Lumber Co., 257n.13
Public Health Services. *See* Health and Medical Facilities
Public Law 280, 145, 274nn.2,3
Puget Sound, 10, 15, 19, 89, 164, 180, 202
Puget Sound Agency, 284n.8
Puyallup Indians, 58, 59, 110, 117, 127, 260
Puyallup River, 71, 73

Quadsac Indians. *See* Kikiallus Indians
Qualley, E. Cornelus, 48
Que Que Kadam (Stillaguamish Indian) (James Dorsey's father), 23
Quileute Indians, 268n.4
Quinault Indians, 113, 133

Rapid City, S.Dak., 211
Raven Boat Company, 137
Ray, Dixie Lee, 186, 195, 271n.5
Razar Brothers Logging Co., 257n.13
Recognition: interpretation of, 185, 186, 279n.6, 280–81n.1
Redthunder, Sharon A., 125, 161
Reedsport, Oreg., 257n.13
Reid, Mary Jane Bell Chamberlain, 141, 194; death, 273n.14
Reid, Oscar George (Esther's stepfather), 6, 8, 9, 33, 35, 141, 144, 194, 195, 235; death, 273n.14
Reservations: Colville, 52; Fort Kitsap, 16, 285–87n.1; Lummi, 16, 95, 106, 117, 254n.1, 256n.1, 285–87n.1; Muckleshoot, 180; Port Madison, 16, 93, 285–87n.1; Quinault, 167; Stillaguamish, 94; Suquamish, 16, 93, 285–87n.1; Swinomish, 16, 27, 285–87n.1; Tulalip, 16, 27, 79, 121, 128, 129, 285–87n.1; Yakama, 52, 53, 54, 95, 124, 148, 160, 178
Richmond, Calif., 34
Riley, Carrol L., 49, 55, 118
Robb, William 23, 28

# INDEX

Roblin, Charles E., 256n.16
Rocaway, Oreg., 41
Roman, Frank, 273n.1
Root, Pamela (Cree Indian), 265n.16
Ross, A. A., 9
Ross, Arnold (Esther's third husband), 47, 52, 53, 90, 95, 119, 124, 129, 229, 249, 254–55n.1; contested will of, 125, 130, 142, 159–64, 184, 192, 274n.15, 277n.9; grandchildren, 52, 53, 54, 124, 125; illness and death, 98, 119, 125, 130, 131
Ross, Esther: auto accidents, 26, 32, 47; birth, 3, 253n.1; death, 242–45; dietary problems, 31, 47, 76, 77, 162, 163, 169, 172, 240; hearing problems, 31, 41, 43, 98; illnesses, 31, 103, 186, 187, 192, 195, 235–41; Indian name, 3; interrupts bicentennial train, 146–54; intervenes in Boldt case deposition, 114–16; intervenes in Boldt case testimony, 119–22; marriage to Fletcher Valentine Carlton, 9, 10; marriage to Walter Allen, 32; marriage to Arnold Ross, 47; paternity of her children, 9, 30, 31, 256–57n.19; physical abuse, 54, 95, 96; reaction to Catholicism, 261–62n.1, 267n.13; religious preference, 191, 249; sues the Department of the Interior, 167, 168, 173, 174, 175; trips to the Capitol, 74–78, 103–106, 131–34, 140–42, 162, 172, 185, 186, 206
Rudd, Patricia D., 223, 244, 250
Ryan, Virginia (Snohomish Indian), 265n.16
Ryser, Rudolph C. ("Rudy") (Cowlitz Indian), 136, 181, 188, 280n.1, 283n.14

Sacramento, Calif., 253n.1, 288n.14
Salem, Oreg., 124
Sam, Johnny (Sauk Indian), 27
Samish Indians, 54, 103, 113, 178; get recognition, 281n.10
Sampsel, Roy H., 25, 138, 139, 147, 149, 150, 154, 155, 166, 174, 179, 249
San Diego, Calif., 141
Sand Point Naval Station, 288n.9
San Francisco, Calif., and San Francisco Bay, 6, 99, 247
Sargent, E. N., 49
Satiacum, Robert ("Bob"), 58, 59, 61, 73, 101, 119, 127, 267–68nn.3,4
Satiacum, Susan, 59
Sauk Indians. *See* Sauk-Suiattle Indians

Sauk Prairie (intertribal meeting grounds), 19
Sauk River, 19
Sauk-Suiattle Indians, 18, 19, 46, 50, 55, 113, 130, 131, 202, 269nn.8,9
Saulnier, Shirley M., 206
Savok, James, Jr. ("Jim"), 212, 213
Sayegusa, Rod, 127, 133, 134, 137, 138, 148, 149, 158, 184
Scandanavian immigrants, 20
Schlosser, Thomas P., 280n.1
Schools: Adventist, 6, 7, 33, 37, 53, 240, 290n.16; Chemawa Indian School, 124; Public, 6, 33, 37, 39, 40, 53, 93, 232
Scott, William, 256–57n.10
Scottsdale, Ariz., 240
Seaboard Lumber Company, 59
Seattle, Wash., 11, 13, 29, 37, 41, 61, 62, 71, 98, 100, 110, 136, 163, 229, 254n.1, 256–57n.10
Sedro-Woolley, Wash., 155
Sehome Park Care Center. *See* Health and Medical facilities
Seneca, M. E., 214, 215
Sennhauser, John, 269n.9
Settler, Homer, 149, 153
SFAC Logging Co., 257n.13
Sheldon, Francis J., 177, 178
Shoalwater Bay Indians, 186, 187
Shockman, Michial D., 286n.1
Shoshone Indians, 65
Siletz, Oreg., 257n.13
Siletz Indians, 65
Silva, Angelina. *See* Johnson, Angelina
Silva, Betsey (Betsy) (Stillaguamish Chief Chaddus's daughter), 3, 4, 21, 253n.2
Silva, Buelah (Louise, "Lula," "Lulu") (John Silva, Sr.'s adopted daughter), 10, 11, 33, 254n.8
Silva, Frank (Stillaguamish Indian) (Esther's uncle), 23, 28, 38
Silva, John (Esther's cousin, adopted son of Frank Silva), 24, 38, 43–46, 49, 56, 57, 61, 62, 68, 70, 71, 77, 80, 82, 83, 90, 91, 119, 182, 280n.3
Silva, John, Sr. (Esther's grandfather), 3, 10, 22, 254n.8
Silva, John (Esther's uncle), 10, 254n.8
Silva, Mary (John Silva's second wife, Angelina's stepmother), 4, 10, 253n.7, 254n.8
Silva, William (Angelina's half brother), 10
Silvana, Wash., 5, 22, 151, 233

Six Nations of the Iroquois Confederacy, 59, 68, 69
Skagit Indians. *See* Upper Skagit Indians
Skagit River, 19, 89
Skokomish Indians, 18, 110, 122
Skykomish Indians, 46, 278n.18
Slaughter, Madge, 236, 289n.1
Slaughter, William A., 289n.1
Small Tribes of Western Washington (STOWW), 84, 96, 98, 99, 104, 106, 112, 133, 134, 136, 137, 143, 155, 158, 164, 167, 170, 179, 189, 202, 264n.3, 269n.7, 271n.5; fishing advisory committee, 97, 112, 113, 127, 128; membership, 97
Smith, Anthony, 116
Smith, Charles ("Charlie"), 87, 91, 217
Smith, George, 161
Smith, Gus, 44, 61, 68, 80, 83, 87, 93, 94, 103, 114, 132, 166, 173, 177, 183
Smith, Jacob L., Jr., 230
Smith, Jessie Carney, 281n.2
Smith, John (Gus Smith's son), 166, 183, 193, 194, 200, 202, 208, 221, 223
Smith, Lena, 118, 121, 202, 214
Smith, Ralph, 284n.11
Smithsonian Institution, 45, 104, 172
Smouse, Donald ("Don"), 132, 133, 189, 194, 207, 228, 250
Snashall, Robert C., 142, 159, 161, 163, 179, 184
Snohomish Indians, 16, 18, 19, 46, 50, 59, 178n.4
Snohomish River, 19, 258
Snohomish, Wash., 47, 202
Snoqualmie Indians, 15, 46, 178, 258n.4
Snyder, Sally, 49, 55, 61
Snyder Act, 176, 211, 274n.5
Sohappy, David, 116
Soholt, Dennis, 202
Soholt, Donna, 61, 158, 193, 199, 200, 208, 221
Southern Christian Leadership Conference, 74
Sovak, James, Jr., 212, 213, 282–83n.13
Spady, Kenney, 242
Spellman, Cardinal James, 67
Spokane, Wash., 62
Springfield, Oreg., 39
Spuzzum Indians, 288n.14
Squaxin Indians, 113, 264n.4
Stanley, Sam, 104
Stanley, W. H., 254n.8
Stanwood, Wash., 3, 4, 11, 20, 21, 32, 89, 121, 122, 254n.1

Stay, Alan C., 126, 136, 137, 148, 164, 179, 217, 271n.5, 273n.1, 286–87n.1
Stennhouser, John H., 268–69nn.4,9
Stevens, Isaac I., 15
Stiles, William A., 269n.9
Stillaguamish Indians, 12, 13, 15, 16, 18, 19, 55, 58; blood quantum, 24, 28, 49, 51, 52, 80, 81, 115, 177, 191, 202, 203, 209, 210, 229, 247, 284n.5; Boldt case intervention by, 113; census and enrollment, 23, 24, 37, 45, 50, 80–93, 189, 190, 192, 202, 203, 204, 206, 208, 209, 210, 214, 222, 247, 290nn.5,6; census and enrollment in 1850, 15; census and enrollment in 1919, 22; first contact, 20; non-reservation, 5; properties, 233, 270n.1, 272n.13
Stillaguamish River, 18, 19, 47, 50, 55, 62, 63, 87, 88, 89, 91, 119, 165, 166, 219, 233
Strickland, Lee, 80
Striegel, Louis, 272n.20, 273n.23
Strimatter, Lester, 268n.4
Suiattle Indians. *See* Sauk-Suiattle Indians
Suiattle River, 18
Sultan, Wash., 26
Sumner, Wash., 98
Superior Court of Whatcom County, 241
SuperSonics, 290n.16
Supreme Court of the Constitutional Government, 67
Suquamish Indians, 271n.6
Survival of American Indians Association (SAIA), 59, 61, 64, 93, 101, 106, 109, 116, 231
Suttles, Wayne, 50
Swanson, Colleen, 61
Swanson, Oscar, 9
Swanton, Ohio, 85
Swenson, Georgene, 266n.2, 281n.6
Swinomish Indians, 122, 271n.6

Tacoma, Wash., 61, 101, 153, 155, 211
Taholah, Wash., 167
Taitnapam Indains, 270n.9
Talbot, Robert M., 90, 91, 131
Tally, Catherine (Lummi Indian), 183, 242
Tatro, LaVaun, 284n.11
Taylor, Michael, 114, 137, 269n.9, 273n.1
Taylor, Theodore W., 77
Thieu, 88
Thomas, Jacob, 289n.15

INDEX    *311*

Thomas, Jim, 236
Thompson, Morris, 130, 158, 166
Thompson River, 288n.14
Thorpe, Grace (Jim Thorpe's daughter), 101
Thorpe, Jim, 101
Three Stars, Peter P., 189, 193, 194, 200, 201–203, 205, 206, 209, 216, 217, 220–22, 249, 282n.13
Tillamook, Oreg., 40, 41, 42, 257n.13
Tlingit Indians, 104, 172
Toledo, Ohio, 75
Tollefson, Thor, 71, 117, 119, 268n.4
Tonasket, Mel (Colville Indian), 107
Toppenish, Wash., 148
Trafton, Wash., 5, 22, 87, 90, 91, 219
Trail of Broken Treaties, 103
Treaties: Medicine Creek, 11, 255n.3; Neah Bay, 255n.3; Point Elliott, 11, 13, 15, 16, 50, 56, 57, 60, 63, 77, 111, 113, 128, 139, 141, 255n.3, 278n.18; Point No Point, 11, 255n.3; Quinault, 255n.3
Trimble, Charles ("Chuck"), 104, 107, 131, 141, 157, 158, 162, 177, 181
Troeh, Chatherine (Chinook Indian), 98, 248
Tsimshian Indians, 172
Tukwila, Wash., 289n.11
Tulalip Bay, 16, 18
Tulalip Indians, 128, 129, 164, 165, 174, 177, 178, 180, 227, 271n.6, 278n.18

United American Indian Fort Lawton Occupational Force, 101
United States Court of Claims, 122
United States District Court for the District of Columbia, 173
United States District Court for Western Washington, 269nn.4,8,9, 286n.1
United States Indian Claims Commission. *See* Claims
United States Public Health Service, 163, 278n.16
United States Supreme Court, 28, 29, 62, 78, 110, 126, 128, 215, 271n.5
University of British Columbia, 50
University of Colorado, Law School, 159, 288n.9
University of Utah, 64
University of Washington, 89, 121
Upper Skagit Indians, 18, 46, 50, 55, 113, 130, 131, 202, 264n.3, 269n.8
Ute Indians, 65
Utsaladdy, Wash., 4, 122

Valley Forge, Pa., 171
Vance, John T., 76, 263n.5
Vancouver, B.C., Canada, 108, 246
Vancouver, Wash., 182, 199, 235
Vashon Grand Portugal Flores Island, 3
Venn, Douglas ("Doug"), 237, 242, 243
Venn, Marie, 237
Ventura, Calif., 141
Veterans Administration, 30

Waidelich, Martin, 232
Walker, Hans, Jr., 285n.20
Ware, Ernestine ("Flo"), 74
Warm Beach, 50, 121
Warm Springs Indians, 172
Warren, Earl, 67, 78
Warrenton, Oreg., 257n.13
Wars: Puget Sound, 16, 18, 289n.1; Vietnam, 65, 66, 67, 81; World War II, 34, 35, 37; Zionists and Arab Nations, 81
Washington, Joe (Lummi Indian), 60, 183, 188, 246
Washington, D.C., 24, 28, 82, 84, 92, 103–107, 115, 125, 149, 154, 174, 211. *See* Ross, Esther, trips to the Capitol
Washington and Evergreen Legal Services. *See* Evergreen Legal Services
Washington Reef Net Owners Association, 268n.4
Washington State Department of Fisheries, 58, 109, 117, 122, 212, 267–68nn.3,4
Washington State Department of Fish and Wildlife, 268n.3
Washington State Department of Game, 58, 109, 117, 122, 212, 267–68n.3, 268–69n.4
Washington State Easter Seal Society, 240, 243, 290n.16
Washington State Sportsmen's Council, Inc., 268n.4
Washington State Supreme Court, 58
Washington State Utilities and Transportation Commission, 236
Watts, Arthur E., 125, 159, 160
Weisl, Edwin L., Jr., 56
Wells, Ardeth, 143, 189
Wells, Nev., 65, 68
Wenatchee Indians, 19
Western Logging Co., 257n.13
Western Shoshone Indians, 261
Western Washington Agency, 43, 60, 85, 89, 105, 138, 145, 150, 160, 184; division of agency and change of name, 284n.8

Western Washington U.S. District Court, 110
Western Washington University, Center for Pacific Northwest Studies, 288n.9
Weston, David P., 149, 216
Weston, Paul, 149
Whitacker, James C., 132
Whitebear, Bernie (Colville Indian), 100, 101, 248, 265n.11
Whiteing, Jeanne S., 173, 181, 224
Wilcox, Ken, 148, 149, 151, 153
Williams, Edward J., 56
Williams, George (Tulalip Indian), 164
Williams, Wayne (Tulalip Indian), 107, 147
Wilson, Buelah (Cowlitz Indian), 167
Winthrop, Wash., 148
Wood, Al, 290n.16
Wood, Joseph F., 29
Woodall, Patricia, 241, 242
Woods, Andrea (Western Shoshone Indian), 261n.9
Wounded Knee, S. Dak., 147
Wright, Benjamin Reuben (Tulalip Indian), 122
Wright, Frank (Puyallup Indian), 97, 280n.1
Wrigley, Paul, 245

Yakama Indians, 59, 110, 113, 269n.9
Yale, B.C., Canada, 289n.14

Zeine, Edward and wife, 90
Zemple, Arnold R., 259n.23
Ziontz, Alvin J. 268–69n.4, 269–70n.9

www.ingramcontent.com/pod-product-compliance
Lightning Source LLC
Chambersburg PA
CBHW020737160426
43192CB00006B/220